DRUMBEAT
of LOVE

Other books by Lloyd Ogilvie

Let God Love You
Life Without Limits
Lord of the Ups and Downs
If I Should Wake Before I Die
A Life Full of Surprises
You've Got Charisma
Cup of Wonder
When God First Thought of You

LLOYD
JOHN
OGILVIE

DRUMBEAT
of LOVE

*The unlimited power of
the Spirit as revealed
in the Book of Acts*

WORD BOOKS
PUBLISHER
WACO, TEXAS

First Printing—November, 1976
Second Printing—July, 1977
Third Printing—October, 1977
Fourth Printing—December, 1977
Fifth Printing—March, 1978
Sixth Printing—April, 1978
Seventh Printing—May, 1978
Eighth Printing—May, 1979
First Paperback Printing—October, 1979

DRUMBEAT OF LOVE
Copyright © 1976 by Word, Incorporated,
4800 West Waco Drive, Waco, Texas 76710

Printed in the United States of America
ISBN 0-8499-2895-8
Library of Congress Catalog Card Number: 76–19535

All Scripture quotations, unless otherwise marked, are from the
Revised Standard Version of the Bible, copyrighted 1946, 1952,
© 1971, 1973 by the Division of Christian Education of the
National Council of the Churches of Christ in the U.S.A., and
used by permission. Quotations marked *The Living Bible* are
taken from *The Living Bible, Paraphrased* (Wheaton: Tyndale
House Publishers, 1971) and are used by permission. Quotations
marked NEB are from *The New English Bible,* © The Delegates
of The Oxford University Press and The Syndics of The
Cambridge University Press, 1961, 1970; used by permission.
Quotations marked Phillips are from *The New Testament in
Modern English,* copyright © 1958, 1959, 1960 by J. B. Phillips;
used by permission of The Macmillan Company. The quotation
marked Berkeley is from *The Holy Bible, The Berkeley
Version in Modern English* by Gerrit Verkuyl. The New
Testament, copyright © 1945 by Zondervan Publishing House.
Quotations marked Moffatt are from *The Bible: A New
Translation* by James Moffatt, © 1922, 1924, 1926, 1935,
1950, 1952, 1953, 1954 by Harper and Brothers.

To   Bruce and Hazel Larson
Fellow adventurers with whom
I have heard and felt the drumbe.
of love

Contents

Preface

My experience of the Holy Spirit has been like a drum-beat. When I met Christ and turned my life over to him, inviting him to live his life in me, the drumbeat began—softly at first, then persistently, indefatigably. The rhythms have never ceased. This is no distant drummer. The indwelling Lord has sounded the cadences of a living pulsebeat from within my soul. In times of challenge and adventure, the beat quickens. When difficulties surround me, the triumphant timbrel rolls in double time. I am never left on my own. If I drift into self-dependence, the beat slows and becomes faint. Alarming! When I dare to trust the Spirit unreservedly, the strong, stereo beat returns in full force. Assuring!

The drumbeat of the Master is love—his love for me, and through me to others. It is his call and recall to the excitement of the new life he lived, died, and was resurrected to make possible, the life he returned to enable from within us as the empowering Holy Spirit.

The Acts of the Apostles is the biography of the indwelling Drummer. This amazing book of Scripture could well be entitled the Acts of the Holy Spirit. It is his story. Luke, the beloved physician, heard the drumbeat. The rousing beat summoned him to the adventure when he met the Apostle Paul at Troas. It uni-fied the orchestration of his immense intellect and sensitivity. The years of missionary activity and expansion of the Church

9

drew Luke into the jet stream of the Holy Spirit's power. The physician and the Apostle were inseparable to the end.

It was in Rome, while Paul was awaiting trial, that the scholar in Luke was impelled to write an account of the birth of the new humanity, the Church. His Gospel captured the events of Jesus' life, death, and resurrection. Acts followed as the chronicle of Jesus' return and ministry through the Holy Spirit. Posterity has been blessed. The fast-moving account leaves us breathless and disturbed. Here is life as God intended it to be lived, and the Church as he envisioned it to be as a channel of power. We can't help but wonder why our lives are so impotent and our churches so ineffective. The astounding, invigorating dynamics of the Holy Spirit have never been more present and available than now.

My study of Acts has deepened the sound of the drumbeat of the Holy Spirit in me. In this book I have tried to share what each event means to us today. I have sought to be faithful to the fast-moving flow of thought and have made an effort to recapture Luke's essential message in each passage. My prayer is that reading what I have written will help you feel a "you-are-there" involvement. If you hear the drumbeat of love I will be gratified and satisfied beyond measure.

I want to express appreciation to Floyd Thatcher, a beloved editor, who has been unceasing in his faithful encouragement of my exposition of the text of the Beloved Physician. Thanks also to my assistant Norma Soll, secretary Esther Bowen, and typists Judy Smith, Carmel Buck, Carole Claussen, Carolyn Weese, and Belva Russell for their tireless efforts in typing the manuscript for publication.

Lloyd John Ogilvie

CHAPTER 1

Prelude to Power

Acts 1

Everywhere I go these days I hear the same urgent appeal from Christians. They want their lives to count. Their greatest fear is that they might live their lives in ineffectiveness, ineptness, or insipidness. They long for a challenge big enough to demand their allegiance, exciting enough to rally their enthusiasm, and crucial enough to warrant their time. A restlessness pervades both clergy and laity today, an impatience with "business as usual" and dull churchmanship.

I hear the stirring among the youth. They seem to know intuitively that life was meant to be more than getting an education, finding a job, marrying the right person, raising a family, gathering the usual security symbols, and settling into the ruts of routine. Even young people who are products of traditional Christian education and culturally conditioned church life are asking, "Isn't God up to something more exciting in the world than this?"

Many of us in the middle years know the same disquiet, for life has a way of applying a very highly concentrated varnish remover to our pretended satisfaction. Something's missing. Beneath the highly polished surface an incompleteness engulfs us. When life has settled down and goals are nearer accomplishment, the greatest burden is boredom. Our churches are filled with middle-aged people who long for something which will give zest and gusto to life. All of the icons of security just don't satisfy.

Last year, when I turned forty-five, my friends took great de-

11

light in sending me birthday cards poking fun at the middle-aged. One card in particular asked some questions by which you could determine whether you had entered the muddle of the middle years. They made me laugh, and then want to cry empathetically.

"When you get up in the morning, does your hair stay in bed?"
"When it's time for a dental check-up, do you send in your teeth?"
"Does it take more than five minutes to wash your stomach?"
"When's the last time you saw your ankles?"
"Are seventy percent of your friends desperate?"

What a hooker that last question was! I had to agree that there is a quiet desperation under the frantic business of many people I know. Christians. Active church people. Blandness in marriage, frustration at work, rage over the inability to change, loneliness which has nothing to do with the absence of people. I hear the ache everywhere. Life is lost in living. We dare not mock the persistent question, "Isn't there more to life than this?"

Senior people can answer the question. They know there must be something more. Retirement often proves to be an unbearable state of uselessness for those who have always regarded their work as their reason for living. Others are forced to face problems in reestablishing relationships which have been set aside with the justification of earning a living. The church casts about to provide interesting and entertaining programs for retired people. Few of the efforts have anything to do with the central mission of the Church. As one man said to me recently, "I've been a deacon in my Baptist church for years. Built a church building, raised money, served on committees. But the one thing my church never gave me was a relationship with Christ that would make my life exciting. Now I have all the time in the world, but don't know what to do that will count. All I'm asked to do at church is usher, fold envelopes, and go on outings with other equally unfulfilled people." Another retired person, a woman who had held a very responsible position in industry, said, "I'm so busy now I don't know how I ever found time for my profession!" I asked what was occupying her time so frantically. Her response included clubs and social activities. But nothing that she was doing to fill the emptiness had anything to do with the needs of people or the strategy of Christ for her life.

In an unguarded moment of openness over a cup of tea, she asked the disturbing question she had wanted to ask for a long time. "Do you think I have fulfilled the real reason I was born?" How would you have answered her? How would you answer for yourself, wherever you are on the journey—young, middle-aged, or in the twilight years?

Don't miss the fact that these uneasy stirrings I've mentioned are occurring among Christians who have been a part of the Church through the years. For many of them the life of the Church has been a part of the syndrome of security. It has given comfort and inspiration, but little challenge and dynamic to life. It is not surprising that among the one hundred greatest events in American history recorded in the *Life* Bicentennial Issue only a parenthetical reference to the influence of the Christian Church was given. We wonder about the next century. The problem is that the Faith has been domesticated to suit our culturally conditioned lives rather than dramatized as the ultimate purpose which gives meaning and direction to all other secondary loyalties. That may have satisfied people in the past, but the restlessness among contemporary Christians in the Church is demanding a freshness, a vitality, an authenticity unknown in recent years. There has never been a more exciting time to be alive than now.

I believe these stirrings are from God! He is creating this sense of unfulfillment and dissatisfaction in his people. I am convinced that we are living in an unprecedented time of potential blessing and power, and this is God's appointed hour to liberate the Church from being a memorial society to becoming a society of movers. Christianity is the movement and the Christian life is adventuresome participation in it. The Church is to be the joyous fellowship of those who will write a new chapter in the Book of Acts. We are not the embalmers of the past but the enablers of the present and the empowered people for a new age.

The Church in America has been locked on the dead center once occupied by the disciples between the Resurrection and the gift of the Holy Spirit at Pentecost. What happened to the followers of Jesus recorded in the first chapter of Acts exposes our greatest need. That's why a study of Acts is so crucial on God's agenda for the Church. We are on the edge of a momentous outpouring of the Holy Spirit. If we dare to experience the same prelude to power the Apostles experienced, we will be ready for

Pentecost, the rebirth of the Church, new fire for burned-out church people, and the expulsive power of uncontainable enthusiasm and excitement.

What Jesus did to get his disciples ready for Pentecost is what he longs to do in you and me. He took a confused, disunified, equivocating band of followers and forged them into a movement. Let's look at how he did it. Luke tells us vividly in this first chapter of Acts.

First of all, Jesus wanted his disciples to be sure of him as the leader of the movement. Luke tells us that he "gave commandment through the Holy Spirit and presented himself alive by many proofs." Our Lord lived and taught among the disciples as the resurrected Savior. My study reveals that the words "commandment through the Holy Spirit" actually mean that he taught them concerning or about the Holy Spirit. He wanted them to know that he was the same Lord who had called them into discipleship, ministered among them, and was crucified and raised for them. But he wanted them to know something much more: that he would always be with them through the Holy Spirit. They had to know this; they had to be sure. After he ascended, he would return. The same Spirit who had dwelt in him, whom they now experienced in this incisive interface of preparation, would return. The Holy Spirit would be the Lord's continuous activity among them, his living presence in the present tense.

That's what we need to know. Christ is alive! He is here with us. He wants to come not just around, or among us, but within us. The Holy Spirit is not some separate scepter, but the glorified Christ, alive and available. The remarkable "Acts," not just of the Apostles, but of the Holy Spirit through them, are available today and are to be everyday Christianity among those who join his movement to change the world.

There is a lot of confusion about the Holy Spirit today. We have fragmented the oneness of God with our trinitarian formulations. The same God who created all things, who called Israel to be his people, and who intervened in history in so many spectacular ways is the same Spirit who was in Christ to reconcile the world and who empowered the disciples at Pentecost. Our statement of the Trinity should clarify our experience of one God: He is indeed our Father; we know that because of what he did for us in his Son; and we experience his presence with us in the Holy Spirit. No wonder the early Church alternatively used the terms *Holy Spirit, the Spirit of Jesus, the Lord,* and *the Spirit* as referring to the same reality, rather than to separate parts of the Deity. The Holy Spirit is the immanent and intimate approach to man of the living God whom we know through Jesus Christ.

The disciples needed to be clear about how Jesus would return, and so must we. God's new age of Pentecost in our time will happen when we understand the Holy Spirit, long for the Holy Spirit, pray for the Holy Spirit, and open ourselves to the Holy Spirit as the contemporary Christ with us and within us.

The second aspect of the preparation of the disciples was to focus the Kingdom of God as the charter and message of the movement. The resurrected Lord picked up the drumbeat of his teaching throughout his ministry. The disciples were called into a movement to proclaim the Kingdom of God. In his message Jesus had clarified that the Kingdom was within them, among them, between them, and coming in the world through them. It means the rule of God in all life. All that exists, all that we have and are, and all that is to be through us must be brought under the Lordship of Christ. The movement into which the disciples were called was to be the Kingdom on earth. It would not be a political kingdom, or a return to Davidic glory, or the Messiah's reign as temporal king of Israel. As participants in the movement of the Kingdom, we are to allow the Lord to reign supreme in all our affairs and to discover and implement the implications of his teachings in every facet of life. There's a purpose big enough for any of us! What is there in our lives, in our church, or in our society that must be brought under his control and guidance? The answers to that question declare the marching orders for the movement. A personal question now aches for an answer: How much of our life is completely surrendered to him? What areas or relationships need to be opened for his guidance, forgiveness, and power? That demands action!

But *when* and *how* are the subjects of Jesus' next preparation for power—timing and strategy. He wanted his disciples to be people who could wait for God, who would allow God to work through them, not people who would work for God on their own schedule and priorities. Can you imagine a more painful

word to speak to these intrepidly urgent disciples than "Wait!"?
They were ready to move! Christ was alive and victorious, and
now was not the time to wait. We all know how they must have
felt. *Wait* is still the most cruel word for our impetuous natures
to hear; yet there are ordained waiting periods in which our Lord
prepares us for what he has prepared. It's difficult to wait for
people to understand or change. Waiting for health in the midst
of sickness is excruciating. Waiting for a loved one's progress
outside an operating room stretches one's faith. But waiting on
the Lord is most difficult of all. We pray for guidance and direction, and we are forced to wait. Why? What is God up to? Then
we realize that it's in the waiting times that he prepares us for the
next phase of our life in him. Until we are fully dependent upon
him, completely open to do his will, and unreservedly willing to
act on his timing, he cannot use us.

The Apostles were told to wait for the promise of the Father.
Jesus had told them that would be when they were "clothed
with power from on high" (Luke 24:49). Worth waiting for!
Yet it's difficult for us to wait; we want everything yesterday, or
the day before that! But God is never off schedule: he is never
ahead or behind time; he is always on time. We can trust that he
will use all circumstances and life's eventualities for his perfectly
timed plan for us. The people who share his movement in history
must dare to believe that.

And what a promise for which we are to wait! Jesus now
gives the qualification for initiation into the movement: baptism
with the Holy Spirit. He reminds the Apostles that John baptized
with water. This outward sign of consecration, the experience of
cleansing, became the initiation ritual of those who joined his
righteous movement. Now there was to be a new kind of baptism.
Just as John's baptism was immersion in the waters, symbolic
of cleansing, the Holy Spirit's baptism was to be immersion in
the very life-giving spiritual power of God. The Apostles were
to be indwelt, empowered, engrossed, and enlightened by the
living God! Jesus knew that no one could be a part of his Kingdom movement and live the life he had lived, doing what he
had done, without a baptism of the Holy Spirit. Like many
Christians today, the disciples knew Christ and were convinced
of his Lordship, but they needed the indwelling of the Holy
Spirit. It's possible to be a believer and not have power; it's

impossible to live the adventuresome life Christ intended without the Holy Spirit.

But the disciples hadn't been listening, nor have we. When they blurted out, "Lord, will you at this time restore the Kingdom of Israel?" they displayed their ineptness and inability to listen. I am thankful for their poorly timed question, for it occasioned the Lord's teaching about how to trust God in the present and about what would be given to us for "now"-oriented faithfulness. The disciples wanted a return to past glory. Jesus helped them anticipate the future.

Recently I walked by a restaurant in downtown Los Angeles called The Pub. In the window I saw a sign announcing the late afternoon cocktail hour usually referred to as Happy Hour: "ATTITUDE ALTERATION TIME—4:00 to 6:00 P.M." was its ambiguous promise. I thought about tired office workers who might take the bait and feel that their attitudes could be altered by some mood-changer. But attitudes are not easily changed, especially when it comes to reverence for the past that blocks out what God wants to give in the present.

Jesus boldly told the disciples that the false glory of the past could not be reestablished and that the future was in God's hands. It was not for them to know the times or seasons appointed by God. What they would be given was far greater. They would receive power when the Holy Spirit came upon them. It would mean intellectual power: they would have wisdom and knowledge. It would be spiritual power: they would have great faith and do impossible things as miracles of the Spirit. It would be emotional power: they would have deep love for one another and people in the world. And it would be physical power: they would have strength and endurance beyond their human potential and capacity. That should have altered their attitude!

But now observe what follows. The power of the Holy Spirit is to be given for a very specific purpose: to be a witness. The word *witness* really means martyr. The energizing, life-giving Spirit is for communication. A further preparation for Pentecost, then, is a commitment to be mediators to others of the grace and hope of the gospel. There can be no Holy Spirit empowering unless we are engaged in being witnesses in the full implication of the word's original meaning of martyr. That implies that nothing can dissuade us from our belief and confidence in Christ.

It also suggests a Cross-oriented love for the people with whom we want to share the good news of Christ's love. That precludes easy evangelism that is nonrelational and cares little for people's needs and growth. How many people in our lives know without any shadow of doubt our forgiving, accepting, affirming love? Witnessing is not just spouting concepts or outlining plans of salvation. It is profound caring for and sometimes suffering with and for people. People are first on God's agenda. They are the focus of the movement into which we are called. The Holy Spirit is not given until we are witnesses!

There are lots of people today who are seeking the gifts and power of the Holy Spirit for their own needs. That's only the beginning. The dynamics of the Spirit are given when we are involved in identifying with others and their struggle.

A woman wrote me to say that she had been in a dry spell spiritually. She was anxiously seeking the power of the Holy Spirit, yet she felt no flow of new life or enthusiasm. I asked her to tell me the names of ten people who needed love. Each one she listed needed wisdom, knowledge, and faith she could not engender in them. But when she got into specific, costly caring she realized that she was saying things beyond her human intelligence and communicating hope beyond her experience. When she was stretched by the demands of loving, she received a profound experience of the Holy Spirit's gift of love. She knew it; so did the people she tried to care about. Her martyrdom did not cost her her life but it did cost time, energy, and privacy. Her reward was an intensive, intimate experience of the Spirit of God. The same will be true for us. Who are the people on your list of ten?

Contemporary "Holy Spiritites," as I call them, want a private experience of the Spirit without pouring themselves out for people or giving themselves away to heal human suffering. Jesus is very specific about the dimensions of our witness. The resources of the Holy Spirit will be given in the realms of responsibility.

These realms of our witness are delineated by the geographical extent of Jesus' challenge: "Jerusalem and in all of Judea and Samaria and to the end of the earth." For us that means at home, among our friends, at work, in the community, throughout the nation and the world. What a shock these areas of geography must have been to the disciples! Jerusalem? The Lord was crucified there! Judea? Where they were rejected! Samaria, among the impure half-breeds? The end of the earth? Gentiles too? It would take years to assimilate that challenge. And yet, the further the witnesses extended, the more power from the Holy Spirit would be given. The same is true for us. No witness, no Spirit!

The next aspect of Jesus' prelude to power for the disciples was dramatic and decisive. He ascended into heaven. This is the confidence of the movement: the assurance of the Ascension. He left them alone, a very startling way to teach! He had told them about it previously. "It is expedient for you that I go away" (John 16:7). How could his leaving them, or us, ever be expedient? Look at it this way. He had to leave them in one dimension to return in a greater demonstration of power. He left as Jesus of Nazareth, resurrected and victorious; he returned as the Holy Spirit, indwelling and ubiquitous. Now he was to be unloosed on all the world. People would meet him not just in Galilee, or on the Mount of Olives, or in Jerusalem, but everywhere throughout the whole world. He left as a risen Savior and returned as the mighty Lord of the Church, his movement to change the world.

Christ always goes away. That's how he forces us to grow. No previous level of growth or insight is sufficient. He will always leave us at one stage of discovery so that our security is never in ourselves or in our own capacity to know him. The absenting Savior is constantly pushing us on to new frontiers. But he always returns in a greater discovery of him than we ever imagined. Moffatt translates the advice given the confused disciples by the angelic messengers: "This Jesus, who has been taken from you into heaven, will come back in the same way you saw him go into heaven" (Acts 1:11). Heaven here does not mean the reaches of the sky but the realm of God. It is not just "up there" but is a quality of relationship with God. From that realm Jesus would return in the Holy Spirit. He would come in the way he went: unpredictably, suddenly, powerfully. In that confidence the disciples left the Mount of Olives and went back to the Upper Room in John Mark's home where they had celebrated the Last Supper and where the resurrected Lord had first returned to them.

It was there that they discovered the relational preparation

for the movement. Note especially that they devoted themselves
to prayer together. More than physical proximity, this means a
spiritual unity. I have always felt that Pentecost happened not
according to a date on a calendar but in response to reconciliation among the disciples. There were deep tensions among
them during and after Jesus' ministry among them. Sharp divi-
sions and conflicts surged among these strong-willed people.
Until they were together on their knees, fully open to God and
each other, the Holy Spirit could not be given. Notice that Jesus'
mother and brothers were there. There had not always been
appreciation and affirmation between them and the disciples or
between them and Jesus. Now a remedial healing was taking
place as a part of the prelude to power.

I have never known a contentious group to receive the Holy
Spirit. Nor have I ever seen a church in which division and dis-
unity prevailed receive the blessing of the Holy Spirit. If we
want power from the Holy Spirit as individuals, we need to do
a relational inventory: Everyone forgiven? Any restitutions to
be done? Any need to communicate healing to anyone? As
congregations we cannot be empowered until we are of one
mind and heart, until we love each other as Christ has loved us,
and until we heal all broken relationships. The price seems
high! But it's a bargain price for what can happen through
Pentecost power.

The election held among the Apostles to determine Judas's
successor provides the final dimensions of preparation for participation in God's new age of the Holy Spirit. Two things
stand out: the qualifications required to be a candidate and the
expectant sense of destiny about the movement to which the
Apostles all had been called. What was required for apostleship
then is basic for anyone who would receive the Holy Spirit
today. The Apostles had to have been with Jesus from the beginning of his ministry and they had to have witnessed his
Resurrection.

For us this means, first of all, an acceptance of what God
did through the life, ministry, and death of Jesus. Preparation
to receive the living Lord as Holy Spirit is a response to his
immeasurable love taught and dramatically imparted on the
Cross. Acceptance of Jesus Christ as Savior does not follow,
but precedes, the baptism of the Holy Spirit. The first step

toward Pentecost is toward Jesus. Until we have made an unreserved commitment of all we have and are, we cannot experience
what he offers as the Holy Spirit.

Also, the Cross looms up between us and the power of Pentecost. Has the Cross been an experience of the forgiveness of
our sin? Have we accepted the assurance of the atonement for
the past, and have we been healed in the depth of our natures
by his gracious love? Do our memories still haunt us? Are we
still imprisoned in guilt, self-justification, or defensiveness? The
Holy Spirit is often sought by people who want to bypass Jesus
and his Cross. It's like wanting a gift from someone whom we
will not acknowledge or befriend. It won't work. I have known
countless people who have drifted into spiritualism or self-
centered optimism who have sought the Holy Spirit without the
message of Christ to guide their lives or the Cross to heal their
personalities.

Equally necessary for apostleship and the baptism and filling
of the Holy Spirit is the witness of the Resurrection. Of course,
that does not mean that we too have been in Joseph's garden or
in the Upper Room on Easter morning! What it does mean
is that we have experienced and realized the Resurrection, not
only Christ's but our own. That means several things. It means
that we must accept God's power to raise Jesus from the dead.
We must be people whose faith is rooted in that central miracle.
Going further, it means that we become people who dare to
believe, and joyously expect, God's intervention in life's impossible situations. He is able to resurrect our feeble efforts and
complexities and do his best in what we think is life's worst.

But now to the core of it. A witness to the Resurrection has
gone through the death and resurrection cycle in his own life.
Paul made clear in Romans 6 that we are to die to ourselves,
our plans and purposes, longings and dreams. We become
dead as far as our own wishes are concerned. Then we can
experience resurrection to the new life for which we were born
and reborn. We become new creatures: the old person passes
away and the new person comes alive. Only that kind of person
has room for the indwelling of the Holy Spirit. Otherwise, the
Holy Spirit has no place to dwell and no freedom to move
within us.

The second aspect of the election which directly affects us, and the final dimension of the prelude to power, is the sense of destiny the Apostles had. They had been called for a very special movement, and they expectantly awaited the power God was about to pour out. When they prayed to God about their ministry and apostleship, it was with confidence and predestined assurance. They knew they were called, appointed, and set apart. And so should we. But don't forget, the Holy Spirit is given for apostleship, not for our pious enjoyment. We can dare to ask for the Holy Spirit because we too have an apostolic calling. Boldness, intrepidly daring prayer results: "Lord, come Holy Spirit, fill us, empower us, use us."

This is the amazing preparation for power Luke describes in Acts 1. No one need be restless, unfulfilled or ineffective again. We have been selected to receive the Holy Spirit. A new day has dawned. We are ready for Pentecost.

CHAPTER 2

The Dynamic Dimension

Acts 2

A sense of need is a gift. The recognition of spiritual
emptiness is a blessing. A realization of the distance between what we are and what we could become is a special grace.
The Lord is never nearer than when he excavates a sense of
emptiness in us. The Holy Spirit can fill only empty hearts.

The Apostles more than met this qualification as they waited
in the Upper Room during the ten-day interval between Jesus'
Ascension and Pentecost. Emptiness? They felt it with devastat-
ing insufficiency. They had experienced a life of high adventure
with Jesus. The power of God had been exposed in his message,
healing, and love. Not even death could defeat that power. And
Jesus had told them that same power would be theirs. The
things he did they would do, and greater things. But now as
they waited despairingly for the fulfillment of his promise of
power, the words of hope seemed to mock their impotence and
inadequacy. It's a terrible thing to have a passion with no
power to live it. Four words express the emptiness prior to
Pentecost. The Apostles were discouraged, dejected, disabled,
and filled with depression.

Was it all true? Had it been a dream? Did Christ really appear after the Resurrection? Were they victims of a wish dream?
Ten days is a long time to wait when the frail thread of hope
is about to break.

Dejection was natural. They needed more than a revered
memory or a remembered message. Only the Savior himself

would suffice. What good would an impersonal power be without him?

A vision without vitality ridicules our disability. We've all known it: a challenge to love when we have little capacity for it, a need to forgive others when we can't even forgive ourselves, a longing for wisdom and knowledge for life's demands when we can't figure out what to do with today, the unsettling needs of people when we have neither faith nor hope to believe that healing can take place.

No wonder depression captured the emotions of Jesus' followers. It grew out of the desperate feeling that they could not be what they had been called to be. Inverted hostility became self-incrimination. What is it for you? What makes you depressed? Human nature, what people do or say, the suffering and sickness in the world? What is it that makes you feel the futility of life? Is it when you do your best and it's not good enough, when you try to make a difference around you and there is little discernible difference, or when you love and little love is returned? I am convinced that depression is not circumstantial or environmental, but deeply personal. It is rage turned in upon ourselves as a result of the disturbing realization that we can't change things in ourselves, in people, or in situations.

The mood in the Upper Room is shared by millions of Christians today. And I say, praise God! An evidence of his gracious love is that he has allowed us to come to this place so that we would be ready for Pentecost. Our efforts to live the Christian life on our own strength have run the long course of self-justification. The repeated commitments to care about people have left us exhausted and depleted. Programs to change society and bring justice have exposed our cherished cultural loyalties and forced us to admit that we cannot follow through on seeking first the Kingdom of God when our security is up for grabs.

My own experience and my involvement with people have led to a deep conviction that may not be theologically orthodox but is experientially validated. There are two stages in becoming a vital Christian. One is our response to Christ by the gift of faith. We commit our lives to him and begin to live for him. We come to grips with his message and the lifestyle it demands. We try to love, forgive, and serve. Then, as a result of the demanding challenge, we are forced to admit that we can't do it; we don't have what it takes. That prepares us for the second step, which must constantly be repeated. Out of power and conscious of our own failure, we are broken. Empty! That's the only way we can hear Christ's words, "Apart from me you can do nothing." Only at that point can we accept the fact that being a Christian is not just following the Master, seeking to live up to a standard of perfection, trying to be faithful and obedient, but rather allowing him to live his life in us and through us. That's what Pentecost is all about.

Recently I attended a meeting of church leaders called together to pray for our nation. The spectrum of theological persuasions was amazing: fundamentalists and liberals, free church and high church, Pentecostals and conservatives. The need of America drove us together. The realization of the ineptness of our churches pressed us to pray. We needed wisdom and knowledge, faith and daring, healing and hope. We needed the Holy Spirit, the Living Christ! The openness of one man broke us open. He told the story of his own experience of receiving power after long years in the ministry. An electricity charged the room. That's what we all needed—the uplifting, enabling, infilling of the Spirit himself! There is no greater need in the whole Church in America.

Some years ago, when I was the pastor of a small band of people in a new church, I used to greet the people at the door prior to worship. Deep, trusting relationships had been forged among us. As I shook hands with each person, I would ask, "What do you need this morning?" A casual observer would think the question ridiculous. Many of the people were prosperous and successful. Yet a sense of spiritual need had brought them together to be an authentic church of seekers and strugglers. As each would share with me some concern or hope and report on progress or difficulty, I would collect all the needs in my mind. The call to worship for the service which followed the greeting was a statement of the kind of needs which had been shared and the availability of the Holy Spirit to meet them. One morning a successful young lawyer grasped my hand and said, "I feel completely drained and empty. I need the Holy Spirit!"

That's what the disciples were saying on the day of Pentecost. What happened first in the Upper Room, then in the courtyard, and finally in the temple courts was an encounter with, and an

infilling by, the Living God himself. They never forgot it. The
experience was so dramatic that it changed their lives and gave
birth to the Church. They were given the dynamic dimension of
the Christian life. Those who had followed Jesus in the flesh
were filled with Jesus in the Holy Spirit.

The aspects of the experience not only describe the event, but
also clarify the availability of the dynamic dimension for us.
Picture it; feel it. Our own Pentecost can happen right now!

The disciples lifted their bowed heads and looked at each
other with awe and astonishment. The stillness of the air was suddenly stirring, in gusts of breeze at first; then in a rush of a
mighty wind like a blast of a hurricane. A violent wind shook the
room. The disciples staggered about trying to keep their footing
like sailors on the bow of a ship in a stormy, high sea. Something was happening. And the disciples were convinced that what
they had been waiting for had begun. How gracious of the Lord
to return in so unmistakable a way! The Spirit of the Lord, what
the ancient Hebrews called the *ruach*—the breath—of God, was
now moving mightily among them. The tornadolike whirr was
unmistakable. The echoing sound was like thunder.

Now the audible sign of the presence of the Spirit was followed by a visible one. A firelike manifestation hovered over the
disciples; then suddenly it parted and a portion flashed in a
tongue-shaped descent on each of the disciples, again a symbol
significant to these Hebrew disciples. Fire was a symbol of the
divine presence, of purifying and refining energy. They had been
promised that they would be baptized with the Holy Spirit and
with fire.

Now it had happened in a way to dispel their unbelief and
coldness of heart. The fire they saw above each other's heads
was confirmed by the fire of warmth and joy they felt in their
hearts.

That's what Luke means when he says, "And they were all
filled with the Holy Spirit." What had come in undeniable, symbolic evidence now came within them. The emptiness was filled.
The Lord took them where they were, as they were: broken,
empty men who needed to be convinced by his presence without, so that they could receive his presence within. Here the
word "filled" (*eplērōsen*) means that, as a container is filled with
water, so the tissues of their brains were actually energized with

the Holy Spirit. New emotions were released and new volitional capacity engendered.

In an unexpected outward expression of this electrifying of the tissue of their inner being they praised God, but not in their own tongue. To their utter amazement they were talking in languages other than their native Aramaic—another sign of the miraculous presence of the Holy Spirit! They had heard other languages from Jews in the Holy City—enough to force them to realize that a magnificent linguistic capacity was now theirs. I can imagine Peter grasping Andrew to have him listen to his adoration of God in Latin and then to listen to John talk in pure Greek. Then other languages flowed with equal facility.

It was this, I believe, that sent the Apostles rushing out into the courtyard and then to the temple. They could tell about what happened to them and praise God in the many foreign languages represented in Jerusalem at the Feast of Pentecost.

Jews from all over the then-known world were gathered in Jerusalem to celebrate the Day of Pentecost. Many had traveled great distances to commemorate the giving of the Law to Moses and to praise God for the ingathering of the harvest. The providence of God had been expressed in both the guide for life and the sustenance of food. Pentecost, fifty days after Passover, was a time for rest and celebration. The streets of Jerusalem, and particularly the temple precincts, were crowded with an international throng of Jews. Luke is careful to enumerate the mixture of Parthians, Medes, and Elamites along with residents of Mesopotamia, Judea, Cappadocia, Pontus, and the Roman district of Asia. Added to these were Jews from Phrygia, Pamphylia, Egypt, Libya. This list is topped off with both Jews and proselytes from Rome, Crete, and Arabia. That multitude represents a lot of different languages and dialects. And each individual heard about the mighty works of God in his own tongue. What a miracle of communication, both for the disciples and for the international listeners. The Spirit was at work in speakers and hearers in a dramatic demarcation of a new age.

I would like to digress long enough to clarify what I think this was. The Scripture says that the Apostles spoke in *other* tongues, not that they spoke in tongues. The gift of tongues— an ecstatic and unbridled expression of praise, in unintelligible language—was a later manifestation of the indwelling of the

Holy Spirit. Luke makes reference to this gift in two subsequent incidents in Caesarea—when Peter preached at Cornelius's house and at Ephesus when Paul laid hands on a band of disciples of John the Baptist. Paul lists speaking in tongues and interpretation of them as specific gifts of the Holy Spirit. His Corinthian letter acknowledges the authenticity of the gift but cautions about its use.

Interest in the gift of tongues in our own day is great, and many people have found delight and release in it. Its public use, with interpretation, allows the prophetic power of God to guide the assembly of his people with a supernatural impartation of wisdom. Privately, a person may pray in tongues and then be given the gift of insight into what God has sought to communicate. Both manifestations are legitimate gifts, but never to be flaunted or used as a basis of self-justification before God or others. In my opinion it is heretical to confuse speaking in tongues as the only undeniable sign that we have received the Holy Spirit or to use the term "charismatic" to describe it. Charismatic means grace-gifted. The Greek word *charismata* refers to all the gifts delineated by Paul in Corinthians 12. On Pentecost it was not speaking in tongues which was given but the gift of communicating praise to God for Christ in other languages.

For the disciples, and for all those who heard, the manifestation of speaking in foreign tongues on the Day of Pentecost was a declaration of the new age of the universality of Jesus. Concretely, the Great Commission to go into all the world was part of the enacted miracle of Pentecost.

People's response to the miracle is very interesting. All were amazed and perplexed and asked each other, "What does this mean?" The Lord had gotten everyone's attention. Others mocked, saying that the Apostles were drunk. Still others, as we shall see, were alerted to the possibility that God was indeed present, doing a new thing. They listened to Peter's speech which followed, and three thousand of them were converted.

What is our reaction? We need to pause to regroup our own personal response to all three manifestations of the first outpouring of the Holy Spirit, the returned Lord Jesus, on his followers. Wind, fire, and the gift of communication—all three are part of what happens when our emptiness is filled by the Holy Spirit.

The wind of Pentecost for us affirms that the gift of being

filled with the Holy Spirit begins with God. The wind of Pentecost is God himself. The Holy Spirit was not created by God for Pentecost. This was not some new aspect of God revealed and released for the first time. The Holy Spirit is the essence of the Eternal God, creator and Lord of all creation, the same Spirit who dwelt in Jesus and is now given to indwell those who believe in him. We are at the center of the truth when we say that the Holy Spirit was and is the resurrected, ascended, reigning Christ, now among and within his committed followers. He had promised the infilling gift: "The Father and I shall make our home *in* you. Abide in me and I in you." Paul later expressed the central reality of the Christian experience when he said, "Christ in you, the hope of glory." The wind, the breath of God, the living Christ, the Holy Spirit are all one. Just as a newborn baby is enabled to breathe in the breath of life by the trained and skilled blow of the obstetrician, so too, when we confess our emptiness and need of enabling power, we breathe in the Spirit and become new creatures.

There's a lot of talk about whether we receive the Holy Spirit at conversion or as a second blessing later on. The question is distracting and confusing because it's based on a fallacious fracturing of the unity of God. All aspects of our conversion, rebirth, infilling, and growth are works of the Holy Spirit. His gift of love frees us to admit our need. His gift of faith enables our initial response to the gospel. His persistent presence liberates us from the idea that we could ever live the Christian life on our own steam. Each time we acknowledge our inadequacy he fills the fresh experience of emptiness with particular gifts we need to carry out the mission and ministry of Christ. When the needs of people and the world break our hearts and the triumphant adequacy of the gospel grasps our minds, that is a particular time when we are baptized by, filled with the Holy Spirit. Previously he has been impinging on our consciousness; now he is the indwelling Lord. The baptism of the Holy Spirit is not an esoteric, special, or separate experience given to a chosen few Christian believers. The rarity of the power of Pentecost in so many believers' lives tells us about them, not God. The Holy Spirit is utterly available. But if we are filled up with our own pride, plans, determination, and self-effort, there is no room left. And if we are attempting only those things we could do on our

own strength, who needs the Holy Spirit and his gifts? When
we get fed up with being filled by the things which do not satisfy
or empower, we are ready to be filled with the Holy Spirit.

The fire of Pentecost describes what happens when the living
Christ, the Holy Spirit, takes up residence in us. Potent words
flow in explanation: conviction, passion, enthusiasm, galvaniza-
tion. All of these are part of the fire of the Spirit in us. The
disciples on the road to Emmaus after the Resurrection spoke of
their hearts burning within them—a foretaste of Pentecost. John
Wesley talked about his heart being strangely warmed. Christians
have been called the fellowship of the flaming heart. Jesus promised that the Holy Spirit would bring to our remembrance all
that he said and did. Inflammatory material—the word of God,
a Cross, forgiveness and reconciliation, defeat of death, resurrection, the offer of new life, now and forever! Flaming convictions of assurance! That explanation alone can account for the
courage and daring of the early Church, and ever since—
passionate devotion burning in the believer for Christ and the
world he died to save. Enthusiasm is inner excitement about
Christ expressed in unextinguishable affirmation of life. Problems become new opportunities to discover the unlimited potential of the Lord. The fire of love leaps out of us to set a fire
burning in others. Warmth of countenance, expression, and words
is an authentic test that the Living Christ's post-resurrection
home is in our hearts.

But there's more to the fire of the Holy Spirit. It also purifies
and galvanizes. John the Baptist's promise that we would be
baptized with the Holy Spirit and with fire is quickly followed
with severe implications. "His winnowing fork is in his hand,
and he will clear his threshing floor and gather his wheat into
the granary, but the chaff he will burn with unquenchable fire"
(Matt. 3:12). That passage not only refers to what happens to
those who do not believe, but also what happens to those who
do.

The chaff in us is burned out by the fire of the Holy Spirit.
Our chaff is anything which keeps us from our Lord or any
other person. It is the attitudes which cripple, the values which
demand false loyalty, the habits which incarcerate us. Our chaff
also includes memories of past failure for which we will not
accept forgiveness and forget; the plans for the future which

could never receive our Lord's blessings. Most of all, it is willful self-centeredness and determination. We are loved just as we are, true, but the Spirit will never leave us there. His work in us is to re-create us in the image of Christ. Once he comes to live in us, he begins to move out into every area of our minds and hearts. He's never finished with us.

Recently I passed through a very difficult and painful period of seeing myself realistically through the eyes of a couple of people I love very much. They pointed out a developing pattern which could cause ineffectiveness in my relationship with them, and possibly others. The only place I could go with the data was to prayer. The Spirit was firm and yet gentle. He confirmed aspects of the criticism and helped me see the insecurity which prompted the pattern. Then he gave me power to do something about it. The amazing thing was that just before this need for change was brought to my attention, I had been feeling very secure and at peace, as if my growing in Christ had finally reached a quiet maturity. Not so! Chaff I hadn't realized was there had to be burned away. And it will be like this for as many years as I have to live on earth. Under the fire of the Spirit the dross will surface and have to be skimmed off to make the metal pure.

Closely related to the burning of chaff out of us is the galvanizing of our relationships by the fire of the Holy Spirit. Welding takes white-hot fire. So do deep, inseparable relationships. The fire in my heart coupled with the fire in yours makes us one. The union is intellectual as we receive the mind of Christ; it's emotional as we feel the warmth of love for each other in spite of hurts or failures; and it's volitional as we make decisions to do his will together. Christ prayed that we might be one. His living Spirit in us is indefatigable in making this possible.

The third aspect of Pentecost was praise. We must never be so distracted by the gift of speaking in other tongues that we miss what the Apostles talked about in many languages: the mighty works of God. Praise is an evidence of the indwelling of the Spirit and is a sign for us that we have received his power. Praise is the antidote to pride, the evidence that we have accepted the fact that all we have and are is a gift. More than that, praise unlocks further power from the Holy Spirit. If we praise God in blessings, the Spirit heightens our joy. If we praise God in difficulties, we acknowledge that he can work in all things. Praise is surrender: it is thanking God that he can use everything to enable us to grow. But most of all, praise is a universal communication. The finest way to share our faith is to tell others about what God is doing in our lives, but not just the successes. When we praise him in the midst of frustration and pain, our witness is undeniable. When efforts to convince people about doctrine fail, it's usually because they can't see and feel the power of praise. The Holy Spirit cannot be contained. He will always break out in praise.

The eager, impassioned praise of the Apostles brought the charge that they were drunk. Peter's response occasioned the first Christian sermon in explanation of a quality of life which had been exposed. Wouldn't it be great if contemporary preaching could be an explanation of the life of church members whose winsome witness prompted people to come to church to find some way of understanding the amazing life they had observed?

Peter got the matter of new-wine excitement out of the way quickly. "Now, listen; you know what time it is," he implied. "It's only nine o'clock in the morning [the third hour of the day]. We haven't had anything to eat yet because we have not yet made our sacrifices; that's another hour away and our main meal is two hours beyond that. We don't have wine without a meal. How can you be so absurd as to say that we are drunk? Something else has happened. Let me tell you."

Immediately he repeated the prophecy of Joel written about 400 B.C., speaking with emphasis the words of God: "And in the last days I will pour out my Spirit upon all flesh." That's what was happening in Jerusalem! The result, according to Joel, would be that "they shall prophesy" (Acts 2:17). These were not to be the wild ecstatic mutterings of the prophet bands of ancient Israel, but a prophecy focused in visions and dreams of what God would do.

The fourth evidence of the Holy Spirit's power then and now is prophecy. This is not just foretelling, but forthtelling, proclamation of truth. The Holy Spirit enables us to see things as they are, Christ as he is, ourselves in his light, others in their need. The gift of prophecy is the capacity to communicate truth with daring freedom and boldness. It's not accusing people for what they are not, but sharing what they can be. The Spirit gives us discernment about what to say and the courage to say it with

love. Without the Holy Spirit we will constantly be in trouble,
saying too little or too much. One man told me recently, "There
are times I wish God would give me lockjaw. I always say the
wrong thing when I try to help people by sharing my faith."
We talked and prayed about this together, asking for the specific gift of prophecy. The Holy Spirit, not a stingy giver, gave
the man sensitivity and empathy. He learned how to listen and
watch for the Spirit's opportunity and judge when the time
was right. A man with whom he works joined our church recently. His conversion and new life are a direct result of my
friend's Spirit gift of prophecy.

Peter not only explained the effusion of enthusiasm as a result of the Spirit being poured out; he went on to use the gift
of prophecy himself. The presentation he gave of the gospel was
to be a pattern of subsequent preaching in the early Church.
He proclaimed what God had done in Christ; then he fearlessly
explained what his people had done with what God had done;
finally he passionately communicated what God did in spite of
what they had done. The life, death, resurrection, and present
power of Christ were all undeletable elements of early Christian
preaching. No wonder Peter's prophecy had the results it did.
The people were cut to the heart and cried out, "Brethren, what
shall we do?" Peter's response has never been improved upon in
centuries of explanation of how to become a Christian. "Repent,
and be baptized every one of you in the name of Jesus Christ
for the forgiveness of your sins; and you shall receive the gift of
the Holy Spirit" (Acts 2:37–38). Familiarity may blunt the
radical nature of Peter's invitation. He asked for nothing less
than for the people to turn around, accept Jesus as Messiah and
Lord, confess sins, be baptized, and fearlessly become identified
as followers of the Master. The result would be that they would
receive the Holy Spirit. Three thousand responded. The same
Holy Spirit who had filled the Apostles now gave the gift of
faith to the new believers.

The final manifestation of the Pentecost outpouring was the
fellowship of the Holy Spirit. "And all who believed were together and had all things in common; and they sold their possessions and goods and distributed them to all, as any had need"
(2:44–45). The Church was born. A new humanity came alive.
God's eternal strategy of reconciliation between him and his

people and of his people with one another was now being fulfilled. Eden revisited, Mount Moriah superseded, Exodus accomplished, a new temple not made with hands, Calvary's sacrifice
realized, the Resurrection victory shared, the Holy Spirit gift
accepted, a new Israel—the Church—born. The drumbeat of
love sounded in the believers' hearts and gave them power to
be to each other what the Lord had been to them.

When night fell over Jerusalem that Pentecost day, a new
creation had begun. The words "communion of the Holy Spirit"
(*koinonia* in Greek) have a fresh impact, carrying the profound
implications that in Christ we are called to love, forgive, enable,
and sustain one another. There can be no true fellowship without
his living presence in us and between us. The Church of the Holy
Spirit is the demonstration in history of God's eternal purpose
for all people. The people in whom the Spirit lives will be constantly broken open to be channels of grace to fellow adventurers in Christ.

The day of Pentecost had begun with the disciples together
in one mind and heart. The Holy Spirit could come because of
that. By the end of the day the fellowship expanded by three
thousand. Luke ends the second chapter of Acts with triumphant
joy: "And the Lord added to their number day by day those
who were being saved." The movement to change the world had
begun, and we have never heard the end of it.

There is no need I have ever heard articulated by individuals
or the Church that could not be met by the Holy Spirit. Our
need for wisdom, knowledge, faith, healing, discernment, and
freedom are his gifts. When he fills us, the fruit of the Spirit intuitively becomes our capacities: love, joy, peace, patience, kindness, goodness, faithfulness, gentleness, and self-control. What
else do we need? The greatest gift of all—the Lord himself! And
that he offers in the Holy Spirit.

CHAPTER 3

You Can Liberate People

Acts 3

The power of Pentecost is for people. What happened
at Pentecost is for the paralysis of the world. The Holy
Spirit, Christ in the present tense, is for the healing of people in
the present age. The excitement and enthusiasm of the infilling
of the Spirit and the birth of the Church was to create a people
through whom the Lord could continue his ministry of reconciliation and healing. A new age was born, Christ was alive in
his people, and they were now equipped to do what he had done
and the greater things he promised—communicating his love
and bringing people to him.

Chapter 2 of Acts is inseparably linked to chapter 3. The
gift of the Holy Spirit was to make the Spirit-filled people a gift
to the world. What happened to the Apostles, to the hundred
and twenty, and subsequently to the three thousand who were
baptized and became part of the Church, was for what the Lord
wanted to have happen through them in people and their society.
No sooner had the Holy Spirit been given than they were confronted by human need focused in the paralyzed beggar at The
Beautiful Gate of the temple.

It always happens that way. The dynamic dimension of the
immediacy and intimacy of the Holy Spirit is to galvanize us
into oneness in the Body of Christ, the Church. Then we are
to realize that the Church was born to be a blessing. The wind
of the Holy Spirit is to pick us up and carry us to people in need.
The fire of the Holy Spirit is to kindle warmth and affection for

others. This consuming fire is to burn out the chaff of judgmentalism, reserve, and exclusivism. The ecstasy of the personal praise unleashed in our emotions is to give us excitement for the ministry of the Spirit through us to others. The passion of Pentecost is for personal caring about people. The rapture is for responsibility.

But the tragedy is that many who are delighted by Pentecost are not ready for the demands of the Pentecostal age. We want to linger in chapter 2 of Acts, enjoying the Holy Spirit and other Spirit-filled people. But such eccentric exclusivism and esoteric enjoyment of others of the Spirit release little of its energizing power for the mission of Christ in the world. The result is a subculture with its own jargon and religious games. The qualifying questions are often, "Are you filled with the Spirit?" or "Are you charismatic?" The questions should be: "Has the Spirit's infilling impelled you to people in need?" "Have the gifts of the Holy Spirit equipped you for ministry?" "Is the fruit of the Spirit of love, joy, peace, long-suffering being fruitful in communicating Christ to others?"

The authentic test of Pentecost is what happened in Acts 3. We must stand with one foot in chapter 2 and the other foot in chapter 3 or we will not be able to remain for long, or walk with the Lord effectively. And that's just what we want to do now in this exposition. We want to discover how to use the power and passion of Pentecost for the paralysis of the world around us.

Acts 3 presents a threefold truth that must be understood through a tripartite thrust and treatment. Our focus will be first on a triumvirate of needs: in ourselves, in the particular people God has placed in our lives, and in our society. Then we will be ready for treatment of the passage through these three significant questions: What happened? Why did it happen? How does it happen now?

When Peter and John were on their way to the temple to pray following the evening sacrifice at 3:00 P.M., they met a habitual beggar who was brought each day to beg from those entering the temple to worship. The contrast of The Beautiful Gate and this pitiful paralytic must have been arresting. According to Josephus, the gate was fifty cubits high. He says, "It was adorned after a most costly manner, as having much rich plates of gold and silver." Made of Corinthian bronze, it was shaped in the form of a vine symbolizing Israel as the vine of God in the world's vineyard. It shone like gold in the sunshine, but the radiance of the metal was nothing to be compared with the Holy Spirit–filled radiance of Peter and John, who were living branches of the True Vine, the Messiah himself. They were incarnate intimations of the promise the Lord had made. "He who abides in me, and I in him, he it is that bears much fruit" (John 15:5).

Little did the beggar know that he was to be the fruit the Lord had promised. Any effective beggar can pick out from a sea of faces in a crowd those who would be responsive to his appeal. This beggar was immediately drawn to Peter and John. The Holy Spirit's love and joy were flashing from their faces. "Surely those two will give me some money," he thought, as he called to them. Sensitized with the empathy of the Holy Spirit, Peter and John had new eyes to see human suffering. The Spirit's gift of love and compassion pulsed through them as they looked at the beggar intently. The crowds swirled past them through the gate, but Peter and John were riveted on the paralytic as if he were the only person with them in Jerusalem. The beggar importuned them, reaching out his imploring hand in the hope of receiving alms. Peter's response has echoed through history as both prognosis and prescription. He told him that they did not have what he wanted but what he needed. "I have no silver or gold, but I give you what I have; in the name of Jesus Christ of Nazareth, walk" (Acts 3:6). He did not offer him fortification for his begging life, but faith for healing and the beginning of a new life. The Greek conveys the meaning that Peter seized the man's soliciting hand and raised him up. Immediately his feet and ankles were made strong. He leaped up and walked, and they entered the temple together. What a vivid picture Luke gives us of those three on their way to worship: Peter and John filled with joy and excitement that the living Christ through the Holy Spirit was at work in them; the healed paralytic expressing the uncontainable exuberance all three of them felt. "And [he] entered the temple with them, walking and leaping and praising God" (v. 8). He leaped with liberty, dancing to express his delight.

Now let's put this first miracle of the Spirit-filled Church

into a very personal context that will make the whole passage
so much more compelling. We must ask, "Who is the lame
man for us?" He is one of three persons; possibly all three at
once. Some of us are like the paralytic in some areas of our
lives. As we read this, we may become aware of an immense
immobility physically, emotionally, or interpersonally. We are
conscious of inabilities, inadequacies, and ineptnesses. We want
to love, but it's difficult. We want to express care, but we can't
get free of ourselves. We long to live a significant life, but we
are cornered by circumstances and people who seem immovable.
Ever feel paralyzed in body or spirit? Is your greatest need
right now most like the paralytic's? You need more than gold
or silver, analysis or surgery, therapy or theology! You need
healing! If that's where you are, let the full impact of this passage be that what happened to that man by The Beautiful Gate
is the beautiful gift God wants to give you also.

Others who read this may have their focus on some person
or persons in their lives who are lame and need healing. For
these the passage thunders a question: Why is it that I have
silver and gold to offer, but have never dared to utilize the
power of the name of Jesus of Nazareth to bring healing? In
the lives of all of us there are people who need Christ more
than they need anything that our silver or gold can offer. To
read and study this passage honestly, we must do what Peter
did: we must direct our fixed attention on them. The power of
Pentecost is for these very people, through us.

The third dimension of what happened there at the temple
is represented in the public paralysis all around us. By public
I mean social and cultural paralysis that results from structural
and corporate evil in our society. If we are to care deeply about
people, we must reach the taproot of the pollution in our communities and nation. How should we pray; what shall we do
about that? The amazing thing is that we have both the power
of the name of Jesus and the silver and gold he placed at our
disposal to heal human suffering. And what have we done with
either?

I hope that by this time in your reading of this discussion
you have brought three things into focus: (1) the paralyzed
dimensions of your own being which need healing; (2) the people who need Christ's healing through you; and (3) the evils in

our contemporary life which cause people to be frustrated and
paralyzed with injustice or inequality. What we will discover
now will empower us for all three. Keep them focused in your
mind indelibly.

This powerful chapter of Acts can be divided into three sec-
tions. Acts 3:1–10 deals with *what* actually happened; Acts
3:11–16 shows us *why* it happened; and Acts 3:17–26 reveals
how it can happen now. Study of these questions will afford us
the full impact of what the Lord wants to do with the paralytic
in us and in the people around us.

What actually happened that day in Jerusalem? Luke, the
physician, is very specific in the use of medical terms to describe the paralytic's congenital difficulty. The Greek word for
feet refers to the base or heels; the word for ankle bones refers
to the socket for the ankle and the heel. "Leaping up" describes
the sudden socketing of the heel and ankle. The bones had been
out of place, and an articulation, a joining or linking, occurred.
The language indicates that the process, which would normally
be corrected by a physician only over a long period of time,
happened in a split second.

The lame man was seized by Peter and pulled to his feet.
Note the elements of the healing. Peter looked at him intently,
prayerfully, as if seeking the discernment of the Spirit on what
to do. Then he proclaimed the name of Jesus Christ of Nazareth as the agent of healing in the man. In this time, the word
"name" actually carried the authority, power, and availability
of the person named. It was as if Peter had said, "The authority of Jesus over sickness, his power to heal human affirmities,
his presence here with us now—by that, rise and walk!" But
note, Peter then took the man by the hand and helped him up.
He made personal contact. He gave a hopeful hand of help!
Then the two dynamic forces were combined, Peter's Spirit-
filled lift and the Spirit of life working harmoniously together.
Both are necessary for healing; the Lord has deemed it so.
The Holy Spirit, the Divine Healer, now is available through
the agent of the Pentecost-powered, willing, expectant, trusting
representatives of the Church.

The amazement of the people prompted the answer to our
second question: why did this happen? The Scripture is clear
that Peter and John and the healed man went into the temple

to worship. The service of prayer took about half an hour. Can you imagine what praise and adoration must have surged from their hearts! The time of prayer gave Peter an opportunity to contemplate the startling, explosive truth that the healing miracle conveyed. The Holy Spirit penetrated his mind with gifts of wisdom and knowledge, followed by deep discernment. The purpose of Pentecost pounded through his thoughts. Christ is alive! He has come to live in us in his Holy Spirit. He is now ready to do through us what he did among us in his ministry. There is something about that name! Jesus! Savior! Healer! All the power of God which we witnessed in him is available to us!

While the three prayed, the crowds outside were ringing with rumor. "The beggar who is always at The Beautiful Gate. You know him! Lame since birth. Well, we saw him walk and leap and praise God! How did it happen? The disciples of the crucified one, Jesus of Nazareth, used his name to heal this man!" No wonder there was a great crowd waiting for them at Solomon's portico when they came out from evening prayers. Peter's explanation to them of what happened tells us irreducibly why it happened.

Peter wanted to make two things undeniably clear as he began to preach. First, there was no human piety or power in him and John which made the miracle possible. He wanted to take the attention off the human agents of the power and rivet the crowd's attention on the Power himself. To do that he pointed them to none other than the God of Abraham, Isaac, and Jacob. They should not be amazed or surprised by what he had done that day; it was but one more in a succession of miraculous interventions for his people through Israel's history. But the startling truth Peter went on to communicate was that the Lord God of Israel had come in his Messiah, who was none other than Jesus of Nazareth, whom they had crucified. What Peter preached was a refined Christology which had been engendered in him by the Holy Spirit. What the Spirit had revealed to him on the road to Caesarea-Philippi, intensified by the experience of the Transfiguration, and confirmed by the power of the Resurrection, now had been punctuated by the exclamation point of Pentecost. That experience completed Peter's knowledge of who Jesus was. As G. Campbell Morgan puts it, "In half an hour after Pentecost, they knew more about Jesus than they had ever known before."* The Spirit had taught Peter well, and now he could use cherished messianic Scriptures to drive home his point. Jesus was the Holy and Righteous One predicted in Isaiah 31:1 and 53:11; Zechariah 9:9; and Psalm 16:10. He was the servant Messiah of the Old Testament prophecy (Isa. 42:1–9; 49:1–13; 52:13–53:12). Yahweh had come in Jesus, whose name means "salvation from sin." The Spirit of the Lord was upon him, and by the same Spirit he did mighty wonders. The Spirit who raised him from the dead was the same Spirit whom they had just seen at work in the lame man.

Now Peter's Christology takes on glorious illumination through the guidance of the Holy Spirit. He calls Jesus the Author of Life. (Other translations of this passage use the expressions Pioneer of Life, Prince of Life, Guide of Life.) John, who was standing by Peter that day, put the same truth in arresting terms when he later wrote his Gospel: "In the beginning was the Word, and the Word was God. He was in the beginning with God; and all things were made through him; and without him was not anything made that was made. And the Word became flesh and dwelt among us, full of grace and truth; we have beheld his glory, glory as of the only Son from the Father. And from his fulness we have received, grace upon grace" (John 1:1–5, 14, 16). That Scripture carries the deep meaning of the title Author of Life. The actual full implication is "file leader," one who takes precedence, one who goes first. What that means to us is that the creative power of God through whom the world was made—the divine logos, the Word of God—is the same One who came as Messiah. He is the source of both life and salvation. He made us and remakes us through redemption. As Author of Life, he is originator, leader, and example. Hebrews 2:10 catches the same spectacular truth: "For it was fitting that he, for whom and by whom all things exist, in bringing many sons to glory, should make the pioneer of their salvation perfect through suffering."

In the light of this truth, Peter is ready to explain what hap-

---

* *The Acts of the Apostles* (New York and London: Fleming H. Revell Company, 1924), p. 32.

pened to the lame man: "And his name [the Author of Life], by faith in his name, has made this man strong whom you see and know; and the faith which is through Jesus has given the man this perfect health in the presence of you all" (Acts 3:16). A name stood for all that one is; therefore, the name of Jesus carried all the power of Creator, Messiah, resurrected Lord, immediate Presence. The name of Jesus released all the power of the Holy Spirit for a specific need. The qualities and power of a person were inherent in his name. By invoking the "name," Jesus' power and authority were called into action and mediated by his living presence in the Holy Spirit.

The miracle of the healing of the lame man had been done with the power and authority Jesus gave the disciples near the end of his ministry. The things he did they also would be able to do. "Truly, truly, I say to you, he who believes in me will also do the works that I do; and greater works than these will he do, because I go to the Father. Whatever you ask in *my name,* I will do it, that the Father may be glorified in the Son; if you ask anything in my name, I will do it" (John 14:12–14, emphasis mine). That's what Peter and John had done that day at The Beautiful Gate. By the name of Jesus, the power of the Author of Life, the man had been healed.

But who had the faith in the name? Peter and John, or the lame man? The answer to that is crucial for the needy people we focused on earlier. *The Living Bible* gets at a very crucial answer in the way it translates Peter's explanation. "Jesus' name has healed this man—and you know how lame he was before. Faith in Jesus' name—faith given us from God—has caused this perfect healing." It was the faith of Peter and John in the name that enabled the release of the power for healing.

That leaves us with an amazing realization: We have been called and chosen, given the freedom to respond to the love and forgiveness of the Cross, empowered by the infilling of the Holy Spirit, and now gifted with the gifts of the Spirit. One of the primary gifts of the Spirit-filled person is faith. The Spirit had given Peter and John this gift that day. That's why the miracle happened!

This gift is given to us. It is ours for the ministry we have with people and their needs. It makes us intrepidly daring in calling for the name to be released in the lives of the lame people all around us. The gift is expressed through prayer. By faith we dare to ask that the power of Christ's love, forgiveness, healing, guidance, and hope will be infused into the minds, emotions, and bodies of the people who desperately need him.

Some years after the healing of the lame man, the Apostle Paul tried to help the Philippians rediscover the authority and power over evil and human infirmity which had been given to them. "Therefore God has highly exalted him and bestowed on him the name which is above every name, that at the name of Jesus every knee should bow, in heaven and on earth and under the earth, and every tongue confess that Jesus Christ is Lord, to the glory of God the Father" (Phil. 2:9–11). That was Paul's creed for the facing of difficulty and for praying for the needs of others.

But can that happen now? That's what we all want to know. It's one thing for Peter and John to heal a lame man. They had known Christ in the flesh; they were fresh from Pentecost. What about us?

The answer to that is given in the last section of Peter's sermon. He clearly declares the messianic age. If the people would repent and accept Christ as Messiah, Lord, and Savior, they could participate in the liberating resources of God released for them through the Messiah. My understanding of Peter's words is that between the Resurrection and Pentecost and the Second Coming of Christ there would be times of unprecedented blessing through the presence and power of the Lord.

You and I are recipients of the promises of this period of blessing. We can realize it through the same response Peter called for from the people that day: "Repent therefore, and turn again, that your sins may be blotted out." That's what we can do to enter into the messianic age. It means turning from our own devices and resources, confessing our independence and efforts to live on our own strength. Peter promises times of refreshing and restitution, the cool balm of forgiveness and joy, the replenishment of our inadequacy with the presence of the Lord.

But it means something more—a great deal more. The promises to ancient Israel for the messianic age are now given to us, the Church, the New Israel. Astounding authority and power are given to us. What Paul prayed for the church at Ephesus, I pray for the Church in America:

> That the God of our Lord Jesus Christ, the Father of glory, may give you a spirit of wisdom and of revelation in the knowledge of him, having the eyes of your hearts enlightened, that you may know what is the hope to which he has called you, what are the riches of his glorious inheritance in the saints, and what is the immeasurable greatness of his power in us who believe, according to the working of his great might which he accomplished in Christ when he raised him from the dead and made him sit at his right hand in the heavenly places, far above all rule and authority and power and dominion, and above every name that is named, not only in this age but also in that which is to come; and he has put all things under his feet and has made him the head over all things for the church, which is his body, the fulness of him who fills all in all (Eph. 1:17–23).

That declares what is available to your congregation and mine. We need not wring our hands in frustration. We are not a powerless minority in the face of evil. We can change the course of history, we can alter the trend of evil in our society, we can liberate people—if we will pray in the name of Jesus Christ.

Prayer is the secret weapon of the Church and Christ's people. Once again focus on the triad of concerns for anything which is crippled in us, the people of our lives and society. How much time have we spent in prayer for them? Have we evoked the name of Jesus for the needs of people and society he has placed on our hearts? When Paul wrote instructions to Timothy on how to unlock the uncalculable riches of Christ, he said, "First of all, then, I urge that supplications, prayers, intercessions, and thanksgivings be made for all men, for kings and all who are in high positions, that we may lead a quiet and peaceable life, godly and respectful in every way. This is good, and it is acceptable in the sight of God our Savior, who desires all men to be saved and to come to the knowledge of the truth. For there is one God, and there is one mediator between God and men, the man Christ Jesus" (1 Tim. 2:1–5).

The urging admonition is that we are to pray for people. At the top of the list are our prayers for people in authority. That means local, state, and national officials. Bad laws and ineffective government are the direct result of inadequate prayer by the people of God. Prayer for the nation in the name of Jesus means prayer for God-appointed people to be elected regardless of party. And it also means that we pray for those who are elected and who hold offices controlling our lives. Good government enables the free preaching of the gospel. We need only to survey history to realize what happens to the Church when freedom of speech and assembly is denied.

There are also specific manifestations of evil which arise in society at particular times which must be confronted with prayer in Jesus' name. Coupled with that is the Spirit-guided action these prayers clarify. Prayer is itself action, and it delineates the specific steps we are to take in the implementation of those prayers. If we were to make a list of officials in government and pray daily for them, I believe we would see results. Then if we made a list of the most crucial problems in our local communities and united as congregations to pray, we would not only experience the intervention of God, but we would begin both to see what we are doing to contribute to the evil ourselves and to discern practical things our Lord wants us to do.

This study of Acts 3 has stirred me deeply. I hope for nothing less for you. There are basic conclusions which leave us uncomfortable.

1. The Holy Spirit has come in a fresh, new Pentecost in our time. Have I received the Holy Spirit? Is my heart his home?
2. I have been called to be part of the Church, the Body of Christ. Have I surrendered my separatistic independence to become one in mind and heart with a fellowship of adventurers in the Spirit?
3. Have I, and have we as congregations, recognized and realized the power that is given to us through the Holy Spirit?
4. Have I utilized the power of prayer in Jesus' name for the lame in myself, in others, and in society?
5. Have I accepted the awesome truth that God will not bypass his people and their prayers and that if I do not pray his blessings will not be given?

The answers to these questions put me in the place of the

beggar outside The Beautiful Gate. I have been asking for things, alms of material blessings. The healing and release of paralysis of Spirit: that's what I need! What of you?

Then, suddenly, I remember that that lame man was not the first paralytic to be healed in Jerusalem. The other was at the Pool of Bethesda. Jesus put the question to him that we all must answer. "Do you want to be healed?" Then he takes us by the hand and lifts us out of our impotence. Now we can see what we are to do. Like Peter and John, we are to be agents of healing in Jesus' name.

CHAPTER 4

From Boredom and Blandness to Boldness

Acts 4

A friend of mine gave me a book with a title which captured my attention: *Blessed John Ogilvie, Martyred in
Scotland.* Though I was not named for him, I was anxious to
learn what this Ogilvie had done to get into trouble. I found
that John Ogilvie had left the Calvinist persuasion to become a
Jesuit priest and that there are conflicting stories about the
nature of his crime. Some say he was caught saying the Mass;
others indicate that he was punished for treasonous plotting
against the life of James VI. Whichever it was, he was hanged
in Glasgow in 1615, the only post-Reformation Roman Catholic
to be martyred in Scotland.

His memory is not dead, however. Recently a man by the
name of John Fagan was healed of cancer by wearing a medal
of Blessed John Ogilvie. Fagan's wife prayed for Ogilvie's intercession, and her husband was cured. The Vatican has now
decided that the miracle did take place, and it seems probable
that John Ogilvie will be raised to "sainthood."

I was left to rethink my definitions of *martyr* and *saint.* Since
the Scriptures clearly designate all believers in Christ as saints,
my beleaguered namesake will not be given any title he did not
have in his lifetime, however misguided his convictions may have
been. As for calling him martyr, I had to reflect a long time on
whether saying the Mass or plotting against James was worthy
of the title.

Another friend gave me an article about the proposed canoni-

47

zation. The heading of the article was the same as the book, only my friend had crossed out three of the words and added another. It now read, *Lloyd John Ogilvie, Martyred*. We both laughed about that. Then we had a very serious conversation about what we would be willing to die for. "Saint" John Ogilvie had stirred up some challenging reflection.

In America we enjoy spiritual freedom. But what if we lost that blessing and it became a crime to be a Christian? If we were brought to trial, what evidence, material and circumstantial, would the prosecutor be able to use to convict us? Most of us would never be brought to trial, much less convicted, because so little about what we do and say could be identified as Christ's power in us.

Why is it that we find it so difficult to talk about what we believe and act on the convictions we hold dearly but never express daringly?

A printer's mistake in a church bulletin was inadvertently on target. The statement, meant to express appreciation to the previous pastors who had served the church, was supposed to have read, "The Christians of this church are deeply thankful for our Pastors Emeriti." A pastor emeritus is one who has recognition and honor but no power. In the bulletin, the words *Christians* and *Pastors* were reversed. The statement read, "The Pastors of this church are thankful for our Christians Emeriti." Not far from the truth except for the word *thankful!* There is no emeritus status for any Christian. We are called by Christ to express his power and communicate his grace. The Christian life is not bland or boring; it's a life of boldness. The blessing of Pentecost was boldness. The early Christians in Acts were marked by the boldness of their Spirit-filled lives.

What a convicting, convincing comparison Luke gives us in Acts 4. Here are two assemblies of God's people, the Sanhedrin and the early Church. Both believed they were being faithful and obedient to the truth. One was protective and defensive; the other was powerful and dynamic. One believed it was appointed to conserve the past, keep the peace, and conserve the status quo. The other believed it was called to communicate the love of God, witness to a miraculous intervention of his power, and to live in the resources of his persistent presence. One was maintained for preservation; the other was maintained by prayer.

One was based on what God had given long before; the other was based on what God was doing right then. One was symbolized by blandness and boredom; the other by boldness. The Sanhedrin and the early Church—what a comparison, indeed! In it we see crystallized two types of Christians and two examples of what the Church can be today. The disturbing questions are: In which assembly would we be most comfortable? If we had to identify our congregation, the Church in America, would it be most like the Sanhedrin or the early Church?

Look at what Luke had to say to spell out the comparison. The Sanhedrin was the highest ruling body of the Jews. It was made up of seventy leaders plus the high priest, who served as president. In verse 5 of this chapter, Luke reminds us of the three groups represented in the seventy. The rulers were the chief priests of the temple. Each was appointed to represent one of the twenty-four courses or groupings of priests who served on a weekly rotation in the temple to perform the sacrifices and maintain the purity and propriety of worship. The elders were the tribal or family heads of the nation. The scribes were experts in the Law and the oral tradition, the accumulated implications of the Law for practice in daily life.

There were two religious parties in the seventy in the Sanhedrin. One was the Pharisees, many of whom were scribes. They were vigilant, nationalistic leaders who felt deeply the responsibility for preservation of the Law, the tradition of the Hebrew people, and the most minute detail of the regulations of their religion. They abhorred foreign domination, admitted the possibility of spirits, accepted the idea of resurrection, and awaited the coming of Messiah, but only according to their carefully defined presuppositions. Most of them had arisen from the trade class and were known for impeccable legalism.

The Sadducees were the landed gentry of the time. They controlled the wealth, owned most of the land, and wielded immense power. Collaboration with foreign conquerors was a necessary evil for the maintenance of their material position. They wanted peace at any price, and the price became exorbitantly high under Roman domination. They wanted no disturbance of the balance of power, the détente they had carefully worked out with the Roman government. As the wealthy aristocracy, they held control of the purse strings and kept them tightly closed around their holdings. Theologically, they were guided by clearly defined convictions which were often in direct opposition to those of the Pharisees. They did not believe in the resurrection, a life beyond the grave, or the spirit realm of either angels or devils. They did not anxiously await, long for, or anticipate the messianic kingdom, for very specific political reasons. The turbulence and conflict that it would bring would surely threaten their financial security. Resurrection became synonymous with revolution. According to Foakes-Jackson, "To the Jew of this time, it meant imminent world catastrophe, in which the powers of the earth would be destroyed and a new order miraculously set up."* This would mean disturbance for those who desperately wanted to keep things as they were. Now we can see why the Pharisees opposed Jesus and the Sadducees abhorred the early Christians. In this light we can understand how the plot thickened in Luke's account of the first trial of the early Christians. It was the Sadducean party which precipitated the conflict and was enraged at what the early Church was, did, and believed. The issues are crystal clear:

They preached the Resurrection.

They proclaimed a living Lord.

They lived by a spiritual power through the Holy Spirit.

They performed miracles which were undeniable proof of their power through the Holy Spirit.

After the healing of the lame man at The Beautiful Gate, the crowds gathered on Solomon's portico with agitated wonder and amazement. Peter clearly identified the source of the healing as the name of Jesus Christ of Nazareth and the release of his power through his living presence with them in the Holy Spirit. He forcefully preached that the Christ, whom the Jews had crucified, had been resurrected and was alive, continuing his miraculous ministry through the Apostles.

When word of what Peter had said reached the Sadducees, they were gripped by fear and consternation. They quickly gathered the temple police, who were stationed about the temple to keep law and order, and the chief priests, whose concern was

---

* F. J. Foakes-Jackson, *The Acts of the Apostles,* Moffatt New Testament Commentary (New York: Harper and Bros., 1931), p. 32.

making peaceful sacrifices to a distant and wholly other God of Israel's past. The Sadducees were the instigators of the arrest after they heard the inflammatory preaching of Peter. *The Living Bible* translation states the issue poignantly. The Sadducees were "very disturbed that Peter and John were claiming that Jesus had risen from the dead." They could have called the Sanhedrin together immediately, but it was already evening by this time, and Jewish law forbade a trial after sundown. Peter and John were thrown into jail. The Sadducees had the hours of the night to gather their forces and be sure that their party was represented in a majority, thus tipping off the balance of power with the Pharisees, when they brought Peter and John to trial the next morning.

The presentation of the case against the two men the next morning was not easy. The lame man was with them as a material witness of their power. Everyone present had been familiar with this beggar who had been lame for forty years and daily had been brought to The Beautiful Gate to beg. Perhaps many of them had been interrupted on the way to worship by his importuning. That he now was healed and able to stand, walk and leap, no one could deny.

But it was the quality of boldness in Peter and John which confounded them. Amazingly articulate, forceful, and daring, Peter and John knew what they believed and were able to state it impellingly, using familiar Scriptures and profound theological formulations. Where did they get this boldness? As the Sanhedrin listened, the Apostles' words were painfully familiar. They had heard them before! They sounded like Jesus of Nazareth whom this very court had tried in the illegal dark of night. Perhaps both Peter and John were on criminal "wanted lists" because of their devoted discipleship to the Nazarene rabbi whom the leaders thought they had destroyed forever.

But Peter and John were so convincingly articulate! Where did they get this learning which in some ways exceeded the most learned expression? They were untrained fishermen, without authorized theological education. No doubt about it—they had been with Jesus. The grammar of the Sanhedrin's surmise is telling. They simply asserted that Peter and John had been followers of Jesus in his earthly ministry. Little did they compre-

hend that the Apostles had been with him the day before healing
the lame man and that the resurrected Lord was with them
right then!

There had to be some way to trap them, to establish some
charge. The Sadducees among the Sanhedrin led the crossexami-
nation, longing to establish evidence which would convince
their fellow party members that Peter and John were worthy of
condemnation or death. Obviously Deuteronomy 13:1–5 was
used as the basis of the trial:

> "If a prophet arises among you, or a dreamer of dreams, and gives
> you a sign or a wonder, and the sign or wonder which he tells you
> comes to pass, and if he says, 'Let us go after other gods,' which
> you have not known, 'and let us serve them,' you shall not listen
> to the words of that prophet or to that dreamer of dreams; for the
> Lord your God is testing you, to know whether you love the Lord
> your God with all your heart and with all your soul. You shall
> walk after the Lord your God and fear him, and keep his com-
> mandments and obey his voice, and you shall serve him and
> cleave to him. But that prophet or that dreamer of dreams shall
> be put to death, because he has taught rebellion against the Lord
> your God, who brought you out of the house of bondage, to make
> you leave the way in which the Lord your God commanded you
> to walk. So you shall purge the evil from the midst of you."

The idea was that anyone performing a sign had to prove that
it was of God and that it was used to honor and glorify him
and to lead people closer to him. That's exactly where the Sadducees failed. Peter and John had done both. They gave God
the glory and called the people to praise him for it.

The hands of the Sanhedrin were tied. The undeniable evidence of the authentic miracle stood before them—the lame
man, well and irrefutably energetic. All they could do was warn
Peter and John and charge them never again to speak in or of
the name of Jesus. What a futile attempt! It was like trying to
reverse the direction of a fast-moving stream or hold back the
undauntable winds of a hurricane. What a pitiful plea they
made to each other: "What shall we do with these men?" Sounds
painfully like Pilate's equivocating exhortation, "What shall I do
with this man you call your King?" (Mark 15:12, *The Living
Bible*). Their frustration is further amplified: "We can't deny

that they have done a tremendous miracle, and everybody in Jerusalem knows about it. But perhaps we can stop them from spreading their propaganda. We'll tell them that if they do it again, we'll really throw the book at them" (Acts 4:16–17, *The Living Bible*).

The threats they leveled at Peter and John were to no avail. The answer both gave was powerful: "You decide whether God wants us to obey you instead of him! We cannot stop telling about the wonderful things we saw Jesus do and heard him say" (Acts 4:19–20, *The Living Bible*). What could the Sanhedrin do with that? If they punished Peter and John, it would start a riot among the people with whom the Apostles had great favor. Everyone was praising God for the miraculous healing of the lame man. More threats, more promises of reprisal—that was all they could do. They released the two men, hoping against hope that it would be the last time they would see or hear anything of them.

Then Peter and John returned to the fellowship of the Church. Here surely is the explanation of the boldness of the early Christians. They gathered together to pray. And what was the content of their supplication? For boldness! In the prayers of the Church we hear the substance and the source of the boldness of Peter and John we witnessed in Luke's account of the arrest and trial of the Apostles.

Let us consider first the substance of their boldness and then evaluate its source in the prayers of the Church. The word *boldness* means lucid and daring statement. In the Greek the word is *parrēsia*, "telling it all" (*pan rēsis*). It is both the conviction and enunciation of undeniable truths. There could be no mistaking the meaning. Boldness is the blunt, almost blatant and defiant enunciation that arrests attentions, compelling people to listen. There is no apology, no faltering, but a "thus saith the Lord" clarity. The Apostles had a sanctified stubbornness. Their hearts were possessed by a great affection, and their minds were directed by a clear purpose declared with liberating freshness. Boldness is rooted in the truth we have realized, expressed in the daily witness, and acted out in undeniable evidence of its implications.

When we review our text in chapter 4 we see the motive for and nature of the boldness of Peter and John.

First, the Resurrection, this essential miracle of God, made
courageous people out of cowards. If death was not an ending,
but a transition in living, they could face anything and endure
everything. Christ's death and resurrection set them free to live
with joy. His words were the drumbeat in their hearts. "I am
the resurrection and the life; he who believes in me, though he
die, yet shall he live, and whoever lives and believes in me shall
never die" (John 11:25–26). Resurrection and life—the two
must be kept together. The fact that Christ arose is one thing,
but that he is with us is something even greater.

The second reason for the remarkable lives of the Apostles
was their experience of the risen Christ. Because he was alive
they could face all of the limitations of life with daring. It was
by the power and authority of his name that they feared no one
and no thing. Peter said, "It is by his authority that this man
stands here healed!" (Acts 4:10, *The Living Bible*).

The third reason was this tangible miracle which had been
performed. They realized that the power of the living Christ
was at work through them. The actual manifestation of healing
quickened their faith.

The fourth motivation was the objective standard of Scripture. In his speech Peter quoted Psalm 118:22 ("The stone
which the builders rejected has become the head of the corner.")
and Isaiah 28:16 ("Therefore thus says the Lord God, 'Behold,
I am laying in Zion for a foundation a stone, a tested stone, a
precious cornerstone, of a sure foundation: "He who believes
will not be in haste." ' "). Jesus was the fulfillment of the prophets of old. He was the foundation stone or the keystone at the
top of a corner, binding the walls together where they meet.
Perhaps Peter meant both ideas. The point is that when we are
founded on Scripture, on something more than our own sub-
jective ideas and feelings, we are able to move forward with
unlimited audacity. Added to the Scriptures of the Old Testament, the objective standard for these Apostles was the life and
message of Jesus. They knew what to do and what to say because
they remembered what he had done and said.

The fifth reason was that they were filled with the Holy Spirit.
Note in Luke's account that there is a difference between being
"full of the Holy Spirit" and being "filled with the Holy Spirit."
The first begins when we surrender our lives and open our-

selves to be the container and transmitter of the living Spirit of God. The second comes for special need and opportunity of ministry and witness with people and in the world. In verse 8 Luke tells us that Peter was "filled." The past aorist passive participle *plētheis*, "filled," indicates an act performed upon Peter, rather than a continuing state, and refers to a promise Jesus had made his disciples: "And when they bring you before the synagogues and the rulers and the authorities, do not be anxious how or what you are to answer or what you are to say; for the Holy Spirit will teach you in that very hour what you ought to say" (Luke 12:11–12). The crucial truth to remember is that the Holy Spirit is both sanctifier and source of special strength. It is by the Spirit's gift of faith that we believe; it is through the influence of the Spirit that we grow in assurance and Christlike character; but it is also by a special outpouring that we become equipped for a unique situation, problem, challenge, or extremity. The worst that can happen to us always brings about the best that the Spirit has to give us. When Peter was "filled with the Holy Spirit," the Spirit took possession of his mind, saturated his emotions, compelled his will and pulsated in his body. That's why Peter and the early Church had boldness! Johannes Weiss says about the early Christians that they had "a tempestuous enthusiasm, an overwhelming intensity of feeling, an immediate awareness of the presence of God, an inconquerable sense of power, and an irresistible control over the will and inner spirit and even the physical conditions of other men—these are the ineradicable features of historic early Christianity."*

The sixth reason for the boldness of the early Christians was not just that Jesus saves but that only Jesus saves. An exclusion led to a bold inclusiveness. When we believe that our Lord is not only the best of good men, or one savior among many, we are filled with an urgency which expresses itself in boldness.

Recently a woman jumped from a burning building many floors down into the net held by sturdy firemen. Later she was asked, "How could you do it? Where did you get the courage?" She answered, "I had to do it. It was my only chance!"

---

* *Earliest Christianity: A.D. 30–150*, 2 vols. (New York: Harper & Row, 1959), 1:42–43.

That's the way the disciples felt. They would agree with
E. Stanley Jones's blunt alternative: "Christ or chaos." The
various translations of the verve of verse 12 are impelling. Moffatt says: "There is no salvation by anyone else, nor even a
second name under heaven appointed for us men and our salvation." *The Living Bible* renders it: "There is salvation in no
one else! Under all heaven there is no other name for men to
call upon to save them." The key word is *salvation,* which actually means healing and health, wholeness and oneness.
Through Christ's Cross and indwelling power we are reconciled
to God, renewed in self-acceptance, released from guilt and
self-justification, reunited with others in accepting love, and
reconstituted as agents of hope in the world. No other religion
or cult can promise that!

Now we can understand boldness: it was clear vision, absolute certainty, strong conviction, and unflinching courage. Contemporary Christians and the Church of our time have no greater
need. How shall we find it? The prayers of the early Church at
the conclusion of chapter 4 give us the secret of the source
of strength.

What an amazing response the Church gave to Peter and
John's report—not fear, nor wavering trepidation, but prayer.
We need to consider this prayer as a model, for it gives an outline of how they sustained their boldness. Note the convictions
which saturated their prayer and supplications.

The undergirding conviction was of the absolute sovereignty
of God over all life. "Sovereign Lord, who didst make the
heaven and the earth and the sea and everything in them. . . ."
The word for "Lord" here is different from the one used else-
where in the New Testament. In this case it is *despota,* meaning "despot," or in its deeper implication, "absolute ruler, final
sovereign, master." There was no doubt in the Church that the
Lord was in charge of all things. Coupled closely with this
faith was the assurance that what was happening to them was
no different from what had happened through the ages. Their
hope was not in men. They had learned that only the Lord was
worthy of trust. The painful difficulties they were facing were
not unlike what happened to David, who had asked their question years before. They were in good company! Based on Psalm
2:1–2 they prayed, "Why did the Gentiles rage, and the peo-

ples imagine vain things? The kings of the earth set themselves in array, and the rulers were gathered together, against the Lord and against his Anointed." It's a great comfort to know that God's faithful people have always been in trouble. In fact, it's a sure sign that we are obeying God rather than men. So what's new about persecution for righteousness' sake? Jesus called it blessed.

But we can deal with that only if we're sure of the next thing the Church prayed. They claimed God's overruling. He had allowed the Cross, but had the final word in the Resurrection. So the Church could pray, "For truly in this city there were gathered together against thy holy servant Jesus, whom thou didst anoint, both Herod and Pontius Pilate, with the Gentiles and the peoples of Israel, to do whatever thy hand and thy plan had predestined to take place." Jesus was not a helpless victim. God was in Christ, there on Calvary with him. What men thought was the worst they could do to get rid of Jesus was used for the best that God could give, because he would never rid himself of man and his needs. God can use anything that happens to us. He constantly brings good out of evil or difficulty. Nothing is meaningless. He has an ultimate plan. We can never drift beyond his overruling intervention.

Those convictions are now expressed in confidence. The rhythms of the prayer quicken. "Now Lord, look upon their threats, and grant to thy servants to speak thy word with all boldness." They ask for more of the very thing that had gotten them into trouble and driven them to prayer. Amazing! But note the reason: "while thou stretchest out thy hand to heal." They were asking God to continue the healings which had caused such consternation. Keep it up, Lord; we're ready! They knew that all power in heaven and earth was theirs through the name of Jesus. Nothing could stop the movement now. "And signs and wonders are performed through the name of thy holy servant Jesus." What a conclusion to a daring prayer. The spectacular events spread across the pages of Acts must all be traced back to praying like that.

The Lord's answer to the prayer was that the room where they were assembled was shaken, an outward indication of the Lord's presence in the Holy Spirit. "And they were all filled with the Holy Spirit and spoke the word of God with boldness."

Again Luke uses the word *filled,* this time in the aorist passive indicative. A special filling occurred and they spoke with boldness. Inflow and outgo were in direct proportion. They were especially equipped for the particular task.

Where do you need the gift of boldness today, this next week? Can you picture yourself as God's bold person there with that situation or person? How would you act; what would you say; what would you dare? Perhaps it's a word or an act of love which inhibition has debilitated, or a witness you have been reluctant to make because of fear or embarrassment or timidity. Or perhaps it's a reconciliation or restitution that must be performed at great cost of pride and prejudice. Or maybe it's taking a stand for what you believe at home or at work or among people whose approval you desperately need. Then too, it may be stepping out in faith to confront some social evil even at the loss of financial comfort or security. Picture that vividly. Then ask for a special filling of the Holy Spirit. He is undeniably faithful. He will give us power to act and speak with boldness, and life will be thrilling again—be sure of that. We will have moved from blandness and boredom to boldness!

CHAPTER 5

Body Life

Acts 4:32–5:16

Very late one evening, I told a friend that I was going down to the church. He playfully, but pointedly, drew attention to the error in my terminology. "Oh, are there Christians meeting together at this hour for study and prayer?"

He had me. What I said was not what I meant. I should have said, "I'm going down to the building where the Church often meets."

To go to church is not to go to a place, but to gather together with a particular kind of people, with a peculiar purpose and a very special power. Avery and Marsh have composed a lovely folk song which proclaims that I am the church, you are the church, and we are the church together; that the church is not its buildings or a steeple, but rather its people.

When you see or hear the word *church*, what flashes into your mind? A building, a denomination, an organization, a cultural social structure? Or do you think of Christ's people?

For Luke, writing his account of the acts of the Holy Spirit, there was no such confusion. The first time he used the word *church*, it was drenched with meaning. He used the Greek word *ekklesia*, which meant those who were called out and called together. It implied both realities for him. The early Christians had been called out, called to the Lord and called into fellowship with each other. Luke's initial use of the word in Acts 5:11 comes at the conclusion of one of his most powerful descriptions of the fellowship of the early Christians. In Acts 4:32—

5:14, he dramatizes the reality of the word in both the quality and qualifications of life which these Holy Spirit-filled people exemplified. He tells us how they lived and worked together: in Barnabas he illustrates what that meant and in Ananias and Sapphira what it should not mean. We are left with a staggering picture of the Church as it was meant to be and a startling presentation of what it is always in danger of becoming.

The most vivid synonym for the word *Church* which is used throughout the New Testament is "the Body of Christ." The company of Christ's people, in communion with him and one another, was the divine agent called to continue his ministry in the world. Paul, declaring this vividly to the Corinthians, compares the Body of Christ to the physical body: "For just as the body is one and has many members, and all the members of the body, though many, are one body, so it is with Christ. For by one Spirit [source] we were all baptized [the experience of the Spirit] into one body. Jews or Greeks, slaves or free, and all were made to drink of one Spirit [the birth of the church]" (1 Cor. 12:12–13).

Then Paul shows how all parts of the physical body are equally essential. The hand, the ear, the eye, the lesser parts of the body cannot say, "I have no need of you." The suggestion is that the members of the Church are mutually dependent in the same way. "If one member suffers, all suffer together; if one member is honored, all rejoice together." That contradicts what a Science of Mind woman said about her ailing leg. "It is sick, but I am not sick. That leg does not belong to me, because I am well." How absurd!

Paul climaxes his example of the Church's being like the body with the triumphant challenge, "Now you are the body of Christ and individually members of it" (1 Cor. 12:12–13).

In recent years, a term has been used extensively to describe the essence of the Church. It is "body life," and refers to what Christians are and what they do as the called-out, called-together people of God. In this passage of Acts, Luke tells us what the body life of the early Church was like. It stands as the irreducible maximum, scripturally and historically, of what we are to rediscover as the authentic Church today. There is no more pressing item on God's agenda for us than to study and absorb this passage, allowing it to be the charter and charge for the Church in America.

Luke tells us that there were three dynamic elements which gave birth to the Church as the Body of Christ. "Now the company of those who *believed* were of one *heart* and *soul"* (emphasis mine). Body life is experienced by those who believe alike, who have one heart and one soul. The three encompass our minds, emotions, and wills. There can be no fellowship without all three. Confusion of belief results in distortion of relationships as 1 John 1:7 clarifies: "If we walk in the light, as he is in the light, we have fellowship one with another." Belief in Christ as a gift of the Holy Spirit galvanized the early Christians in thought, affection, and life purpose. They believed that Jesus was the Christ, that God had raised him from the dead, that he was present with them in the Holy Spirit, that he was their absolute Lord of all life, and that their purpose was to share his love with each other and the world.

It's amazing how we have fragmented these basic elements today. No wonder there is little body life in most congregations. Our minds, hearts, and souls often are not one! Unified beliefs are essential for any congregation. But intellectual agreement on a statement of faith can be sterile conceptualism without the expression of relational warmth. We all know Christians who think alike but have little love for each other or concern for mutual needs.

But to be of one soul goes even deeper. The soul is the life verve in us. When Christians are of one soul, it means that the Holy Spirit who lives in each has brought unity of direction and goals. We breathe the same "life breath" spiritually and are guided in a unified functioning together.

How does that happen? It is important to remember that the unity of belief, affection, and direction in the early Church had come as a gift of the Holy Spirit. The effusion of Pentecost had produced the effectiveness of the fellowship. It was a miracle. People are not naturally of one heart and soul. Everything in our sinful, willful, human nature works against that. We cannot produce or program fellowship. I often smile when I see an announcement in a church bulletin that there will be a time of fellowship after a church service. That's an audacious assumption! There will not be fellowship during or after the service unless the Holy Spirit has made us of one mind and heart. There may be a social hour of pleasant conviviality, but fellowship will be a gift.

Luke goes on to describe the result of being of one heart and soul. There was a complete lack of defensiveness, protectiveness, or individualism. "No one said that any of the things he possessed was his own, but they had everything in common." That implies that the Church was a fellowship of people who believed that all they individually possessed belonged to the Church for the common good of all. This was not forced equality but voluntary sharing. They had everything in common because they had Christ and his unifying spirit in common. The Greek word for fellowship, *koinonia,* has as its root the word *common.* Paul ended his trinitarian benediction which delineated the ways God has of being God by "the Communion of the Holy Spirit" (2 Cor. 13:14). Again the word is *koinonia.* Through the Holy Spirit we are fellow participants in Christ and in a life of mutual love, sharing, and caring. A Korean learning English said, "Fellowship is 'fellows in same ship.' " He was getting close.

We are told that there was not a needy person among those early Christians. Why? Because those who had possessions sold what they had and brought the proceeds to the Apostles to be distributed among those who had need.

Body life in the Church is expressed in the way we care about each other. All that we have is given as a gift to us for each other. Each time we have communion in our church an essential part of the celebration is the special offering for the deacon's fund, which is distributed to those in need. One church I know about allows people to put in and take out monies when the collection plate is passed at communion. The "haves" and the "have-nots" are equally blessed!

Now note the outward expression of the body-life *koinonia* of the early Church. The Apostles gave their testimony to the Resurrection with great power. There was consistency between the life and message of the Church. What they proclaimed they exemplified. The quality of their fellowship did not contradict what they preached. They had become their message.

All this made possible the essence of body life: "Great grace was upon them all." That's the supreme expression of the Church as the Body of Christ. Grace, the Lord's uninvited favor, flowed among them and through them from the Spirit to each other. Affirmation, esteem, enabling acceptance was experienced and expressed. It was a gracious Church living under the shadow of the Cross. Each person knew that he had been saved by grace, healed by grace, and nurtured in grace. Grace became the life blood of the Body.

No sensitive churchman today can read this account without being forced to wonder what happened to that quality of life through history or where his own congregation is in comparison with it. Institutionalism has built fine buildings, but have we built great people? We have well-organized programs and slick brochures, highly trained professionals and carefully defined procedures. Luke's account mocks our lack of gracious caring and costly sharing. His illustrations of those in the Jerusalem church who exemplified and contradicted its body life force us to look at ourselves honestly.

The body life of the Church is personified in a Levite from Cyprus named Joseph. He was a cousin of John Mark, whose home had provided Jesus and his disciples the Upper Room for Passover. Subsequently it became the site of Pentecost and the central meeting place of the Apostles as the infant Church grew. Joseph was a wealthy man. Through the influence of the Apostles, he heard the gospel and responded with the commitment of all that he was and owned. Obviously the influence of the Holy Spirit, coupled with the warmth and acceptance in the body life of the church, resulted in a gratitude which he expressed by selling a piece of property and giving the proceeds to the Apostles for the needs of his fellow members of the Body of Christ. He had experienced a penetrating personality transformation which produced a magnanimous generosity. This earned him a new name symbolic of his new life in Christ.

The Apostles nicknamed him Barnabas. The name is filled with symbolic meaning. In Hebrew this would have meant *bar* ("son of") *nebhû'āh* ("prophecy") or "son of prophecy." The Aramaic was *bar-newahâ'*, meaning "a son of refreshment." The gift of prophecy in the early Church made a person profoundly aware of what the Spirit of the Lord was saying to individuals and the Church. It was a "thus saith the Lord" clarity and urgency. A New Testament prophet could see what should be done because of what God's Spirit was miraculously unveiling to him in his prayers. The Hebrew and Aramaic converge on a central meaning. The Word of the Lord, boldly and lovingly declared, brought prophetic direction and refreshment.

But Luke leaves little to the imagination about what the name Barnabas meant to the Church and how Joseph expressed it. In a powerful parenthesis he uses the Greek words *huios parakleseos*. The same basic word is used by Jesus to describe the ministry of the Holy Spirit: "And I will pray the Father, and he will give you another *Counselor,* to be with you forever, even the Spirit of truth" (John 14:16). Here the word *parakletos* is used to mean "one who is called to one's side to help, one who strengthens and enables one to stand." In John's first letter to the early Church the same word is used for Jesus' intercessory ministry with the Father: "If any one does sin, we have an *advocate* with the Father, Jesus Christ the righteous" (1 John 2:1). The idea becomes clear: the paraclete is one who helps, exhorts, encourages, intercedes, and empowers. Joseph had distinguished himself for all these qualities. Thus the King James Version translates the Greek of Luke's parenthesis about him as "Son of consolation," the American Standard Version as "Son of exhortation," and the Revised Standard Version as "Son of encouragement." All these translations are reaching for a clear interpretation of what Luke was trying to express. Joseph earned a magnificent title. His life was like Jesus' reconciling ministry with the Father and like the Holy Spirit's ministry within the believer. He was an exhorter who could be with people in such a way that they could see and hear the next steps of their growth in Christ. He was a counselor who tenderly expressed the forgiveness, acceptance, and viability of Christ's love. But he was certainly an encourager, one who imparted and imputed courage and daring in others. As an encourager he could affirm people, help them to be delighted in themselves, and dare to be the persons God called them to be. All of this was expressed so loudly in what he did that people were open to hear what he was saying.

One of the most memorable examples of Barnabas's encouraging ministry was with John Mark, recorded later in Acts. Mark had defected during the first missionary journey with Paul and

Barnabas. When it came time to make a fresh journey to preach the gospel, Paul refused to take Mark along. Barnabas interceded for his cousin, and, when Paul persisted in his refusal, he took Mark and worked with him. The great Christian leader and author of the first written Gospel who Mark became owed much to the encouragement Barnabas communicated to him.

Every time Barnabas is mentioned in Acts, he is bringing encouragement. His ministry with Paul, his faithfulness to the Apostles in prison, and his constant affirmation of the new Christians indicate that he lived up to the name he was given. We wonder if he was naturally an encourager. Probably not. Rather, this quality must have been the result of the grace of Christ in his life.

What happened to Barnabas can happen to us. In fact, if Christ has not made us encouragers, there is real question about the depth of our salvation and the extent to which we have trusted our relationships to him. The world around us is filled with discouraged people who desperately need encouragement. Mates, children, friends, fellow church members—all need encouragement.

The ministry of encouragement is actually the most effective way of teaching and communicating hope for people. We all know our shortcomings all too well. But who knows our struggles and our efforts to be faithful to what we believe? An encourager is aware and sensitive to what people around him are facing and attempting to be. He draws alongside a person and communicates by action and word that he understands and cares. A conversation, a phone call, a letter, a commitment to share the load will enable a person to feel loved and want to find out what Christ is saying to him in his need and what he should do.

Body life is the fellowship of the sons of encouragement. There is no new name we need more than this one given to Joseph. We are to be the Churches of the Holy Encouragement. We belong to the Paraclete himself and we are meant to share his strength, hope and courage with each other. We are to stand with each other, liberating each other with Christ's love and energizing each other with his immense availability.

Paul clarifies how this is to work in Ephesians 4 as he reminds the Ephesians who they have been called to be: "I . . . beg you to live a life worthy of the calling to which you have been

called, with all lowliness and meekness, with patience, forbear-
ing one another in love, eager to maintain the unity of the
Spirit in the bond of peace. There is one body and one Spirit,
just as you were called to the one hope that belongs to your call,
one Lord, one faith, one baptism, one God and Father of us all,
who is above all and through all and in all." He then goes on
to explain the gifts given to each for the work of ministry in
the world. Each of us is given a different gift at different times
for particular ministries with people and society. Next, he shows
how this works for the unified functioning of the body life:
"Rather, speaking the truth in love, we are to grow up in every
way into him who is the head, into Christ, from whom the whole
body, joined and knit together by every joint with which it is
supplied, when each part is working properly, makes bodily
growth and upbuilds itself in love" (Eph. 4:15–16).

Then, with a triumphant "therefore," Paul spells out how encouragement is expressed in the Body:

> Therefore, putting away falsehood, let every one speak the
> truth with his neighbor, for we are members one of another. Be
> angry but do not sin, do not let the sun go down on your anger,
> and give no opportunity to the devil. Let the thief no longer steal,
> but rather let him labor, doing honest work with his hands, so that
> he may be able to give to those in need. Let no evil talk come out
> of your mouths, but only such as is good for edifying, as fits the
> occasion, that it may impart grace to those who hear. And do not
> grieve the Holy Spirit of God, in whom you were sealed for the day
> of redemption. Let all bitterness and wrath and anger and clamor
> and slander be put away from you, with all malice, and be kind
> to one another, tenderhearted, forgiving one another, as God in
> Christ forgave you (Eph. 4:25–32).

That passage is not only an explanation of body life but a
challenge to dare to express it. Here is encouragement in Jesus'
style and by the power of his name.

But the body life of the Church which Luke described in Acts
had not yet reached the grand level of Paul's rhetoric. With
appealing honesty, Luke tells us that not all the Church could
be called sons of encouragement. As a matter of fact, two were
just the opposite. They were a son and a daughter of discouragement. Just as Barnabas was under the sway of the advocate, the

Holy Spirit, Ananias and Sapphira came under the influence of the adversary, Satan himself. In the account of their deceitful deed we witness the battle between the Holy Spirit and Satan for the future of the Church.

Nowhere in Scripture does the word *but* so effectively signal a comparison and prepare us for a contrast: "But a man named Ananias with his wife Sapphira sold a piece of property, and with his wife's knowledge he kept back some of the proceeds, and brought only a part and laid it at the apostles' feet" (Acts 5:1–2). We are forced to find ourselves in the comparison. Barnabas or Ananias—with whom do we identify?

There is a fascinating story that comes out of the Theodore Roosevelt presidency. A reporter of a Washington newspaper was observed by a friend reading through the Bible. Since reading Scripture was not a usual practice for him, his associate asked him why he had become so religious. "I'm looking for the name Ananias. The President denied a statement today as untrue and relegated the person who made it to what he called the 'Ananias Club.' Someone told me I could find the name in here."

The Ananias Club! No more demeaning term could be used. Yet there are churches that become just that, and some of us could be considered as honored members.

Ananias's name means "Yahweh is gracious." No one ever contradicted his name more forcefully. His wife's name was Sapphira, which means beautiful. Yet her consent and collusion with her husband was anything but beautiful. The actions of both were brash denials of the body life of the church they pretended to share. Their sin has been the greatest threat to the health of the Body of Christ ever since.

Careful examination of Luke's account clarifies that these two equivocators wanted to emulate the sharing mutuality of the fellowship without the cost. They wanted prestige and privilege without the price. The gift of Barnabas which exemplified this spirit of sharing in the early Church had brought him recognition and a prestigious new name. Ananias and Sapphira wanted the same honor and esteem. They sold a piece of their property, and it was while they were preparing to lay the proceeds at the Apostles' feet that Satan prompted them to desire the best of two worlds: their Church's accolades and their own acquisitive-

ness. They would pretend to give all the proceeds while in fact
holding back a portion for themselves. There was no regulation
that they had to give it all. The Church would have been delighted if they had honestly said that they had sold their property
and were giving a portion of it to the fellowship. But the virus
of pretense had infected them.

When Ananias presented their pretentious gift, Peter had the
x-ray vision of the Holy Spirit to see into his soul. His own
scrapes with "ol' Scratch" had made him ever so sensitive to
satanic influence. In a flash of insight and discernment that was
a gift of the Holy Spirit, he not only saw what Ananias was
doing but what it would do to the Church. Satan wanted to
destroy the Church at all costs. He had paid the high price for
that by buying Ananias's soul.

Peter's words cut and sting: "Ananias, why has Satan filled
your heart to lie to the Holy Spirit and to keep back part of
the proceeds of the land? While it remained unsold, did it not
remain your own? And after it was sold, was it not at your disposal? How is it that you have contrived this deed in your heart?
You have not lied to men but to God" (5:3–4).

No wonder Ananias had a seizure and died! The shock of
exposure was too great for his heart. Unable to take the trauma,
he reeled under the psychic blow to his ego and fell dead before the Apostles' feet, his carefully conditioned gift in front of
his dead stare. The young men of the Church wrapped his body
and carried him out for immediate burial.

Sapphira didn't fare any better. When she came to the Church
she expected the cheering honors of the fellowship. Instead, she
was confronted with Peter's penetrating interrogation. He gave
her a chance to repent, but her heart was sealed around the
diabolical intrigue. Peter's final question uses a very exposing
term. He had asked Ananias why he had lied to the Holy Spirit.
Now he wanted to know why Sapphira had agreed with her husband to tempt the Holy Spirit. The word in this context means
seeing how far one can go in resisting the Spirit without retaliation. But she had pushed the Spirit too far! Peter knew, and now
so did the whole assembly she and Ananias had wanted so desperately to impress. Her reaction was as excruciating as her husband's. She too had a seizure and died.

What does this disturbing event teach us for our understanding of body life? And what does it mean for us and the Church today?

First of all, it tells us that pretense is one of the greatest problems for the Body. The sin of Ananias and Sapphira was that they pretended. They wanted to enjoy the love and acceptance of the "one heart and soul" fellowship while they pretentiously withheld themselves. They were one thing outwardly and quite another inwardly. They were not wholeheartedly open to their brothers and sisters in Christ.

Second, this startling account tells us that acceptance of the Holy Spirit means accountability to the fellowship. The Holy Spirit constantly breaks us open to one another. There can be no exclusive, private relationship with the Holy Spirit which allows us to live unchecked by the fellowship.

Ananias and Sapphira thought they could pretend with the Church and keep the power of the Spirit. Peter was bold to declare that they had not lied to men but to the Holy Spirit. What he meant was that the sin began in their hearts. Long before they had lied with their pretense, they had lied to God himself. In fact, they were no more open to God than they were to the fellowship.

Third, this story tells us that committed Christians can be influenced by Satan. It is possible to be unsettled and confused by his overtures. He is always subtle. He uses a good to keep us from our best. At all costs, he wants us to be stunted in our growth in Christ. As a liar and the author of lies, a master of duality, he wants to fragment our inner life from outward action.

Christians today can become tools in Satan's hands to manipulate and distract the Church from its glorious purpose of being the Body of Christ. Whenever body life grows in power and depth, Satan will attack; be sure of that. Criticism, gossip, inhibition, divisiveness, and cautious reservation can all be traced back to his influence.

But most of all, in the context of the above three implications of this passage, Luke has forced us to consider a fourth: the way we withhold ourselves from others. All that we have is a trust. The Holy Spirit releases all the resources of God into the life of a believer so that, in response, he can release all of his resources to God. Then in turn, the Spirit utilizes those surrendered resources for the needs of the people in our lives—not just our lands, but our love and affection, our caring and assistance, our listening and sharing, our comfort and courage. Any time we withhold ourselves in refusing to give affirmation and assurance, we sin first against the Holy Spirit and then against the family of God. Whenever we have resources in material wealth—in wisdom or insight, in memories of our own defeats, as well as discoveries which could help another person to hear what God may be saying to him—and refuse to put them at the Spirit's disposal, that's sin!

Imagine what could happen if complete unreservedness took hold of our congregations, our families, our friendships! What if we gave ourselves away as if in each person we were meeting our Lord? Consider how we would live and talk and act if we gave ourselves away in the complete assurance that the Holy Spirit, the resourceful replenisher, would give us what we need. That's the secret Ananias and Sapphira missed. They felt they had to keep something for themselves. If they didn't watch out for themselves, who would? The point is that they did not want to be in a position of need where only the Holy Spirit and the gracious, giving fellowship of the Church could sustain them. At heart they were stingy receivers!

The result of what happened to Ananias and Sapphira is seen both within the early Church and among the people in Jerusalem. Great fear, that is, a powerful awe and wonder, came upon the Church. The implied truth is that the fate of these patron saints of equivocation forced others in the Church to search their own hearts. We are sure that many had done what these two pretenders had done—perhaps more. Each member of the Body, of the whole Church, was forced to ask, "In what ways am I withholding myself and what I have and creating the impression that I have given my all?" The same question rankles in us.

The real source of "great fear" was that the Church had to come to grips with the fact that the Body was under attack. Satan abhorred this Spirit-filled evidence of a new humanity. And each person realized that he could be the weak link that could burst the chain of defense against evil. It had almost happened to Peter; it had happened to Judas; and now it had happened in two of their intimate, trusted friends in the fellowship.

We cannot read this passage without asking, "Lord, is it I?" His answer is incisive. The Lord says, "We know, don't we? You and I live in your heart. We know where you have said 'No!' to me and 'Yes!' to withholding tactics with people who need you."

My response is to take a clean sheet of paper and write out the names of the people and the situations in which I have been pretending to a love and concern I am not enacting. Then I am prompted to consider my relationship with my church. Now I must write out the ways I am reserving myself, holding out what I have and am from the fellowship. What kind of church would I have if everyone acted as I do? Dare to take that kind of inventory!

Now, look for a moment at what happened to the people around the Church. Verses 13 and 14 seem directly contradictory, actually proclaiming two aspects of a whole truth: "None of the rest dared join them, but the people held them in high honor. And more than ever believers were added to the Lord, multitudes both of men and women." What that means is that the qualification for being a part of the Church was undeniably clear. It now meant something to be a member of the Body. Those who wanted an easy, unchallenging, undemanding fellowship were self-excluded. The Church stood for something! As a result, it was given greater power. The healing and preaching ministry was all the more effective. "And more than ever, believers were added to the Lord." The Church grew both in quantity and quality. It has always been so, but now more than ever, people are searching for churches which believe something, proclaim the truth with gusto, and exemplify love and caring with passion.

Now there is a final thing which must be asked and answered as a result of this impelling passage. Can the dynamic fellowship of "one heart and soul" be experienced in large congregations, great worship services and big study groups? The answer is no, at least not at first. That's why the Church in miniature, a diminutive Church in the small group, is so crucial to the Lord's strategy of renewing the contemporary Church. In addition to the inspiration of congregational worship and the teaching of classes and study groups, every person needs to be a part of a caring fellowship no larger than twelve. In our church we call these "enabler groups." They exist to do just what the name implies and what this passage of Acts we have studied promises. It is in such groups that we can know each other, share mutual joys and sorrows, encourage the hopes and dreams of each person, study the Word of God together, and experience the power of the Holy Spirit in prayer. These groups are part of the new order of Saint Barnabas which is growing in our church. As people are learning what it means to be sons and daughters of encouragement, the church on a whole is blessed. It only remains to be seen what will happen to our whole congregation as the contagion of wholeheartedness spreads.

This study of Acts 4:32—5:14 leaves you and me with some marching orders. We have all been called into Christ and into fellowship. We can never rest until our churches are "one heart and soul." We must seek to find the contemporary expression of having all things in common. And the Ananias in all of us must be exposed so that we can become Barnabases in attitude and action.

CHAPTER 6

A Life That Demands Explanation

Acts 5:17–42

Listening to the news on my car radio early one morning, I was startled by an amazing contrast between an incredible news item and the incongruous commercial which immediately followed it. The newscaster was obviously as alarmed by what he was reading as I was by what I heard.

A few weeks ago posters appeared all over California billing a meeting in Waldport, Oregon, at which there would be a speaker representing beings from outer space. At the meeting itself, the three hundred people who attended were told that there was a camp on an unspecified site in Colorado at which people could prepare for departure to an unidentified flying object bound for outer space. The speaker's message was that people from earth would have to sell their worldly goods and discard their personal relationships. Their souls would be saved by a UFO which would carry them to a fuller life on another planet.

In response, one man had sold a $5,000 fishing boat for $5; a woman had given away a new van. Another man gave away 150 acres of land, all his farm equipment, and three children to his friends. A mother received a card postmarked in Colorado informing her that her son was preparing to leave the earth. A young hippie gave away his guitar, purported to mean everything to him. Along with many others, they had headed for the site in Colorado. Apparently the pilgrimage, made of young and old in a broad spectrum of personality types, was growing.

Why this response? Many of the people said they were in search of a fulfilling life and hoped to find it on another planet!

I was jarred back to reality by the blaring horns of the cars behind me inching along the freeway. The news item had so captivated me that I had not moved ahead in my line of traffic. As I looked at the impatient expressions of the drivers around me and looked ahead at the miles of cars in antlike formation crawling into downtown Los Angeles, I began to wonder what it might be like on another planet! At such a moment, one wonders what life might be like without congestion, pollution, crime, and an anxiety-drenched society. But would it be any better? And how did these escapees from the realities of life on earth think that it would be any better in outer space?

I was brought down to earth by a prerecorded commercial which had, I am sure, been prearranged on the broadcaster's schedule days before. The contrast to the news report was ludicrous. A woman's lovely voice, backed up with magnificent strings, sang, "This is the life! This is the place to go! This is the place to grow. . . . California!" Then the punchline: "California Federal Savings."

Indeed! Perhaps both outer space and California had been oversold. Both alleged representatives from outer space and singer with the sumptuous sound had made an offer they could not back up. Neither Mars nor California, much as I love my adopted state, could offer life as it was meant to be lived. Geography, physical conditions, environmental surroundings, the right people, or adventuresome challenges do not add up to the abundant life.

It's interesting how advertisers and opportunists of all kinds use the words *the good life* to sell everything from beer to suburban living. They know how to touch the raw nerve in all of us. In one week I found 360 uses of *life* in advertisements. We all join the chorus to sing the lusty words with gusto, "I love life and I want to live!"

But what is life and what does it mean to live with a capital *L?* Some of us have been given the privilege of tasting and touching all that we are told will bring happy living and have found the promises oversold. No place, position, personality, prowess, prosperity—or even person—is able to pull it off for us. There is still a longing for something more. Even the

pilgrims to outer space, if they ever get there, will find that after
the fascination dims, they still will be searching for authentic life.
Our quest for life is not new. It has been aching in the heart
of man for a long time. That was the voracious hunger of people in Jerusalem when the Church was born. The reason for the
eager response to the early Christians was that they modeled and
mediated a quality of life which was attractive, magnetic, and
powerful. People who heard them talk about their new life in
Christ, empowered by his living Spirit, wanted what these
Christians had found. Their vibrancy, their love and acceptance
of each other, and their indomitable vision and purpose created
a hunger in people to taste the quality of life they exemplified.
The life they were living with the resurrected Christ and with
each other demanded an explanation—and a response. The
indicative mood of the Church's life created an imperative mood
of response. People wanted to live the way the Christians were
living. And what a response! Believers were added to the
Church, healing power was unleashed, and Jerusalem was shaken
by a pervading spiritual revival.

That's precisely why the two Apostles were thrown into prison,
I believe. It was not just the message they preached, but the
magnificent life they were living! The Sadducees were jealous and
angry. They had sternly warned the Apostles to speak no more
in the name of Jesus and they had disobeyed. There was nothing
left for the Sanhedrin to do but lock them up. But they could
not lock up either the truth they proclaimed or the Lord they
obeyed. The proud Sadducees had miscalculated the power of
both.

Late at night an angel of the Lord opened the prison doors
and brought the Apostles out. An angel is a messenger, an
emissary of the Lord sent to accomplish a particular task. But
what this angel said was more important than what he did,
astounding as those unlocked doors were to the Christians. He
unlocked the prison doors and what he said unlocked the
Apostles. It was a confirmation of what they had been doing and
a challenge to continue without reservation. It must have been a
stirring moment: a clear word of direction from the Lord. They
had been on the right track; now they were to move ahead with
all stops pulled out! The Lord knew the need for life in the
hearts of people.

It is not surprising, then, that the admonition of the angel was a propitious, emboldening call and recall to the central message and mission of the Church. Here was an unpolished, unambiguous directive which left no doubt about what they should do and say. It has stood as the undeniable purpose of Christians and the Church ever since. If we want an objective standard by which to measure our lives or the effectiveness of our churches, it is here in the angel's mobilizing commission.

"Go stand in the temple and speak to the people all the words of this Life" (Acts 5:20, RSV). Note the capital *L*. The Apostles were to speak not just about life, but about *new* life, and this new Life in particular. The King James Version says, "Go stand and speak in the temple to the people all the words of this life." *The New English Bible* translates the heartening words, "Go, take your place in the temple and speak to the people about this new life and all that it means." J. B. Phillips is even more straightforward, catching the urgency and inclusiveness: "Go and . . . tell the people all about this new life." Here were marching orders to go offer the grandest gift the Lord had to give for the greatest need the people had. Go take your stand. Tell people about Life. Don't leave anything out. Tell them all about it!

The word *life* is used thirty-six times in the New Testament in reference to Christ and the dimension of living he revealed. We need to recapture the power-packed meaning if we are to do what the Apostles did. We have been unlocked from our own prisons of fear, inhibition, ambiguity, and confusion. Like the Apostles, we too have been delivered to declare and dramatize life.

First, *life* is a synonym for the Lord himself. To tell all about this new life begins with him. "In him was life, and the life was the light of men" (John 1:4). The witness of the early Church was clear. "That which was from the beginning, which we have heard, which we have seen with our eyes, which we looked upon and touched with our hands, concerning the word of life—the life was made manifest, and we saw it, and testify to it, and proclaim to you eternal life which was with the Father and was made manifest to us" (1 John 1:1–2). There was no other adequate way to put it: Jesus was life—God's life incarnate and the impartation of what he intended life to be. In Christ we see what God is like and what we are to become.

Second, *life* was the synthesis of what Jesus came to be and do. There are three self-disclosing "I am's" in which Jesus declared himself as the Life. "I am the bread of life" (John 6:35) —the essential basis of nurture and sustenance. "I am the resurrection and the life" (John 11:25)—through his resurrection we are given the quality of eternal life. "I am the way, and the truth, and the life" (John 14:6)—the way to fellowship with God, the truth about God and his nature; and the life of God in history and in the mind and heart of a believer. All of this is summed up in Jesus' own delineation of his purpose. "I came that they may have life, and have it abundantly" (John 10:11). The abundant life encompasses a new level of existence. Beyond plant, animal, and human levels of life, there is a totally new dimension of creation. It is life lived by his limitless power, guided by his love, expressed by his grace, and totally indestructible by death. This is the triumphant truth Paul expressed to the Corinthians. "Therefore, if any one is in Christ, he is a new creation; the old has passed away, behold, the new has come" (2 Cor. 5:17). In light of that declaration we can feel the intensity of James's comparison: "You do not know about tomorrow. What is your life? For you are a mist that appears for a little time and then vanishes" (James 4:14). Bishop Jeremy Taylor said, "God hath given to man a short time here upon earth. Yet upon this short time eternity depends."

Third, the word *life* in the New Testament is symbolic of what happens to a person in relationship to Christ. Jesus is life, incarnated life, and now imparts that life to those who will receive him. In his own message he promised that he would make his home in us. Remember the old hymn? "If you want joy, real joy, let Jesus come into your heart." Exactly! Paul put it plainly: "Christ in you, the hope of glory" (Col. 1:27). Irenaeus would have agreed. He said, "The glory of God is a man fully alive." Paul explained to the Galatians how this full life had happened to him: "I have been crucified with Christ; it is no longer I who live but Christ who lives in me; and the life I now live in the flesh I live by faith in the Son of God, who loved me and gave himself for me" (Gal. 2:20). For Paul, Christ was himself the source of this new life. There is a blunt conclusion to the symbol of life as the description of what happens to us. John wrote the Church: "He who has the Son has life; he who

has not the Son of God has not life" (1 John 5:12). John
Henry Newman leaves us with the same unsettling truth. "Fear
not that your life will come to an end, but rather that it shall
never have a beginning." That beginning comes from having the
Son through a realization that he has always had us. Hebrews
10:20 declares that Jesus is "the new and living way." Indeed he
is! We can sing with the chorus at the close of *Faust:* "The un-
attainable has become an event."

The cycle of death and resurrection is the key. We die to our
willful control of our life and we are resurrected to a new life as
Christ lives his life through us. It doesn't matter how long we
live but whether we find the life in the midst of living.

Fourth, *life* is the balanced symmetry of our relationship with
one another. We often speak of the "life" of a church or the
"life" Christians share together. Because of Christ's life in a
believer, there is a totally different quality to that believer's
relationship with fellow believers. Christ's love, forgiveness,
esteem, and hope become the basis of our union. A part of the
proclamation of the Christian life is the miracle of fellowship,
unity, and oneness. Since most people's problems come in their
relationships, often the most forceful aspect of presenting the
gospel is to share with people what happens when Christ's grace
is the basic ingredient in our attitudes and disposition. There
can be no question that the effectiveness of the early Church in
evangelism was caused by the love the Christians shared. "My,
how those Christians love one another!" was the telling response
of the world. Jesus had promised that "by this shall men know
that you are my disciples, that you love one another."

All of these four aspects are focused in the angel's instruction
to the Church, then and now. They are undeletable dimensions
represented in "all the words" of this life. "Don't leave anything
out," the challenge seems to imply. "Tell the people all you know
about life!"

That's what we need to hear and obey in our "lust for life"
world. Our task is not to argue, philosophize, speculate, cajole,
but to live a life that demands explanation. Is there anything
about us that would force people to say, "Now that's living!
That's the way I wish I could live!" When we consider sharing
our faith as imparting life, what a difference it makes. Then
the emphasis is on Christ and not on theories about him that we
try to force upon people.

"All the words of this life" must become our own experience. Christ must become our life, our consuming passion, purpose, and power. This means spending time with him in prayer so that he can reshape our personalities around his own. It means that we continually renew our experience of new life in him by allowing him to guide our decisions, attitudes, words, and expression. And it also means that we grasp with daily freshness the meaning of this death and resurrection for our problems and concerns. That alone will give us a life that demands explanation.

The Apostles' release and appearance in the temple demanded an explanation. Luke, breaking into the intensity of his biography of the Acts of the Holy Spirit, presents the consternation of the Sanhedrin in comic relief.

Imagine—the Sanhedrin was gathered in glorious array ready to try and sentence the Apostles. Officers were sent to bring the Apostles before them. We can feel the frustration they experienced when the report came back that the prison was still securely locked but the Apostles were not there! While they discussed this with befuddled alarm, an even more unsettling report was brought to them: "The men whom you put in prison are standing in the temple and teaching the people." How could the Sadducees explain that away? They did not accept the existence of the spirits or interceding influence from God. How did those Apostles get free? There was nothing left to do but arrest them again and proceed with the trial.

There is a penetrating meaning for us. If we are to live a life in Christ that demands explanation, it's not only the observable quality of our lives, but evidences in our lives that must show there is a power at work in us. People must be forced to wonder and then to know that there is something more than personality prowess or healthy maturity, that there is something, Someone beyond ourselves enabling us to live the life that attracts attention.

It's how we live in life's pressures and potentials that makes people wonder what hidden inner resource has released us from the prisons of life. People should be saying, "He could never have done that on his own strength!" or, "Where does she get the patience and love she always seems to have regardless of what happens or people say?" or, "What is it about him that frees him of the hang-ups that keep me incarcerated in compulsive patterns?"

I heard a man explain the influence of a television producer who is a member of our congregation. "I watched him for months. It was not so much what he said. We hear a lot of people in our industry talk about some new fascination over a philosophy or religious idea. Neither was it the way he reacted in crises, though he is consistently strong and calm. But that could have been explained by his healthy childhood or successes in the industry. No, it was more than that. It's the way I feel when I'm with him. Long before I asked him about what he believed—and note, I had to ask him—he made me feel of value, like I was the only person alive when he talked with me. He is so free! But I sensed he had not always been like that. I just had to find out what made him tick! Finally, late one evening at an after-production party, I got him in a corner and said, 'Hey, friend, you are something else! How did you find what you've got?' Then he told me about Christ in the most unreligious, nonpious way I've ever heard. I didn't feel the way I usually do when people talk about Christ; in fact, I didn't want him to stop! We've talked a lot since then. I've made a start; I can now say that I'm a Christian. Church people usually turn me off. But this guy was irresistible!"

That should be happening to all of us constantly in our relationships. Our task is to know Christ so well and to grow so deeply in him that we don't have to sit around worrying about how to witness. If we allow our Lord to live in us and spend our energies cultivating friendship with him, we will be witnesses. Be sure of that! The Lord himself will position people in our lives because he knows we're ready.

But most of us find sharing our faith difficult. Perhaps the reason is in the answer given to a man who asked, "Why is it that so few Christians can talk about what's happening to them in their faith?" The pointed reply was, "Maybe it's because there is so little that's happening!"

I suggest that we need the same reorienting challenge that was given to the Apostles and a release from some prison of the past or present to back it up. The two must always be kept together: the Lord's clear word and the undeniable evidence in our lives of an opened prison door.

Look at the results in the Apostles' lives when they were brought before the Sanhedrin and were pressed again to explain

A Life That Demands Explanation 81

why they persisted in following and proclaiming Christ. In
Peter's answer we see the result of the visitation of the angel and
the miraculous release.

There was *courage:* "We must obey God rather than men."
We cannot speak "all the words of this new life" until we are
free from all secondary loyalties and securities of an old life.
It is relevant to us that Peter had risen above the entangling
web of dependence upon approval and safety. Now he could
speak a decisive word to people bound up in the constricting
chains of tradition and cultural religion. What a tragedy when
our need for acceptance by people who do not know Christ is
so strong that we cannot dare to live and share the only hope that
will set them free. How many Christians can say, "We must
obey God rather than men"? Can I say that? Can you?

There was *clarity.* Peter once again enunciated the essential
elements of the gospel. In a sense, he did just what the angel
commanded, not only in the temple but before the august Sanhedrin. Fearlessly he said, "We are witnesses!" But not to himself or his accomplishment—he witnessed to Christ! He uses
two words to describe what Christ meant to him. Christ is
Leader and Savior. The word *leader* is the same Greek word
he had used before in witnessing to the Sanhedrin, translated in
Acts 3:15 as Author of Life. Here it seems to have a different
feel and intention. The Greek word *archēgos* translated as "pioneer" in Hebrews, is closely related to an Aramaic term for a
strong swimmer, often a part of a crew on a vessel. If anything
happened to a ship and the turbulent sea prevented getting
through the rocks and reefs to shore, this member of the crew
would tie a rope around his waist, dive into the angry sea, and
swim ashore. After firmly attaching the rope on shore, he would
assist the others to climb the rope to safety on land. Christ was
that kind of lifesaver for Peter. He had been the Savior for all
mankind and was now helping mankind to safety. The Big Fish-
erman knew; it had happened to him! That's why he could talk
so forcefully about repentance and forgiveness.

Then there was *confidence.* The interceding angel and the
persistent presence of the Holy Spirit assured Peter that the
Apostles were not alone. The Living Christ was the unseen but
strongly felt witness. No wonder he could say, "And we are witnesses to these things and so is the Holy Spirit whom God has

given to those who obey" (Acts 5:32). There's nothing we can't attempt, no needed witness we should fear to give, if we are backed up by the Living God himself!

But last of all, there was a condition. Peter clearly says the Holy Spirit is given to those who obey. Obedience is the secret to spiritual strength. We must obey what Christ has said in his message; we must obey what comes to us from reading his Word; and we must obey the deep inner voice of his guidance for particular situations and relationships. How do you know if you're being obedient? I find it helpful to ask myself the following questions:

1. Am I living consistently as much of Christ as I know?
2. Am I living out the implications of what I discover daily in the Scriptures?
3. Am I refusing to do what I feel I should to be faithful to Christ? Has he already told me more than I acted on?
4. Am I consciously inhibited from speaking about my Lord because of fear of rejection or of being considered foolish, unintellectual, or uncultured?

The power of the Holy Spirit is released by obedience. There is no other way. We cannot expect the joy and energy of his infilling if we are saying "No!" to what we know from our prayers we should do.

Obedience is like a thermostat. It opens the flow of the Spirit for the needs around us. The cold of the world calls for the heat and warmth of the fire of the Holy Spirit within us.

The last section of Acts 5 focuses on the influence of the "words of new life" on one of the most honored and respected members of the Sanhedrin. Gamaliel was considered the greatest teacher of that time. He could see the irrefutable evidence of God's Spirit at work in the Apostles. When the rest of the Sanhedrin was enraged (the word used here actually means "sawn apart," or "torn asunder"), he spoke of caution about the Sadducees' determination to execute the Apostles.

Don't miss the amazing turn of events Gamaliel engineered. He saved the early Church! Think what would have happened if the Apostles had been killed! There is no question in my mind that the Spirit of God touched that great scholar as Peter forthrightly proclaimed Christ. After deflecting the rage of the

Sanhedrin with a reminder of previous movements that ran their course and flickered out, Gamaliel said something which otherwise would have seemed absolutely incongruous to them: "So in the present case, I tell you, keep away from these men and let them alone; for if this plan or this undertaking is of men, it will fail; but if it is of God, you will not be able to overthrow them. You might even be found opposing God!"

Gamaliel was an angel unaware. He was a spokesman for God without knowing it. The unseen angel in the first portion of the section opened the prison doors. Now here was a respected leader opening a new door; he was being used by God without his knowing it—or did he know? In a way, I think he did. He was obviously moved by the Apostles. His God-hungry spirit responded to theirs.

The point of this for us is that we never know who is watching, listening. What if Peter had cowered under the pressure of the Sanhedrin and had not spoken "all about this new life"? Gamaliel would not have been impressed!

Our responsibility is obedience. The Lord will put the Gamaliels of life in the right place at the right time. Trust him for that!

One last thing needs to be said about this passage. We have seen what obedience to the angel's admonition had done in the lives of the multitudes in Jerusalem and for Gamaliel in the Sanhedrin. Now observe and feel what it did for the Church itself. After the Apostles were beaten and charged, they "left the presence of the council, rejoicing that they were counted worthy to suffer dishonor for the name" (5:41). The Amplified New Testament says they were "dignified by the indignity." They rejoiced because they had been faithful. The flush of delight in God and one's self after a time of obedience seems to be the Lord's way of saying, "Well done, good and faithful servant!"

Joy is the undeniable mark of the new life. We are not expected to be perfect, or never fail, or be free of life's pressure problems. But joy should be the identifiable evidence that Christ is alive in us and we are facing reality with his guidance, interceptions, and undiminishable strength. It's a joy that no circumstances or situations can produce, either in outer space or in our problematic world. A joy-filled life will always demand explanation. And we will be ready. We have been released from the prisons of a life which is not life at all, to live a new life in Christ and to tell all about it to those God has made ready to listen.

CHAPTER 7

Not for Sale at Any Price

Acts 6:1–8:3

A short time ago, in a period which we were all reluctant to acknowledge as a time of economic recession, many executives were searching for work. A cartoon in a national magazine painfully capsulized their plight. Two well-dressed, immaculately groomed, alert and dynamic Ivy League executives were waiting outside the personnel office of a company. Both had signs hanging around their necks. One hopeful executive had a sign which read, "For sale." The other outdid him. His sign read, "For sale—at any price!"

I laughed—at first. Then I was forced to reflect on some of the people I know personally who have had to sell themselves— their priorities, as well as what they believed—not just for a job but for popularity, peace, or relationship. Then the question which is often asked in business negotiations flashed before my mind: "What's your price?" Does everyone have a price, some point when convictions, concerns, and commitment become secondary? The cartoon was not very funny after all.

The same week I saw the cartoon, I walked through a display of precious art objects which were about to be auctioned to the highest bidders. One famous painting, however, was not for sale. It was a "come-on" to attract people to come to the auction. Beneath it, delicately placed in a gold frame was a sign whose embossed letters spelled out the message "Not for sale, at any price."

An experienced buyer who stood beside me admiring the

painting was not impressed by the exclusive sign. "Huh! Everybody and everything has a price. It just takes a while and a
lot of money." I was left to reflect on that!

Then I thought of the two kinds of Christians represented
in the two signs "For sale at any price" and "Not for sale at any
price." I wondered a bit about the fact that one had hung on
an available executive and the other on an unavailable work
of art. The signs should be switched!

Stephen was a man who was not for sale at any price. An
exposition of Acts 6 and 7 gives us the ingredients of what takes
a man off the market and gives him courage and convictions by
which he can live, or dare to die, if need be. Luke brings Stephen
to center stage in his drama of the Acts of the Holy Spirit. The
scene is brief but the results of what Stephen did and said are
eternal. It would not be an exaggeration to say that if he had
not played his part well, with obedience and faithfulness, Luke
would have had little more to write except a dull conclusion
about an innocuous sect of Judaism that didn't last long enough
to be given a name. Without Stephen there might not have been
a break with Judaism, a world expansion of the Church, an
Apostle Paul, or a faith vital enough that the followers of Jesus
would eventually be called, with a mixture of admiration and
rage, "the Christians." In fact, if it hadn't been for Stephen, I
probably would not be writing this, and chances are that you
would have little desire to read it!

Luke prepares his readers carefully for Stephen's entrance by
describing a problem in the Church which had to be handled
with discernment. Two distinct types of Jews responded to the
forceful proclamation of the gospel by the Apostles in those
early days of the birth and growth of the Church. There were
the Palestinian Jews who were descendants of those brought
back to Jerusalem by Nehemiah and Ezra after the Dispersion.
They spoke either Hebrew or Aramaic and were proud of their
exclusive and impeccable observance of their undefiled tradition.
Then there were the Hellenists, Jews who had descended from
those who had been victims of the Dispersion under the captivity
of Babylon. Their numbers were swelled by others who had
been drawn away from Palestine by economic and business pur-
suits. These latter, though they had settled throughout the Mediterranean world and beyond, had never lost their love for

Jerusalem and the temple. The passion of "this year in Jerusalem" burned in every Jewish heart, however far persecution or enterprising had driven them. Often these Hellenist Jews, who spoke Greek and were ingrained with Greek culture, would remain in Jerusalem after a pilgrimage back to the Holy City. But they were never fully accepted as equals by the Palestinian Jews.

This long-standing tension was healed among the Jews of both groups who became new people in Christ and shared the love of the Church's fellowship. Well, almost! Some of the Hellenists complained that their widows were being slighted in the distribution of the shared benevolence of the fellowship. The offerings of the believers were given to the Apostles for allocation to those in need. Somehow, the Hellenists felt their widows were not being given a fair share and that the Palestinians were being given a preference—a little problem which forced the Apostles to face a big concern. As the Church grew into the thousands, the Apostles were spending all their time with administrative problems and had little time for preaching the gospel. The seemingly insignificant frustration led to a very significant solution. They recommended that the Church elect seven deacons to "serve at table." By that they meant more than what a waiter does at a restaurant today. A "table" at that time meant a place where a money-changer did his collecting or exchanging of money. The deacons were elected to oversee the distribution of the monies and provisions to the needy among the fellowship. And all of those elected were Hellenistic Jews. That should have stopped the squabbles among the ladies! Little did they know that their contention would bring about the election and ordination of a Hellenic Jew who would change the course of history.

His name was Stephen. He was not only head of the list of new deacons, but was to become the leader of a new movement which would shake the infant Church out of the cradle of Judaism and scatter the seed of the gospel to the fertile soil of the Gentile world—all because he was a man no one could buy, at any price.

Luke prepares us for the magnificent thing Stephen did by first telling us about the mighty man he was. Long before we witness the flow from the watershed event of his life, Luke paints

a word portrait of what the Lord can do in, and give to, a man
to make him unpurchasable.

We are told that Stephen was "a man full of faith and the
Holy Spirit." The two dimensions belong inseparably together.
The greatest gift of the Holy Spirit is faith. It is the gift that
makes all other gifts possible. This gift not only liberates a
person to respond to the gospel, but frees him to dare to believe
that all things are possible through Christ. Faith first produces
the new life in Christ and then a new life of daring in the believer.
The Holy Spirit in Stephen had given him the courage to surrender his life to Christ and then to anticipate expectantly
Christ's intervention in all situations. The power of faith produced a viable relationship between Stephen and the living
Christ. Whatever else we admire about this fearless, unpurchasable saint, we find the ultimate taproot of our admiration in his
audacious faith.

Next, we are told that Stephen was "full of grace and power."
The word *grace* has tremendous implications here. Stephen had
been healed by Christ's unlimited, unmerited, unearnable love.
He was a released man. Defensiveness, self-justification, and
competitiveness were gone. Graciousness became the discernible
trait of his personality. He had the disposition of Christ. Faith
had gotten him started, grace had kept him growing, and power
was the result. Our world has tarnished the meaning of the
description *a powerful person*. For Luke it meant that Stephen
had the capacity to communicate the gospel impellingly, the
liberty to lead people into a relationship with the Savior effectively, and the power to produce healing and hope in physically
and mentally depleted people. Stephen was a rare combination
of administrator, preacher, and teacher. But the administrative
position to which the Church ordained him only served as the
Lord's launching pad for detonating him into the orbit of
teaching and preaching.

That Spirit-ordained orbit was his own synagogue in Jerusalem.
Fortified by the signs and wonders that put an exclamation
point behind everything he said, Stephen went to the synagogue
of the Freedmen to preach the gospel. This synagogue was the
special place of worship and fellowship of Hellenistic Jews in
Jerusalem. Its membership was made up of Jews from Alexan-

dria, Cyrenia, Cilicia, and Asia. It was customary in that synagogue to raise and debate religious issues which were captivating the people. The Jews who listened to Stephen had not anticipated being almost captured by the persuasive rhetoric and message he proclaimed. In their response, Luke tells us something more—a great deal more—about Stephen's Christ-centered character: "They could not withstand the wisdom and the Spirit with which he spoke." Again we encounter an aspect of his charismatic, grace-gifted life.

Stephen had the gift of wisdom. That means that the indwelling Spirit gave him great understanding and insight, coupled with discernment. He was able to understand the deep mysteries of God's nature and his purposes for his people. The Spirit gave him thoughts beyond his intellectual capacity and lucidness beyond his learning. The Greek-oriented and trained Jews of his audience were startled and amazed at his wise and penetrating presentation. No wonder they could not withstand it! It was the Spirit of God speaking through him.

Don't miss the progression through which Luke has taken us in his character study of Stephen. The Holy Spirit was alive and at work in Stephen. That gave him the gift of faith to appropriate the gospel and accept Jesus as Lord. This conviction produced his character. He became a grace-oriented, gracious man in Christ, which gave him the power to implement Christ's will in the world around him. Wonders and signs resulted. What he subsequently taught and preached was impelling and irrefutable. He could not be dissuaded or bought off. Nothing the leaders of the synagogue could do or say could diminish his determination or confuse his clarity. After listening to him, no one wanted to try.

Except one. Among the Cilicians in the synagogue was a brilliant Pharisee from Tarsus, the principal city of Cilicia. He had been brought back to Jerusalem by the Sanhedrin to spearhead an attack on the indomitable and troublesome followers of Jesus. Trained under Gamaliel and one of the master teacher's most brilliant students, he now listened with rage to Stephen's declaration that the Messiah was the crucified Jesus of Nazareth. The Pharisee's name was Saul of Tarsus.

Two men with a mission—Saul and Stephen: human intellect

and brilliance confronted Holy Spirit-inspired wisdom and knowledge. Both Hellenistic Jews, each had a passion he could not sublimate nor subdue.

If my supposition is correct, Saul, a Cilician, was a member of the synagogue of the Freedmen and was at this time already engaged in his assignment of destroying the Church. Surely he was there not only to hear Stephen speak, but he was among those who could not withstand the deacon's wisdom and spirit. Nothing enrages an arrogant intellectual more than to be defeated in the arena of his expertise. Add to that the excruciating embarrassment of confrontation with and defeat by a leader of a movement he had been brought to the city to expose and destroy. But Saul too was a determined man who also could not be bought at any price—not even the price of embarrassment before his own synagogue!

It is my belief that Saul was the mastermind behind the scheme to destroy Stephen. He had to find a way. He recruited people to lie and say that Stephen blasphemed the temple and contradicted the Commandments of Moses. The trumped-up charge was carefully worded when Stephen was brought before the council, the Sanhedrin: "This man never ceases to speak words against this holy place and the law; for we have heard him say that this Jesus of Nazareth will destroy this place, and will change the customs which Moses delivered to us" (6: 13–14). It was an old charge, not unlike the one leveled at Jesus himself. But it was very accurate and very false at the same time: Stephen did not cease to speak, that's true; but he did not speak against the holy place or the law, he simply spoke for Jesus and a new life in him as Messiah. He did not claim that Jesus would destroy the temple, but that God was greater than any place built by men. He did say that Jesus enabled a new quality of relationship with God by repentance and forgiveness which would supersede old, worn-out practices of man-made religion.

The Sanhedrin could not understand a man like Stephen. He could not be threatened, bought off, nor punished into subservience. All they could do was listen and look spellbound. Luke tells us, "And gazing at him, all who sat in the council saw that his face was like the face of an angel" (6:15).

There's the capping phrase of our character study. What did

the Sanhedrin know about angels? Think what expression on
Stephen's face must have held the attention of these ecclesiastics.
Resoluteness, determination, vision, brightness more than human
brilliance shone through those piercing eyes coupled with
warmth, love, and irresistible entreaty. The angelic face would
not allow their eyes to turn away. All that Luke has told us about
the characteristics of Stephen's charisma was focused in his face.
The people around us can always read our hearts by our faces.
The inner things we live with will show upon our faces. The soul
is dyed with the color of its commitment. What happens to a
man's face when the light in his heart goes out or no flame has
ever been set to blaze? Our countenance is connected to our
character and our character to our communion with the living
God.

No palm-reading medium is necessary to know a man. Look
at his face!

Strange, isn't it, that the Sanhedrin was trying Stephen for
opposing Moses. Yet they were startled by his face that was
strangely like that of Moses when he returned from Sinai. "Moses
did not know that the skin of his face shone" (Exod. 34:29).
It's also worthy of note that when this same council tried Jesus
they had to cover his face (Mark 14:65). In Stephen's countenance did they see the same face shining through?

But who reported this amazing fascination with Stephen's
face? Who there would have dared expose the Sanhedrin's
gravitation to the glory that flashed from his features? How did
Luke find out about this? Who told him? Who else but Saul,
who was to spend the rest of his life haunted by those eyes?

But that day before the Sanhedrin, what Saul saw on Stephen's
face was blocked from reaching his heart. His commission to
destroy the followers of the Nazarene had been awarded because
of his vigilant commitment to the Law and strict observance of
the customs of Israel. Like a lawyer trying his first case, Saul
was determined to win at all costs. He would not be dissuaded,
however brilliant either Stephen's face or his rhetoric was. He
had a test case! If he could expose Stephen for blasphemy
and do it according to Deuteronomic Law, he would have a
precedent for the subsequent destruction of the sect. Deuteronomy 17:2–7 fit his predetermined assignment perfectly: Stephen
had, in Saul's judgment, transgressed the covenant and was serv-

ing another god, this Jesus of Nazareth. Now Saul was in the process of fulfilling the requirement to inquire diligently, though he needed nothing more to convince him that Stephen was guilty. The Pharisee of Tarsus was already gathering authentic witnesses to enact Moses' prescribed punishment. Stephen's death by stoning was sealed in Saul's heart.

He must have been a bit impatient when the chief priest asked for Stephen's defense. "What more do we need?" Saul must have thought in dismay. Stephen's magnificent review of Israel's history in the light of Jesus as the Messiah must have impressed Saul's mind, steeped as he was in Israel's history and ordered by Greek learning. He must have admired the breadth of Stephen's knowledge of Scripture. But truth is inflammatory to a person set on a determined course. Saul was not only attracted but repelled as Stephen got too close to the raw nerve in him. Saul must have been relieved and fiendishly refortified in his plan when Stephen finally got around to drawing the net on the implications of the truth he was expanding. He knew if he waited long enough Stephen would paint himself into a corner from which only he, Saul, could lead him out for execution!

When Stephen declared prophetically that the leaders of Israel to whom he spoke were "stiff-necked people, uncircumcised in heart and ears, who always resist the Holy Spirit," Saul knew that he had written his own death warrant. Indignation flared as Stephen used the sacred names of the Messiah, the Righteous One, and referred to angels. The Pharisees were enflamed by the first and the Sadducees were angered by the other. The two parties of the Sanhedrin were galvanized into a singular, enraged determination: get rid of Stephen!

Now Saul could step back and let the dam break and allow the polluted waters of hatred to inundate Stephen. The Sadducees and Pharisees of the high court were so enraged that they ground their teeth against him. Like a pack of ravenous wolves, they gnashed their fangs in readiness to attack.

Stephen felt the danger, the overwhelming hatred. What could he do now? Nothing other than he had done all through his brief life in the Savior. He called for help! He looked up and knew that the Lord was with him. "But he, full of the Holy Spirit, gazed into heaven and saw the glory of God, and Jesus standing at the right hand of God." What else can that mean

than that his eyes of faith, strengthened by the Holy Spirit, had
a vision of the power of God focused on the Lord Jesus? He was
not alone. The Lord was faithful to his promise. In a triumphant
affirmation of faith Stephen cried out, "Behold, I see the heavens
opened, and the Son of man standing at the right hand of God"
(7:56). That confession of confidence contained all that he had
tried to say about Jesus and the one thing the leaders of Israel
abhorred most. To say that Jesus was the Messiah of the Jews
was one thing; to claim that he was the Son of God was worse;
but to give him the title Son of man was more than they could
tolerate. To them that meant that Jesus was the Savior of the
whole world. The term "Son of man" encompassed the Ezekiel
passages and signaled that God's Messiah would save all men,
not just the Jews. Loss of exclusiveness and the depreciation of
their own distinct identity as God's only people is what they
feared most. If Jesus was Son of man, that spelled the beginning
of the end of their priority and special privilege, and signaled
that he would lead Israel in being the agent of salvation for all
nations!

No wonder they cried out! They wailed in erratic, wild, jeering shouts of hatred. The truth had cut too closely. They stopped
their ears. Then with uncontainable rage, as if by one great
command, they rushed together upon him. Who gave the signal
for united rushing and beating? Was it Saul? In Acts 26:10 he
gives his own confession of his voting power in the Sanhedrin.

To engineer a death sentence and oversee an execution as
an observer is no mean accomplishment. Saul did just that. After
Stephen was beaten by the enraged officers themselves, there
was no stopping their death-determined will. He was bound and
dragged outside the city walls. (After all, the law commanded
that no blood be spilled in the sacred precincts!) They pushed
him over the wall and down into a pit in which he would be
stoned. Saul stood by, keeping everything in good Deuteronomic
order. The witnesses against Stephen, according to the rule, were
to be the first to throw the stones. They took off their outer garments to be free from any encumbrance. These witnesses were
carefully checked by Saul as they put their garments at his
feet. He watched as the first heavy stones struck Stephen's face.
That face! It still had the same radiance, confidence, and love
Saul had observed earlier. Then he gave the signal for the mob to

join in the mass release of their pent-up hatred and frustration.

Saul could not imagine how a man could pray at a time like this! He was utterly amazed when he heard Stephen's strong, courageous voice cry out, not for mercy or to compromise his beliefs in the hope of saving himself, but in prayer to his Lord. Saul's heart was now a bit ambivalent. What was it about this Stephen? His name, *Stephanos* in Greek, meant "crown," and now his crown was the unmistakable radiance which hallowed his face.

As the stones rained down upon him, Stephen prayed, "Lord, do not hold this sin against them." Then he died. The crowd was silent. In that moment the potent compound of relief, guilt, fear of death itself, and the uneasiness of having taken judgment into their own hands filled the air.

And Saul stood by consenting to Stephen's death. Once again he looked on Stephen's face. Now bloody and broken, it still radiated love and forgiveness. We can only wonder what went through Saul's mind. I imagine that he was forced to wonder what kind of a movement he had been called in to eradicate. One thing is certain: from Stephen's death he knew that he was not dealing with ordinary people. No threats or promised acquittal would dissuade them. It would be a difficult, nasty, bloody business blotting out the Church, he was sure of that. But pride mingled with religious hatred finds distorted expression, and now that Saul had started the persecution there was no turning back! But he would never wash Stephen's face from his mind or his words from his heart. They were like a goad within him against which he compulsively had to kick. And kick he did, as he went from house to house, ravaging the Church, dragging believers from their houses, and committing Jesus' followers to prison. Saul had to succeed in his assignment!

In order to appreciate fully the meaning of Stephen's martyrdom, we need to live in the skin of both the members of the Church and of the one who persecuted them.

The questions the followers of the Master must have asked are on our lips. Lord, why did you let this happen? If you were there with Stephen, with all the authority and power of the living God, why didn't you intercede and save him? Is praying only for strength and never for deliverance? The question echoes through the ages and resounds in our own hearts. Why do good people suffer? Why do potential leaders like Stephen get snuffed out just as their flame blazes most brightly?

That's what the early Church must have asked as they huddled behind locked doors for fear they would be next, or in prison wondering why they were not spared in the name of Jesus. Stephen was the hope of the future of the Church. He was a leader of a new wave of leadership to follow after the Apostles. Was there hope for future generations, or would they all come to the same end? Just as we do, the early believers overestimated the power of their enemies and underestimated the power of the Lord. He was not finished; he had barely begun.

But getting inside the feelings of the Church must be combined with getting inside Saul. The memory of Stephen's death, reinforced by the courage and strength of all the Christians he persecuted, rumbled about in his mind and heart. The Lord of the movement he was trying to stamp out was closing in on him. On the way to Damascus to rout out and persecute the followers there, Saul was possessed by the memory of Stephen and the inextinguishable fire he had witnessed in the Master's men and women. That indelible impression had begun a civil war within the vigilant Pharisee. He was ready to respond when the Lord himself intercepted him on the road and revealed himself undeniably alive. What if Stephen had been a man who could be bought at the price of safety or survival?

But go deeper—much deeper. The persecution of the Church in Jerusalem caused believers to scatter throughout Judea and Samaria and, later, to all the then-known world. Stephen's message had declared the independence of the Church from being a sect of Judaism; now his death forced an independence of the Church from Jerusalem. This was the beginning of Christianity's thrust out into the Gentile world where the Church would be forced to see that Christ was the Savior of the whole world. And the one who had executed Stephen would become the acknowledged new leader of missionary Christianity.

The moving of the Lord! He's always there making good out of evil. He took the very one who sought to destroy him and made him the greatest declarer of the gospel. Years later Paul was able to say with love and admiration, "Stephen, thy witness!" How little did Stephen know that his death would be a mighty wind that would blow the seed pod open and plant a seed not

only in the heart of his chief opponent, but across the world
to bear millionfold harvest through the centuries.

Paul's first sermon after his conversion was an amazing replica
of Stephen's message before the Sanhedrin. The germ of Paul's
theology had formed that day in the council. But Stephen's
character and resultant countenance were forever an example to
Paul of what Christ could do in a man.

Years later, Augustine wrote an answer to the deepest questions in our hearts as to why the Lord allowed Stephen to suffer
and die. The gracious Master of men was willing to work
within the confines of the human nature he had come to redeem.
Augustine explained it plainly: "If St. Stephen had not spoken
thus, if he had not prayed thus, the Church would not have
had Paul." The blood of the martyrs is indeed the seed of the
Church. Little did Saul know as he guarded the coats of the
witnesses who stoned Stephen that day that he soon would wear
the mantle of Stephen himself!

In reality, Stephen was a man who could be bought, and it
had been for a high price. The transaction was completed long
before he confronted Saul in the synagogue, the council, or the
stoning pit. He belonged to the Lord, and Calvary was the price
He had paid for Stephen. That's why Stephen could not be
bought off. In a profound way Stephen had paid the price for
Saul. That death eventually led Saul to confront Jesus' death
and to confess that he had been purchased with the blood of
the Cross.

In *The Robe,* Lloyd C. Douglas describes Stephen in the
hour of his death. Holding one hand high, Stephen shouted,
"I see him! My Lord Jesus—take me!" When Stephen fell among
the stones which had been hurled at him, Marcellus turned
from the brutal scene and looked at a soldier standing near
Stephen. The soldier nervously commented that he had heard
Stephen say he thought someone was coming to rescue him.
Marcellus corrected the soldier. Stephen *had* actually seen
someone coming. The soldier ventured, "That dead Galilean,
maybe?" Marcellus replied, "That dead Galilean is not dead, my
friend! He is more alive than any man here." And so was
Stephen a few moments after.

The account of Stephen's martyrdom leaves us with some
convicting conclusions.

The first is that the Lord does not offer us safety, but he

does offer us strength. Our task is obedience to Christ. That may lead to difficulty but he will give us power to stand in the midst of all that befalls us.

Second, a person who has been purchased by the blood of the Cross cannot be sold for any human price. The Lord's forgiving love convinces us that we belong to him and are not available for resale. That confronts us with a question. "If I belong to Christ, is there a price at which I am willing to be resold to a high bidder?" We all know the bitter experiences of being up for auction. But we also know that the Lord never lets go of what he has purchased at the high cost of the Cross. He steps in repeatedly to reclaim his possessions and we know we are his again.

Third, this passage tells us that our Lord is unrelentingly working out his purposes through the worst things that happen to us. He is not absent in difficulties. He will use them to bring us into deeper fellowship with him. But, also, he will use what we go through to reveal to others what he is able to do in the excruciating pressure of their own lives.

Lastly, we can't help wondering what we would have done. We would probably have sold out—unless we had had the same gifts of the Holy Spirit Stephen had. We are forced to ask with life-or-death urgency, "Have I allowed the indwelling Spirit to give me the gift of faith to trust Jesus completely and to dare unreservedly? Have I accepted the gift of grace in order to become a truly gracious person whom no manner of evil can defeat? Am I open to being a riverbed for the flow of the Spirit's power to enable me and others to experience the immeasurable, motivating, innovating vitality of God for each situation? Is there evidence in my life and speech that I have the gift of wisdom? Can I look deeply into the mysteries of God and have knowledge of him and discernment of his guidance for myself and those around me? Are there signs and wonders trailing my footsteps— people loved, healed, introduced to the Savior, alive and on the way in him? Am I the one who can step into the breach of frustration and impotence and bring the hope of the Lord? But most of all, would anyone see in my countenance the face of an angel?"

If not, why not? Did the Lord do for Stephen what he is unwilling to do for us? Hardly.

The point is that Stephen did not start out with a strategy to redirect the course of history. Most great men of history never did. Their obedience to Christ, multiplied by the Holy Spirit, equaled the accomplishment of an unbelievable blessing God was patiently waiting to give through a willing channel.

On a human level Stephen was not naturally any greater than you and I. The difficulties he went through brought out what the Lord had worked into his character.

If we are willing to be as open to the Holy Spirit as Stephen was, then we will be trusted with the kind of difficulties and challenges he was. But we won't see this as trouble; we will be able to allow life to happen to us fully. Instead of resisting reality, we can befriend it, knowing the Lord will use it. That could make all the difference for you and for me for today and all tomorrows.

It will be in those times of pressure and pain that we will be forced to pray Stephen's prayer, not for our dying, but for our living: "Lord, receive my Spirit." And instead of negating and hating the people who cause us difficulty or frustration, we will be able to pray, "Lord, forgive; don't hold it against them!"

Our prayer needs to be: "Lord, give me your Holy Spirit; pour into me faith, grace, power, wisdom, and freedom to believe you can do signs and wonders in and around me. Then give me whatever challenges you can use to bless others and expand your Church. And I ask only one thing more. May at least one person see in my face the face of an angel. There are lots of Sauls who are watching, Lord. Help me to obey and be faithful!"

CHAPTER 8

While in Hollywood, Don't Miss Samaria!

Acts 8:4–25

The corner of Hollywood Boulevard and Vine Street was made famous years ago by radio broadcasts which emanated from there. Tourists from around the country still go to this intersection expecting to see Hollywood in action, but many are disappointed. There aren't any stars lingering about waiting to give autographs. "Man on the street" broadcasts are nowhere to be found; there are no movie companies with cameras grinding out a new movie. Hollywood Boulevard is equally disappointing to visitors who expect to find movie personalities hard at work. One man from Iowa expressed the disappointment many star-struck visitors feel: "So this is Hollywood?"

On top of one of the buildings at Hollywood and Vine there is a billboard which redirects the attention of tourists. The movie industry can be observed in the studios and tours are available, it explains. The bold letters of the advertisement say a lot more than the sponsors intended: "While in Hollywood, Don't Miss Hollywood." The intent is to encourage people to witness the major attraction of the movie industry while in Hollywood.

I got to thinking about how that sign would look on top of the church building of Hollywood Presbyterian Church just a few blocks away. I had been grappling with Acts 8:4–25, the startling story of what happened to the new Church in Samaria, and how much our people and all contemporary Christians need what happened there. That made me envision a billboard which would focus the deepest need in our own lives, our church, and most other churches I know about. "While in Hollywood, Don't Miss Samaria!" Or put even more directly, "While enjoying the life of Hollywood Church, don't miss what happened in the Samaritan Church." Change the geography, put the name of your church in the sign, and you will be on target. The most profound need in most American churches is for what happened in the Samaritan church.

"Don't Miss Samaria!" Those words kept coming back to my mind as I considered Luke's account of Philip's visit there to preach the gospel and be obstetrical overseer of the birth of their church and, subsequently, Peter and John's pediatric guidance for the growing fellowship of believers. There are two distinct aspects of ministry in the city of Samaria: Philip's preaching of the living Christ, and Peter and John's visit to lay hands on the people so that they might receive the Holy Spirit. There are churches in America that need both the preaching of the Word and the infilling of the Holy Spirit, but the most obvious need is for the latter. There are churches which have heard the Word preached for years and yet evidence little of the power, joy, and liberation of the Holy Spirit.

This is no less true of individuals who have heard the good news of Christ's atoning death and his resurrected glory told over and over again. Many have responded and committed as much of themselves as they know to as much of Christ as they have learned. But the intimacy, intensity, and intervening power of the Holy Spirit is lacking. They have missed what happened in Samaria!

Prompted by that urgent consideration, let's look at the Samarian church. Several questions guide our exposition and ache for some explanation. Are there two steps in becoming an empowered Christian? Why didn't Philip's preaching of the Word give the Samaritans all they needed? Why was it necessary for Peter and John to come to lay hands on the new believers so that they might receive the Holy Spirit? And, much more personally—is my church, your church, most like the Samaritan church before or after the Apostles' visit? Is my life exemplified by life before or after Philip, or before or after Peter and John's ministry?

Some background is necessary. After the martyrdom of Stephen and the persecution of the followers of Jesus in Jerusa-

lem, the Church was forced to scatter for safety in the regions
of Judea and Samaria. Jesus' ascension promise was coming true.
His people would be his witnesses in Judea, Samaria, and the
uttermost parts of the earth. And that's exactly what they became.
"Now those who were scattered went about preaching the Word"
(Acts 8:4).

Philip, one of the newly elected deacons, went down to a city
of Samaria. That's significant! The Samaritans were half-breeds,
people whose pure Hebrew blood had been mingled with other
nations through intermarriage. At the time of the fall of the
Northern Kingdom in 722 B.C., many Jews were killed. Some
were carried off by their captors. The Assyrians repopulated the
region from around their empire, and these colonists intermarried
with the remaining Jews. The Samaritans, the descendants of
these mixed marriages, were abhorred and hated by Jewish pur-
ists. That issue was focused in Jesus' ministry. His love and concern for all people was expressed by his activity among the
Samaritans. The woman by Jacob's well in Sychar expressed the
bleeding wounds of prejudice between the Jews and Samaritans:
"How is it that you, a Jew, ask a drink of me, a woman of
Samaria?" When Jesus wanted to astound his disciples about
caring love, he used a "good Samaritan" as the central character
of one of his most telling parables. In substance he was saying,
"Even a Samaritan, whom you have been taught to demean,
showed greater caring than a Hebrew priest or Levite." The fact
that Jesus would use a Samaritan in this way shows how deeply
ingrained the prejudice against the Samaritans had become.

And yet, here was Philip preaching the gospel in a Samaritan
village. Historical honesty forces us to admit that this was not
point one in a carefully outlined strategy of the early Church
for the expansion of the fellowship to the world. Persecution
prompted it; scattering motivated it. The followers of the resurrected Lord were equally amazed that their zeal for Christ superseded ancient prejudices. Without thinking about it, they shared
the good news wherever they went. They couldn't help it. Their
joy spilled over on Jews, half-breeds and Gentiles alike. They
didn't stop to ask the questions which would later haunt the
Church: "Does a person first have to become a Jew to receive
Christ? Is Christ's salvation for the revitalization of Judaism or
is it hope for all men, all over the world?"

Those theological questions didn't seem to occur to Philip. He simply found himself in Samaria and did what was now more natural than breathing, sleeping, or eating: he preached the love and forgiveness of Jesus Christ. Luke has told us already that Philip was among those who were of "good repute, full of the Spirit and of wisdom" (Acts 6:3). The word for "repute" is really *martyr* or *witness*. Philip was a good witness to Jesus because the Spirit was in him, providing the wisdom he needed as a communicator. He proclaimed Christ. The Greek word used is *ekērussen*, from *kerusso*, meaning "to proclaim as a herald." What he proclaimed was the *euaggelizo*, the good news of the gospel, the Kingdom of God and the name of Jesus Christ, that is, the power of his death and resurrection. Once again, as was the case with Stephen in Jerusalem, Philip's preaching and witness were accompanied by mental and physical signs and wonders. Unclean spirits were cast out, people were healed, and Christ's love liberated people to accept love and forgiveness. Joy filled the city.

Luke again uses literary comparison to heighten an understanding and appreciation of a character as he contrasts Philip with Simon the magician. Prior to Philip's visit, Simon had held the city under the spell of his personality and magic. Luke tells us that he amazed the nation of Samaria, saying that he himself was somebody great. The people's response was, "This man is that power of God which is called Great" (8:10). But when Philip came among them, preaching not himself, but Christ, they experienced a greater power than magic. Before their very eyes they saw people transformed by the resurrected Lord. Even Simon believed, and, along with others, he was baptized. But there was still something lacking in Simon, as we shall see. For him and all the new believers in Samaria, the preaching of the gospel, conversion, and the experience of grace was not enough. There was an incompleteness, an unfulfillment. They had received the gospel intellectually and had begun, with human effort, to live it. But Philip had left a crucial dimension out of his proclamation. In fact, his proclamation of half the gospel had left them half healed.

What was missing? There have been many conjectures. My conclusion is that Philip had not been personal enough with the Samaritans to tell them his own struggles to live the gospel without the regenerating power of the Holy Spirit. Any preacher or witness to Christ who proclaims the matchless wonders of salvation without making clear the crucial necessity for the Holy Spirit to live within us and give us the power to live the new life, has given his listeners hope without healing, potential without power to live it. We can know the facts of what Christ did without having the enabling power of what he is doing. It is obvious from Luke's account that Philip preached Christ, the Kingdom of God, and the necessity of a water baptism of repentance (Luke is usually very clear about what was preached), but nowhere does he mention that Philip told about Pentecost and the necessity of receiving the Holy Spirit in order to have the motivating, driving power for the new life in Christ—an experience of present, vital contact. Philip left out their need for the quickening life of Christ in them to animate their discipleship, the kindling fire to give a glow to their witness.

It is there between Philip's eloquent proclamation of the gospel and the visit of the Apostles that we find the contemporary Church and most Christians longing in limbo. Great multitudes had intellectually accepted the truth but did not have uplifting liberation of the Spirit of the Savior they had accepted. The same is true today.

Look around us. There are churchmen who faithfully follow the message and example of the historical Jesus. Some of us are among them, feeling the excruciating plight of trying to be good Christians. Some of us can outline the plan of salvation impeccably: man's need in sin; God's action in Christ for forgiveness; full acceptance of the Cross and dedication to follow Christ; study, worship and prayer as basic to growing in Christ; the importance of sharing Christ's life with others. Church pews are filled with people who have done their best to respond and who come to church Sunday after Sunday, longing to get enough vision and vitality to live another week. But in between, we suffer the embarrassing exposure of our impotence to deal with life's demands, conflicts, and challenges. Many of us would have to admit that, in essence, there has been little change in our attitudes, little transformation of our characters, inadequate power to live in our relationships, and insufficient courage to apply what we believe.

Halford Luccock said pointedly: "Many a church bears the

name of Christian though it is without the gift of the Holy Spirit, and the presence or absence of that gift is closely related to the power or impotence of a church. It is so easy for a church to have all its forms in order and its pedigree intact, and yet lack the present life of God."*

Allow me to be blunt. The contemporary proclamation of the gospel helps us cope with what has been but does not help us contemplate what could be. Most of us could not make it without the often-repeated assurance of Christ's love and his forgiveness for our mistakes, goofs, and misfired intentions. The affirmation of an acceptance by the Savior is like water to a thirsty man or food to one who is famished. What would life be without it? But what could life be with the indwelling power of the Holy Spirit? Why do we hear so little about that? The Church is like an obstetrical clinic which assists birth but does not enable newborn babies to breathe in the breath of life. The result is lots of Christian babes out of the womb, but not fully alive!

I want to develop a working postulate as to why this was true in Samaria. Philip had been born into Christ in the Pentecost-powered Church. He had heard the gospel from the Apostles and had experienced the living Christ in the Holy Spirit. For him intellect, emotion, and will had been united in a response to Christ and the faith. In the warm fellowship of the apostolic Church he lived with the shared enthusiasm and excitement of the church alive. His commitment to Christ and reception of the Spirit of Christ had been one unified experience. That is why he was known as one "full of the Holy Spirit." What he had missed was the necessity for proclaiming the absolutely irreplaceable dimension of the Holy Spirit in his preaching of the whole truth of the gospel. He preached an authoritative, evangelistic message about the Messiahship of Jesus, the Kingdom of God, the saving name of Jesus, but left out the secret of living and growing—the Holy Spirit. Yet, God was faithful to bless all that Philip proclaimed. It was through the initiating influence of the Spirit that people responded so enthusiastically. But at no point did Philip say honestly, "Now, you are going to have difficulty

---

* Halford E. Luccock, *The Acts of the Apostles* (New York: Harper and Bros., 1938, 1942), p. 145.

living out what you have believed. You will face times of deep disappointment with yourselves and others. You will be frustrated and disturbed by your own inadequacy. That's when you will need the Holy Spirit, Christ alive, the same Lord whose death and Resurrection, Messiahship, and Lordship you have accepted. Don't try to live this new life without the Holy Spirit. It will bring you to despair and anguish!"

Peter and John knew this. They had been through the experience of trying to live the admonitions of Christ without the assuring presence of Christ. Pentecost had ended the anxious period of human effort. That's why, when they arrived in Samaria, they could discern immediately from their own experience what was missing, what it was that ached for completion. The Samaritans needed the Holy Spirit!

My conviction is that in the interim between Philip's preaching and the visit of Peter and John the telltale signs of humanly propelled Christian living were already evident. The wilting of the bloom on the bud was obvious. The frail roots needed to be transplanted from the shallow ground of human adequacy into the fertile soil of the limitless moisture and nurture of the Holy Spirit. That's why, undoubtedly, Peter and John told the Samaritans about the Spirit's power to regenerate—to actually change their lives—and sanctification—to make them like the Savior in character, attitude, and action. Intellectual assent was now coupled with acceptance of the Holy Spirit.

This account does not set up a system of how the Holy Spirit is given to believers. We must continuously resist saying that the Holy Spirit is not given at conversion. Conversion is itself a gift of the Holy Spirit. As we have noted previously, no man says that Jesus Christ is Lord except by the Holy Spirit. Paul was very clear about that (1 Cor. 12:3). But to say Jesus Christ is our Lord, our strength and our sustainer—that is often a realized confession after a person has tried to live the Christian life on his own resources and failed. That's when the same Spirit who enabled the first step picks up a defeated Christian and empowers him. Then, when he gets involved in Christ's ministry with people, the special gifts of the Holy Spirit are given and the fruit of the Spirit is evident in his life.

That's what happened in Samaria. The new Christians had been baptized into Christ. Then they were baptized by the Holy

Spirit. One baptism was the result of their repentance; the other, the result of the Spirit's regeneration. The two need not be separated, but in the Samaritan village they were, and, as experience teaches us, so have they been separated in history. But never more so than now.

I think of churches I know which are receiving the power of the Holy Spirit. In each case there has been a renewal in the life of the pastor. The nationwide revitalization of clergy taking place today has in most cases come through experiences that have enabled the clergy to admit their own need and allow what they are preaching to get into their own lives.

A leading pastor serving a strategic Episcopal church confided in me recently: "I had run out of steam. My church was moving along casually with business as usual. Each year I had come up with clever brochures to raise money, interesting topics for classes in my church which would attract attendance but not upset anybody, fascinating sermon topics to entertain people. I was tired out, dried up inside. The people seemed satisfied, and I'm sure I could have gone on that way for the rest of my ministry. Then last spring I had to come up with a Pentecost sermon to celebrate Whitsunday. I started my study at the beginning of the week with a ho-hum, here-we-go-again obedience to the liturgical calendar. But that same week I had a terrible crisis in my family. One of my children was in deep trouble. I desperately needed help to cope. My study of the Holy Spirit had reminded me of God's immediate and intimate power, and I specifically prayed for the Holy Spirit in my own life. The answer came the Saturday night before I was to preach. I felt impelled to share with the congregation that Pentecost could happen today and that the Holy Spirit, the Living Lord, could intervene in our needs. There was an electricity in the sanctuary. The whole service was different! The Holy Spirit was there! That day marked the beginning of a movement which has set my church on fire."

Then I am reminded of an outstanding Presbyterian church where I took part in a conference recently. A letter from one of the church officers sounded as if it had come from the Samaritan church. "Something happened to us last weekend. We all have believed in Christ for years. We are very orthodox, as you know. The gospel is preached from our pulpit and our church school is soundly biblical. But during the conference a lot of us realized that we had grown dull and satisfied. If we ever had a deeply personal relationship with Christ, you would never have known it, we were so cold and proper. Then when we heard about the power available in the Holy Spirit, many of us realized that we had been trying to be good Christians on our own verve. As a result of the conference, we've got a new church around here! The chance to open up a bit about our own needs and to hear Bible studies on the blessings of the Holy Spirit seemed to be the magic combination. It's a bit frightening to think about what we've been missing. The only time we had even heard the words 'Holy Spirit' was in the pastor's benediction. Now as a result of what's happening in our Session, he never presents the plan of salvation without telling about the necessity of receiving the Holy Spirit."

What this church officer wrote I have seen incarnated in thousands of church people over the years. It has led me to a disturbing conclusion: It's possible to hear the gospel, take part in church activities, and be a faithful contributor without the experience of a vital living relationship with the Spirit of God. We can pray prayers without talking to God; we can teach and learn truth without being transformed by the truth; we can work for Christian causes without being healed ourselves; we can read the Bible and live with messed-up relationships; we can hear about the power of the Spirit and live inhibited, intransient lives.

Last spring, at a committee meeting, a prominent member of my church leaned over and whispered a request. "I need to see you. When you have a free hour, give me a call." When the man came in to see me, he said, "I feel I'm missing something. I have been reading Acts and listening to tapes about the Holy Spirit, and I feel that's what I need. Many of my friends think I should go to a Pentecostal pastor and talk to him about it, but I think maybe you can help me. Acts 8 has gotten to me. I think I must be like one of those Samaritan Christians." We talked at length as I tried to plumb the depths of his life to see what inhibitions or problems might be holding him back. To my surprise, I found none—just a fine, healthy churchman feeling there was more than he had experienced. Then, in the quiet of my study, I laid my hands on his head and prayed for the power of the Holy Spirit to fill his life. That was a new beginning for him. But the same Spirit for whom we prayed has led him into serendipities he never anticipated; and the gift we asked for came, not in some ecstatic emotion, but in new warmth, power to love, fresh insight into Scripture, and prophetic vision of what can happen through him and others in his church and in his work. This man is in his late forties, and he contradicts the notion that little personality change can take place during middle age.

A woman twenty-five years this man's junior talked to me a few summers ago at a youth conference. What she said forced me to reevaluate our church school program in American churches. She said, "I've heard the Christian message for years. I have memorized Scripture and can give the steps of salvation in my sleep. I can tell what a teacher or preacher is going to say after he opens his talk. But this week I've heard something new. The Holy Spirit really bugs me. Do you people really mean that the Spirit can live in me and that I can get personal help? There were always two worlds before: my little, worried, lonesome world and the unreachable world of great truths I've heard talked about but could never feel." We made a covenant that I would pray for the Holy Spirit to reveal his power to her. Her part of the bargain was to pray ten minutes each day and consciously surrender her problems and concerns to him. I saw her recently at a college chapel service where I spoke. The transformation in this young woman was a beautiful gift from God. She was dynamic and gracious, and her enthusiasm was contagious. This young Samaritan had received the Holy Spirit! What happened to her I long to have happen to young people whose church school experience has vaccinated them from realizing the real vitality of the Christian faith.

I have come to believe that the possibility of receiving the Holy Spirit by believing Christians depends upon one ingredient or a combination of ingredients. There is usually a need which we cannot fill ourselves, or a challenge which goes beyond our wisdom and strength, or a sense of unfulfillment in our Christian experience. Christians on the move are rarely free of all three of these circumstances. If we do not recognize them, we have probably checkmated God or have walled off the influence he is exercising in our hearts. I don't know of a dynamic Christian who is completely free of a burning sense of need. The secret of Christian living is that the closer we grow to Christ, the more we long to know more of him; the greater we sense his strategy, the more we need and pray urgently for the Holy Spirit.

But never must we pray to receive the Holy Spirit for our own comfort or pious pleasure. Luke concludes his story of what happened in Samaria by presenting another telling comparison with Simon the Magician. Simon becomes the patron of people who want the spiritual power of the Holy Spirit for personal aggrandizement and not for involvement in Christ's ministry. His sin was that he wanted the Holy Spirit for personal ends, as one more bit of magic to add to his bag of tricks. Seeing what power had been released in people after the Apostles had laid their hands upon them and they had received the Holy Spirit, Simon offered the Apostles money, saying, "Give me also this power, that anyone on whom I lay my hands may receive the Holy Spirit." Note that he did not confess his own need nor his desperate need to love others and help them; rather, he wanted the superiority and prestige of being able to give the Spirit to others. You can be sure that if he offered money to get the gift of mediating the Holy Spirit, he would expect the same, and more, from other people.

Peter's stern answer to Simon was more than a rebuke to a magician. It stands as a warning to all of us who want spiritual power without paying the true price, which no amount of money can attain: "Your silver perish with you, because you thought you could obtain the gift of God with money! You have neither part nor lot in this matter, for your heart is not right before God. Repent therefore, of this wickedness of yours, and pray to the Lord that, if possible, the intent of your heart may be forgiven you. For I see that you are in the gall of bitterness and in the bond of iniquity" (8:20-23).

Strong confrontation, that! For us, it means that we cannot expect the Holy Spirit's power until we have opened our hidden hearts to the Lord. Simon had said that he believed in Christ and was among those who were baptized. Yet his inner life was still untouched. In it were bitterness and compulsive patterns of rebellious self-will. Simon was still in charge of Simon. He wanted a spiritual high while his heart was still low-down; he wanted gush without grace through repentance and forgiveness.

Simony is a word which comes from that spiritual sickness. Historically, it meant the buying and selling of position and office within the Church. But there is also a subtle simony in all of us. We all would like to have a spiritual radiance without repentance. We want Life without having to change our life-style. Hidden sins; fantasies we could never tell anyone; broken, hostile relationships; determined patterns of thought that con-tradict the gospel; habits; selfish attitudes which emaciate the people around us—all these lurk within most of us, while at the same time we say we want Christ as Lord of our lives and his living Spirit as the power of our living. We are willing to pay handsomely for the worst and best of two worlds—not only money, but religious activity, self-generated goodness, oblations of overactivity, and manipulative kindness—all so we won't have to let down the moat bridge of the castles of our carefully protected, secret hearts. But the very things we hide are the point of entry for the Holy Spirit. When we confess them, accept for-giveness, and turn them over one by one, the Spirit takes their place. As in the room swept clean of demons in Jesus' parable, there must be something, Someone, to fill the emptiness. Only his Spirit, the Holy Spirit, can do that!

But I can't help being deeply shocked at Simon's reply. He remains immovable in his determination to coexist with both himself and Christ as lords of his life. Instead of changing his heart and repenting, he says, "Pray for me to the Lord, that nothing of what you have said may come upon me." What he said has been repeated by all of us. "Friend, I can't—I won't—change, but pray that the Lord won't judge me and will bless me anyhow!" The Holy Spirit cannot be given in response to that. Could this be the reason there is so little Holy Spirit power among Christians today? Some people have never heard what the Holy Spirit can do in their lives, and that's a sorry commentary on churches and preaching. But what about those of us who have heard about the grace and gifts he will impart and still are not filled with the Holy Spirit? Could it be there's no room?

All of this is why I say, don't miss Samaria. While in Holly-wood, or Houston, Des Moines or Junction City, or wherever you live, don't miss Samaria. What happened there is for all of us and our churches. Philip has been working for a long time. Perhaps it's time for the Apostles to come with the Holy Spirit.

Simon, watch out! The price is high—more than all your silver. It's confession of need, repentance, a new daring. But look at what happened in Samaria. That's worth everything. Don't miss it!

CHAPTER 9

The Secret of an Exciting Life

Acts 8:26–40

I want to share with you what I believe is the secret of an exciting life. People who have discovered it are some of the most attractive, winsome people I know. They sparkle and shine with an identifiable radiance. Their lives are distinguished by an eagerness and earnestness. They have zest and zeal. I believe I have discovered this secret, and it's the source of the unquenchable enthusiasm I feel about living.

The mysterious origin of this vitality is traceable to two words: *guidance* and *obedience*. This triumphant tandem is the belief that the Holy Spirit actually can guide our thoughts and that obedience can appropriate his power to do what is guided. The overwhelming wonder stems from the amazing fact that the Holy Spirit can put into our minds ideas, insights, possibilities, and directions which we would never have conceived or dared contemplate without him. He knows not only the past and present, but the future; not only what we need, but what we will need; not only our own concerns, but those of others. And he has chosen us as channels to do his work in the world. The Holy God, creator of all, Savior and Lord, will use.you and me! We can cooperate with him in accomplishing his plans and purpose in people and situations.

R. H. L. Sheppard found this secret. He said, "Christianity does not consist in abstaining from doing things no gentleman would think of doing, but in doing things that are unlikely to occur to anyone who is not in touch with the Spirit of Christ."

When I first read these words, it was like taking hold of a live wire. I couldn't let go. A current of electricity surged through me; "That's it!" I thought. There's the secret: not just abstinence, but affirmation. A Christ-honed conscience can guide our morals, ethics, and personal behavior. That's maintenance, but what of adventure? That begins when we love the Lord with our minds and dare to believe that he can invade the tissues of our forebrain to guide our thinking, imagination, and will. When we are filled with the Holy Spirit, there is an inspiring indistinction between his thoughts and ours. He becomes the Lord of our intelligence, the generator of the mind's potency for possibilities we never dreamed could be. Couple that with the will to act on what he guides, and you have the secret of exciting living.

That's what made Philip the man he was. He was guided by the Holy Spirit, and he was obedient. In Acts 8:26–40, we discover why he was so effective. He was Spirit-directed, and serendipities occurred wherever he went. He did and said what he was told, a man under orders. Our consideration of this passage of Scripture is to uncover how the Spirit wants to work in and through us today.

Verses 26 and 27 are astounding. They show us that when the Spirit controls our minds, we are open, ready, available. An angel of the Lord gave Philip very clear orders to "rise and go toward the south to a road that goes down from Jerusalem to Gaza." Note that he did not ask why or what he was to do when he got there. Most of us would have wanted a detailed briefing with everything planned down to the last minutiae. Not Philip. He had discovered the secret of an exciting life: "And he rose and went." Dynamic Christian living is capsulized in these five words. The fact that he rose, or got up, says to me that he had been sitting down; or, more consistent with Luke's intended message, I imagine he got up from his prayer knees and went to do what he was told. Philip was a God-called, filled, guided, sent man of power.

Don't miss several very crucial things about these verses. One, God does guide his people. He can get through to us by implanting thoughts and directions. In this portion of Acts Philip is instructed by an angel and later by the Spirit. The names are interchangeable: an angel is a messenger of God; the Spirit is the immediacy of God at work in the mind and soul. The point, however, is that Philip was a cooperative person who could both hear and respond to the influence and instruction of the living God. That same possibility exists for you and me.

But also observe a second insight. Philip was given just enough guidance to change his plans and go in a new direction. What trust and flexibility! The Lord guides us both *into* and *in* the situations he has prepared for us. It takes raw courage to obey in one without being sure of the other. Often we are given just enough guidance to take the first step. Philip obeyed because he believed that the Lord knew what he was doing and he could leave the results to him.

Now penetrate the meaning of the passage further. Philip was not just given direction on the way to go, but when to go. The issue of his obedience was the Lord's timing. He did not need to be told that the road from Jerusalem to Gaza went south. Just as a person in Los Angeles would not need to be told that Route 405 goes south to San Diego, so too Philip did not require a geography lesson. The crucial issue was when. The Greek word which is translated "south" in our text usually means midday or noon. ("At noon" is offered as a footnote alternative in the Revised Standard Version.) The Lord wanted Philip on that road at a particular time for what he was preparing. I am utterly amazed that Philip did not say, "Midday, Lord? On that sun-blistered road in the desert? You must have something very important in mind for that. You'd better level with me about what you're up to."

Perhaps the reason many of us miscarry in the great things God has prepared is because we miss his timing. Think of the opportunities we have never experienced because we were immobilized on some dead center waiting for the "big picture" before we would do the Lord's will. Philip didn't wait.

Luke's words "and behold" in verse 28 are more than a transitional phrase. They are the author's exclamation point. He wanted to stress the point of the Lord's accurate timing for a holy hookup of two people he wanted together. It is as if Luke were saying, "And look! Don't miss what happened because Philip obeyed!"

The startling fact is that Philip's willingness to be positioned on that road at that time and place made possible the miracle of the transformation of a human being! Guidance is relational. It grows out of a relationship with the Holy Spirit, and it usually results in the blessing of a relationship in which he wants us to be his person and to communicate his love and hope.

The Spirit's timing was perfect that day on the desert road to Gaza. The Secretary of the Treasury of the Candace Dynasty of Ethiopia was also on that road. Luke paints a vivid portrait of the man, giving us both his outward circumstances and his inner condition. We can picture this African leader riding in his stately chariot surrounded by the accoutrements of his position and power. He was a eunuch who had risen to great influence serving the Queen of Ethiopia. But all the outward manifestations of courtly pomp did not satisfy the longings of his inner being.

That hunger brought him under the influence of monotheistic Judaism. Perhaps some of the Jews who had been flung to the distant regions by persecution or trading opportunities had introduced him to the dynamics of their belief in Yahweh and an ordered life based on Moses' Law. It seems certain that he had become a proselyte Jew. His longing for truth and reality had prompted him to make a journey to Jerusalem, the center of Hebrew religion and culture. We are told that he had come to worship. The Greek means that he was on a pilgrimage.

Everything Luke tells us about the Ethiopian indicates that he was not a satisfied pilgrim when he left Jerusalem. The temple, the sacrifices, and the rehearsal of ancient customs had not fed the spiritual hunger in him. But the Lord knew his need. He had brought him to Jerusalem, not for what he could find there, but for what he would experience on the road home with a young man who had the clarity of the gospel in his head and the fire of the Holy Spirit in his heart. Philip and the Treasurer of Ethiopia met on the road by the Spirit's design. The eunuch's disappointment with Jerusalem was to be superseded by the Lord's appointment.

The story moves quickly. Philip is given the next stage of guidance. He had been open to go; now he was to understand why. The same willingness which got him on the Gaza road at the right time also got him up into that pretentious chariot of the Ethiopian. When he saw the chariot moving slowly ahead of him, the Spirit spoke to him—again the remarkable power of God to break into thought and conceive an idea! The Spirit said, "Go up and join the chariot." The Greek words unlock the astounding admonition; in the first aorist passive imperative mood here, they mean "join yourself to, be glued to." The impact is clear: Philip is to get next to this awesome-appearing leader, glue his concern on him, focus his total attention on him, become united to his need. We wonder if Philip exclaimed within himself, "Lord, now I know why you sent me here at this moment!" We cannot be sure, but what we can discern is that in keeping with his Spirit-enabled responsiveness, he probably prayed as he was climbing into the chariot, "Lord, use me. Tell me what to say. Make me sensitive, open, contagious."

Underline the thought that some prayer like that must have been prayed by Philip because of the obvious way the Spirit guided what and how he spoke. The guidance of the Holy Spirit is never more effective or evident than when he uses us to communicate the love and forgiveness of Christ to another. Allow the Spirit to use what he did in Philip to thunder a stirring thought in your heart: He can guide what we are to say in the situations and relationships into which he has led us!

Philip clearly received the gifts of wisdom, discernment, and bold faith. There was an infusion of empathy and insight.

Note the progression of the Spirit's guidance. In each step we discover what he wants to give us.

First Philip listened. The Spirit's most sensitive guidance is often what and when *not* to speak. Philip had the fruit of the Spirit in patience. He did not climb into the chariot and begin a prewritten oration about salvation. Instead, as he listened, he overheard the Ethiopian reading from a scroll of the prophet Isaiah which he had probably purchased in Jerusalem. He was reading the words over and over again. The same Spirit guiding Philip was guiding the eunuch to one of the most crucial passages of Hebrew Scripture, the 53rd chapter of Isaiah, the clear prediction of the suffering Messiah: "As a sheep led to the slaughter or a lamb before its shearer is dumb, so he opens not his mouth. In his humiliation justice was denied him. Who can describe this generation? For his life is taken up from the earth" (Acts 8:32–33).

Hearing this, Philip asked a question. That was the second step of the Spirit's guidance. What genius he was given! Instead of saying, "An Ethiopian like you probably doesn't understand what Isaiah is talking about. I've been sent here to straighten you out!" Philip questioned with authentic concern. He got into the Ethiopian's "space" and felt with him the longings of his heart. Note that Philip was neither put off nor overly impressed with the man's stature or wealth. His question was drenched with love and tender helpfulness.

Only the Spirit can help us to come alongside another person and catch the impact of what he is thinking, going through, or hoping for his life. Gentle questions guided by the Holy Spirit communicate interest, esteem, affirmation, and encouragement of another person. I have witnessed hundreds of people come to the experience of Christ through initiative love expressed through persons who genuinely wanted to know about them and their needs. Friends, fellow workers, "chance" acquaintances at parties have felt the impact of grace through inquiring questions that helped them know that someone cared, was interested in them, and had something to share, but in the context of their particular concern.

Now move on in our look at the Spirit's guidance of Philip. He knew his Scriptures. As a fulfilled Hebrew, he knew both the hope of Isaiah and the completion of that hope in Jesus, the Messiah. Philip moved right out onto the edge of discovery to which the Spirit had guided the Ethiopian. He neither changed the subject to get to something on his agenda, nor did he redirect the conversation to present Christ in his own favorite fashion. The most effective way to present Christ is to pick people up where they are in their search for reality in some religion, philosophy, cult, or contemporary spiritual fad.

The other day a woman was expounding to me the virtues of transcendental meditation. She told me about being given a mantra, or magic word, to repeat in her twice-daily, fifteen-minute meditation. A mantra is defined as a thought, the effects of which are known. The word, she said, led her into deep identification with herself and reality. I affirmed her search. Then the Spirit gave me a question which a thousand hours of planning and preparation for that conversation could never have prompted. "Does the word you are using put you in touch with the limitless power that created the universe?" Immediately she wanted to know my word. More than a mantra! The name of

Jesus Christ! But she could never have heard me or subsequently given her life to the Savior and learned to pray in his name if I had not taken delight in her and her urgent search for peace. The Spirit can and does guide our conversations. And yet that evening when I was getting ready to go to the party at which I met this woman, I had no idea what the Spirit had been preparing. I had felt impelled to go in spite of my desire to have an evening at home. Someone once said, "Stop praying and the coincidences stop happening."

The fact that Philip knew the Isaiah Scriptures indicates that the Spirit had been preparing the way long before he received guidance to "rise and go." I am convinced that Philip's instruction in the Scriptures before he accepted Christ and was filled with the Spirit and his later instruction in the fellowship of the Church under the scripturally astute Apostles was for this moment with the eunuch.

What an exciting thing it is to realize that the Spirit is unbound by time or space! He can use the preparation of the past for present effectiveness and is ubiquitously on the move to utilize what's happened for what he wants to happen. That's the mystery of the guided life.

The Ethiopian's response to Philip's targeted question indicated that his previous pleas for help had gone unheeded. He responds to the question with a pitiful question of his own that is really a plea. "How can I, unless someone guides me?" He had been to Jerusalem for help. The greatest Hebrew scholars of the time were there. If he was reading the passage repetitiously, as Philip's question suggests in the Greek, surely he had been reading and asking questions in Jerusalem. Philip utilized the moment. He helped the Nubian pilgrim understand that the one about whom Isaiah spoke was the Savior of the world and could be his Savior. Philip told him the good news of what God had done in Christ and then what that meant in his own experience.

Lastly, note that Philip's guidance from the Spirit liberated him from pushing the man. He did not feel impelled to close the deal with urgent sales techniques. He trusted the Spirit in the eunuch. When they came to a pool of water, surely Philip saw the water beside the road before the potential convert did. But he waited, and, I'm sure, he prayed. How much more last-

ing is a conversion which has been motivated from within by
the Spirit rather than manipulated from without by a ritual
compulsion.

When the Ethiopian asked to be baptized, it is obvious that
repentance and symbolic baptism of dedication had been a part
of Philip's Spirit-worded message, but as an offer to be received,
not as an obligation to be fulfilled. Listen to the Spirit-prompted
longing in the Ethiopian! "See, here is water! What is to pre-
vent my being baptized?" This was surely God's movement. The
eunuch was baptized and entered eternal life, the now-oriented
abundant life, for which Jesus, the Lamb of God about whom
he had been reading, had died and was raised up to give him.
God had had the pilgrim from Ethiopia in mind all along: in
a creche in Bethlehem, a Cross on Calvary, a Spirit-empowered
church in Jerusalem, a vulnerable, leadable deacon, a road to
Gaza, Scriptures written hundreds of years before, the water
beside the road and a baptism into life. The Lord who made the
universe and redeemed it is alive doing all things well!

But not without you and me as irreplaceable channels of his
love and power—that shakes me a bit! The Lord of all creation
has ordained that he would do his work through us. Our seeking his Spirit's guidance and obeying what he wants us to do
and say is the way he works to bless the world.

That necessitates getting acquainted with the Spirit and dis-
covering how to listen and respond. Nothing is more crucial
than that—for ourselves, for people around us, for the Church,
for a society aching for solutions to problems only the Spirit
can unravel. Bonhoeffer was on target: "Only he who believes
obeys and only he who obeys believes." * We cannot grow in
belief unless we obey what we have been guided to do as implications of what we believe already. Guidance and obedience
must be kept together.

Now, to nail down what this passage has said to us today, we
need to identify the building blocks of an exciting life in this
account.

The first is that Philip was a man "full of the Holy Spirit"
(Acts 6:3) and therefore could be guided by the Spirit. Prepa-

* Dietrich Bonhoeffer, *The Cost of Discipleship* (New York: Macmillan, 1960), p. 54.

ration for the Gaza road began when the Spirit took possession
of his mind long before. Our capacity to be guided is in direct
proportion to our consistently faithful receptivity to the true
Spirit in our own minds. If we have previously allowed him full
access to our thoughts, he will guide us particularly in the present. It's easier to steer a moving vehicle than one that is stopped.
If we are on the move in the Spirit, he can guide us more easily.
So the first step to becoming a guided person is to ask to be
filled with the Holy Spirit.

Many present-day Christians miss out here. We go to God
for guidance about problems or people as if we could plug in
and out of the flow of intellectual wisdom. Repeatedly we wring
our hands, asking, "Lord, what do you want me to do?" Often
when we seek guidance, it's a sure sign that we are out of it!
The Lord wants to get us to the place where we are constantly
in touch with him, allowing our minds to channel his thoughts
and direction. Then he can guide us naturally, momentarily,
persistently. Getting guidance then is not a crisis. He has been
working in us before the crisis occurs. If we are constantly
besieging him with some new indecision which has occurred because we have been out of fellowship with him, we will not be
open to the surprises he has prepared for the world around us
through us.

The second building block I see in this passage is that Philip
trusted the Spirit and did not try to distinguish between his own
desires and the Spirit's direction. There was a glorious indistinction between his thoughts and the instructions of the Spirit.
Philip did not say what most of us would say: "I wonder if the
idea of going down to Gaza is my own idea, some foolish whim
of my fancy, some compulsion to get away from where I am."
He dared to believe that the Spirit within him could be trusted.

So often the self-condemning mistrust we have of our insights
and ideas blocks out the guidance the Spirit is giving. If we
have surrendered our minds to him, we can dare to honor our
thoughts.

Paul knew the secret. He distinguished between the mind set
on the Spirit and the mind set on the flesh. *Flesh* is a biblical
word for a humanity separated from the love and power of God.
A mind set on the flesh is one dependent on human training,

learning, experience, and insight. In that light, consider the distinction Paul makes in Romans 8:5–8:

> For those who live according to the flesh set their minds on the things of the flesh, but those who live according to the Spirit set their minds on the things of the Spirit. To set the mind on the flesh is death, but to set the mind on the Spirit is life and peace. For the mind that is set on the flesh is hostile to God; it does not submit to God's law, indeed it cannot, and those who are in the flesh cannot please God.

But the person in Christ is liberated from that. His mind belongs to Christ and is indwelt by his Spirit. Now reflect on Paul's description of a person who has received the mind of Christ:

> But you are not in the flesh, you are in the Spirit, if in fact the Spirit of God dwells in you. Anyone who does not have the Spirit of Christ does not belong to him. But if Christ is in you, although your bodies are dead because of sin, your spirits are alive because of righteousness. If the Spirit of him who raised Jesus from the dead dwells in you, he who raised Christ Jesus from the dead will give life to your mortal bodies also through his Spirit which dwells in you (Rom. 8:9–11).

That does away with the feverish frenzy to decide what is our selfish thought and what is the Spirit's guidance. Bottom line summation gives us the total truth: "For all who are led by the Spirit of God are the sons of God." That means you and me, praise God!

The Lord has given us reliable checkpoints for evaluating the authenticity of what we feel prompted to do or say. Here are some questions I ask myself: Is it consistent with Christ? Does it contradict his message in any way? Will it express love and bring the ultimate good of all concerned? (Note, I say *ultimate* because often we are guided to do hard things which bring temporary pain or conflict but are part of our own or another person's growth.) Will it bring me into deeper fellowship with Christ? Can I do it with him beside me? Are my motives pure? Is it manipulative? Will it extend the Kingdom? Will I be able to look back on it, free of guilt, self-incrimination, or regret?

Added to these questions is the assurance that if we fail or misfire, there is forgiveness and a chance to begin again. So why not trust the Spirit to guide us?

That leads us to the third building block. Being led by the Spirit requires a sensitive third ear in our minds. We need to say constantly what Samuel prayed: "Speak, Lord, for thy servant hears." That prayer is the motto of an exciting Spirit-guided life.

It is the secret of the adventure. The Spirit prompts us to think about something or someone. Most of us find our greatest concerns involve people. We want what is God's maximum for them. That's where a very special gift is given to a Spirit-filled person. The gift of prophecy enables us to know what God is doing in people and their circumstances. It is penetrating x-ray vision to see beneath the surface. But it is always coupled with clarity about what to do and say. God is not a God of confusion but of peace (1 Cor. 14:33) in the imparting of this precious gift.

The prompting of the Spirit's guidance comes in practical ways. Say this; write that letter; make that phone call; send that gift; make that visit; do that act out of love with no thought of reward. To refuse is fatal.

The fourth and final thing I've learned from Philip follows naturally: God's results are dependent upon our response. What would have happened if Philip had said he would rather stay in Jerusalem with the fellowship of the Apostles? The early church historian Eusebius claims that the Ethiopian, whom he calls by the name of Indich, became a Christian leader and brought the good news of the gospel to Ethiopia and was the founder of a strong church which grew there. Not only Indich, but Ethiopia was at stake in Philip's response.

We know that is true from our own lives. We have seen the results of what cooperating with the Spirit can mean for us and others. But we also know what happens when we refuse. We are painfully aware of the existential truth that God will not by-pass his chosen human agents. He has willed it so. If we resist, havoc—or what's worse, dull mediocrity—results.

I think of a father and daughter who were deadlocked in hostile silence after a family conflict. Both were wrong. The man prayed that the Lord would straighten out his daughter. One day he felt the Lord say, "Go to your daughter and apologize for your judgmentalism." The Lord knew someone had to break the bind. The father refused and the drawn swords continued, with the father continuing to pray that his daughter would change. Then one day this faithful church officer was reading his Bible and came across Paul's words, "Fathers, do not provoke your children to anger, but bring them up in the discipline of the Lord" (Eph. 6:4). Then the Spirit said to the man, "If you do not do what I have told you to do, you will not grow in the Christian life." Finally he did what he was told and healing resulted. His confession brought openness and confession from his daughter, and the two were reconciled.

A woman I know was almost hysterical about what was happening to her daughter and her grandchildren because her son-in-law didn't believe what she did. He couldn't escape the nagging with which she pressed her urgent desire for his conversion. One day, thinking about the situation, a new thought invaded her mind. "Be to your son-in-law what you hope he will become. Leave his conversion to the Lord. Stop sending tracts and literature. Think of five things you like about him, emphasize them and affirm him." From the time she dared to accept that guidance, things began to happen in the young husband's life.

A young single woman said an amazing thing: "Now that I believe God can plant thoughts in my mind, I have begun to follow orders. I can hardly believe the results. When I am guided to speak to people and say what I am led to say, they keep responding, 'That's just what I need to hear today!' The other day I called a friend who was on my mind. He was in deep trouble. 'How did you know I was having problems?' he asked. I didn't know, but I felt I had to call."

Recently a friend of mine had my wife on her mind. She couldn't let it drop. "Lord, what do you want me to do?" she prayed. That day she had a "chance" conversation with a medical doctor whose specialty is the disease my wife was battling. He asked if it would help if he called us to give encouragement. Now it just so happened that the young doctor had been a member of my congregation in Winnetka. On the phone he began by saying, "Remember that young resident who attended your church in Winnetka? Well, I'm here in Southern California now, and I've learned that you may need me." He was a great help and gave us timely advice on the very day we desperately needed it. God had arranged the whole thing because he loves us!

About the same time, a woman from Bethlehem, Pennsylvania, learned from my wife's old prayer group in Bethlehem that she needed prayer. This woman had been through the same sickness, had survived, and was completely cured. Later she accompanied her husband on a business trip to California. She visited my wife in the hospital on a day when she most needed encouragement that she would be well. She walked into the hospital room and announced, "Mary Jane, I am here on behalf of your old prayer group. They meet at 8:00 in the morning each day to pray for you. They sent me as living proof that you will lick this disease!" An angel, but not unaware!

Some time ago, a student in my church began practicing the presence of the Spirit. He had the usual personality and relational problems an emerging young man faces. He tried an experiment. He yielded the development of his personality to the Holy Spirit and asked for specific guidance on what to say and do in tough teenage problems. Already a Christian who had opened his life to the Spirit, he now asked for guidance and found a deep peace and new confidence. He moved out in daring to be the person he felt guided to be, breaking the bind of adolescent inversion and insecurity. Tenseness left, and he actually felt the Spirit working through him.

I wish a man I visited recently had learned that as a young man. He is in a chronically sick marriage. He prays about it constantly, and together he and I have prayed for it also and for him. But he has received more light than he is willing to walk in. The prayer he prays is that the Lord will solve the sexual difficulties in his marriage. For him the intimacy of sex is a vital expression of sexual desire; for his wife it is an expression of response to tenderness and warmth in the total ambience of their life together. The Spirit has been at work, however. Some creative reading about women's needs and some counseling have helped him. The Spirit has been trying to teach him some very basic things about the marriage relationship—that gratification is not his right; that giving sensitive, tender affirmation is his responsibility. Finally one day he yielded his mind to the Spirit to prompt what love required of him. He has dared to follow instructions. Each time he is given an urge or a nudge from the Spirit to do and say the gracious loving thing, he is obedient. Recently his wife said, "Instead of a penthouse panther, I've got a lover! I don't know what happened, but I like it. My husband has changed. I can't analyze it, but somehow he knows how I'm feeling and does those things he never used to do. He's got some kind of perception that helps him know what I need even before I tell him."

These stories of real people dramatize the secret of an exciting life. Added to them are countless examples of wisdom, direction, vision, and creativity I see mediated in the church by people who are under the Spirit's guidance. Things which no amount of human intelligence alone could develop are envisioned and realized. At work, people are finding capacities to solve problems and greet the possibilities of the future as never before. They are open to the guidance of the Spirit. And I am amazed also at the remarkable things that can happen when people get the needs of a city on their minds and ask for the Spirit's guidance there. The Lord of the intelligence is giving strategies for solutions which would never occur without him.

The secret of an exciting life is really no secret at all! It's written across the pages of the Book of Acts. And you and I are to be the subjects of the new chapter God wants to write today.

CHAPTER 10

Here's the Way!

Acts 9:1–31

I had a conversation with a leading senator about the future of our nation. He asked me a very penetrating question. "What do you feel is the greatest need in our country?" My response was immediate, "For the Christians in America to discover the power of prayer and for the Church to become a praying fellowship."

He pressed me for an explanation. I told him I believed the power and guidance of God were available for our nation if the people of God would unlock the limitless resources of intercession for our leaders and the problems of our nation. His retort stung. "You'll have to make Christians out of the Christians before that will happen!"

The senator was reaching for something. I encouraged him to go on. "Well," he said thoughtfully, "the name *Christian* is so culturalized it no longer means very much in America. People use it to indicate what they are *not* more than what they are! We need some new name to describe someone who really knows Christ and lives out his faith. If people who call themselves Christians staked their lives and their ethics on Christ, I agree, this nation could be turned around."

I thought a lot about that afterward. Long before the followers of the resurrected Christ were called Christians, they identified themselves and were referred to by a very descriptive phrase that expresses the essential meaning of being in Christ. They were called "those belonging to the Way." That vivid designation cuts to the core of what I feel the senator was trying to express. But we do not need a new term; we need to return to the original one. The early Church exemplified a quality of life in fellowship with Christ, each other, and the world that earned the compliment. Before they had carefully worded creeds, elaborate church organization, and professional clergy, Christ's people startled the world with the consistency of belief and behavior and the congruity of the ethos of Christ and their ethics.

It was not unusual that the followers of Jesus, steeped in Hebrew Scripture, should be called "those belonging to the Way." The Hebrew *halakah,* meaning "walk, or manner of life," summarized God's direction for his people and the nature of obedience to his Law and guidance. Man's way and God's way are referred to repeatedly in Scripture. Surely the early Church was familiar with David's declaration, "This God—his way is perfect" (2 Sam. 22:31). Many of them had been immersed in the Hebrew prayer book of the Psalms and had prayed, "Teach me thy way, O Lord, and lead me on a level path" (Ps. 27:11). "Make me to know thy ways, O Lord" (Ps. 25:4). "Commit your way to the Lord" (Ps. 37:5). They knew that God's way had been given to Moses. "He made known his ways to Moses" (Ps. 103:7). Isaiah had also been clear about the way. "This is the way, walk in it" (Isa. 30:21). The difference between man's way and God's way was engraved with the prophet's admonition: "Let the wicked forsake his way and the unrighteous man his thoughts" (Isa. 55:7), and with Jeremiah's challenge, "Let us examine our ways and return to the Lord."

The term *way* was also used in human relationships. To obey a leader or hero was to follow his way. The Old Testament has repeated references to people being obedient to, or departing from, the way exemplified or modeled by a respected person.

It was in this context that the disciples of Jesus of Nazareth heard the authoritative self-disclosure of the Son of God. "I am the way, the truth and the life" (John 14:6). They found in him not only the clearly delineated way of God for man, but the carefully demarcated way to God. The purpose of his whole ministry was declared by the unbelieving but shaken leaders of Israel in a fulsome compliment which indicated that the usage

"Way of God" was common parlance: "Teacher, we know that
you are true, and care for no man; for you do not regard the
position of men, but truly teach them *the way of God*" (Mark
12:14, emphasis mine). If only they had believed what they
said!

But the disciples believed it, and never more than after Pentecost and the infilling of the Holy Spirit. With the Lord's indwelling power they not only believed the Way, they followed
the Way, lived the Way, and irresistibly shared the Way. The
living Christ was their way to God, their way to live, their way
to relate to each other and their way of life in the world. No
wonder they were called "those belonging to the way."

In that light, I wish I could have reworded my response to
the senator. The greatest need in America is for Christians to
become followers of the Way.

Luke is very ready to help us understand the Way and to
live in it. In Acts 9:1–31, Luke not only uses the designation
for the first time, but in the unfolding drama of Saul's conversion and the ministry of the Church to him he gives us a powerful presentation of Christianity as the Way. Each phase of the
story describes what the Way is like and gives an inventory to
discern the extent to which we too have begun and progressed
on the Way.

Three personalities dominate this passage: Saul of Tarsus,
Ananias of Damascus, and Barnabas. The first shows how the
Way begins; the second how it grows; and the third how it is
deepened. Saul reveals how the Way happens to us; Ananias
depicts how the Way is effected through us; Barnabas challenges us with how the Way works between us. That progression gives us a handle on this powerful passage.

It was the dynamic of Christianity as the Way that had un-
raveled the tightly bound-up, compulsive legalism of Saul of
Tarsus. The "Hound of Heaven" was tracking him as Saul vigi-
lantly tracked down the followers of Jesus in Jerusalem. An
uneasy, guilt-motivated self-justification dominated his determination to wipe the Church from the face of the earth. Little
did he know when he accepted the assignment of the Sanhedrin
to purge the city of the Church that he would be so unsettled
by the courageous and indomitable quality of life they lived.
Stephen's death had carved an unforgettable memory on his

granite heart. Then, as he dragged the believers from their homes, persecuting some and imprisoning others, he could not deny his indignation, fired by rage, leaving the ashes of remorse in his psyche. After he had ravaged Jerusalem, his uneasy spirit searched for new expressions of his turbulent anger. Learning that many of the Jesus people had scattered to Damascus, he obtained an order from the chief priest to continue his merciless mission there.

It was Saul's idea to go to Damascus, not the Sanhedrin's strategy. But behind his plan, a greater plan was at work. The same Lord who had arranged his exposure to the vital faith of the Church was beginning to draw the net around him. He was playing for big game in Saul. The distorted lump of clay had already been thrown on the potter's wheel and the experienced hand of the Potter was about to mold it.

It takes six days for a caravan to reach Damascus. These were difficult days and bleak nights for Saul to think, remember, and wonder. His revered teacher, Gamaliel, had been conciliatory to the Church, contradicting the indignation Saul felt. Who was right? What was it that made these people who loved Jesus what they were? Saul had never seen courage and fortitude like that! Was his cause justified? Why did they make him so angry? Why did they bother him if he was right? As Saul swayed back and forth in the saddle, the heat of the sun beating down on him and his steed was matched by the burning cauldron inside his mind and heart. Contradictory forces were pulling apart the rigid order of his sanity.

At the moment Saul was at the breaking point, just outside of Damascus at high noon, lightning flashed. He and his traveling companions were thrown to the ground. Quivering, Saul clutched the ground, seeking safety. Afraid to look up, he buried his head in his arms. The lightning was quickly followed by the thunder of a voice. The tone, a magnificent combination of authority and assurance, rumbled with judgment and grace: "Saul, Saul, why do you persecute me?" Everything in Saul's alarmed inner being formed his frightened response, "Who is this?" And then he blurted out, "Who are you, Lord?" The word for *Lord* here is really "Sir," indicating that Saul did not suspect who his thunderous arrester was. Feel what Saul must have experienced when the answer came: "I am Jesus, whom

you are persecuting." Now the thunder clapped in Saul's soul!
Imagine what it must have been like inside this tumultuous
man's mind to hear the voice of the very one whom he said
did not exist, whose people he had mercilessly tortured and
executed.

The Lord's instructions to the stunned Saul were impelling:
"Rise and enter the city and you will be told what you are to
do." These were orders to one who was used to giving orders,
instruction to one whose life had swaggered his unteachable
arrogance. Saul shook with awe and anxiety. His soldiers stood
speechless. They too had heard the voice but saw no one.

It was some time before Saul dared drag himself to his feet.
Then he opened his eyes. He was blind! He staggered about
helplessly, crying out in anguish for help. Now look at him—
the mighty Saul being led by the hand into the city which
shuddered in fear of his arrival!

The Potter's hand was now on the clay. He had allowed an
outer physical manifestation of Saul's inner spiritual benighted-
ness. Saul's blinded eyes were as sightless as his soul. For three
days he lived in the tomb of darkness with his attention driven
inward. Before he could see again, he would have the eyes of
his heart enlightened. He had to deal with two undeniable realities as he sat helpless: Jesus Christ truly was alive; and Saul
had persecuted him by what he had done to his people. All his
learning and skill was marshaled to grapple with the unsettling
truth that Jesus was the Messiah his followers said he was.

Saul had a decisive encounter with the Way himself. The
people belonging to the Way had been used to bring him to the
end of his own way and now he was confronted with the "new
and living way," the resurrected Lord.

Many of us wonder if a Damascus Road experience is necessary to become a follower of the Way. Few have had that kind
of dramatic encounter with the Lord. But that's not the issue.
The real questions are: Have we ever been brought to the end
of our resources? Have we ever felt completely helpless without the Lord's healing? Have we ever made an unreserved surrender of all we have and are? Have we felt the persistent pursuit
of the Lord? In what ways are we persecuting the Lord or his
people? How are we resisting his overtures of love and forgiveness? The Lord reaches each of us differently. But many of us
are like Saul in his blindness. We know the Lord is alive, but

we can't see. We sit in darkness. It's not how dramatic an encounter is that's important; it's how decisive our response has
been. I am convinced that the Lord is not prejudiced in his
blessings. He wants all of us to know him intimately and to be
filled with his power incisively. The secret of Saul is available
to all of us. If we don't have the assurance of Christ that made
him the giant he later became or the convictions that gave him
the contagious personality he would have, then perhaps we have
never allowed Christ to bring us from the end of our own
self-will to the experience of the new creation.

Note how this happens from Saul's experience. Christ is always the initiator. We search for him, or we resist him, because
he has made the first move. Saul was brought to the end of
himself—his own resources, cleverness, learning, and arrogance.
And so must we be. The reason so few of us have a dynamic
beginning on the Way is that we have not allowed the trauma
of what happens to us to bring us to the realization of our need.
Many of us would have sat blind in Damascus without even
asking what the Lord wanted to happen in us through what
was happening to us. We have all had our Damascus Roads—
some, many of them, without realizing that the calamities
around us are an outward manifestation of the confusion within
us. The dark night of the soul is to break the compulsive syndrome of independence, arrogance, and frustration. Before Saul
chose Jesus, he was chosen, singled out, prepared, confronted.
That's the good news of the Way of the Lord: "You did not
choose me; I chose you!" Later in the passage we learn what
the Lord had in mind. He said Saul "is a chosen instrument of
mine to carry my name before Gentiles and kings and the sons
of Israel" (9:15). And so are we.

A decisive encounter begins the Way. Next we see what it's
like to live the Way. Ananias incarnates that. The Lord's strategy was to bring Saul to the desperate ragged end of Saul at a
time and place in which he could show him the Way. At the
carefully prepared moment, the Lord appeared to one belonging to the Way—Ananias, whose name means "Yahweh is
gracious." Ananias was called to live out his name and the
name of the movement to which he belonged. The conversation between him and the Lord gives us both a description of
the Way and a profound insight into prayer.

It started with the Lord's approach. Prayer begins with the

Lord. Our desire to pray and seek guidance is the result of the
movement of the Spirit in us. He calls our name! The exciting
life on the Way is listening for his call.

Now note the second step: availability. Ananias's response
is magnificent. "Here I am, Lord." That's how to react on the
Way. Here I am; here is my mind, my heart, my willingness,
my guidable disposition. We can't get very far on the Way without that. Prayer is not lofty rhetoric; it's availability, reporting
in for duty, expressing readiness for anything.

Next on the Way is our assignment. Prayer ought to result
in clear direction of what we are to do. But the assignment is
not always easy, nor in keeping with our preconceptions. The
instruction to Ananias fractured his prejudices. The last thing he
could have imagined the Lord would tell him to do was exactly
what he was ordered to do. "Rise and go to the street called
Straight, and inquire in the house of Judas for a man of Tarsus
named Saul; for behold, he is praying, and he has seen a man
named Ananias come in and lay his hands on him so that he
might regain his sight" (9:11–12).

Saul!? The name sent a chill through Ananias. Saul was not
only feared by those belonging to the Way, but he had become
the symbol of evil and persecution. I got an insight into how
Ananias must have felt from reading the account of the capture
of Adolph Eichmann by the Israelis in Argentina and from seeing the Jews' passionate hatred of the Nazi executioner vividly
portrayed in the play *The House on Garibaldi Street* by Isser
Harel. One of the Jews assigned to guard Eichmann after the
capture felt his skin crawl with indignant rage, intensified by
terrible memories. Something like that feeling must have been
in Ananias's heart when he received the Lord's assignment to
go to the one whom he hated so fervently as an obstruction
to the Way.

This leads us to the next aspect of life on the Way: attitude
adjustment. Prayer does that. The Lord turns us around. We
are now able to see through his eyes the people we have negated
or castigated. Ananias was free to question the Lord. I'm sure
we don't have the full record of the whole exchange. But finally
the Lord got through to Ananias what he had in mind for Saul,
and, in that light, he obeyed.

That's true allegiance to the Way. How graphic Luke is for

us: the same Lord who gave Saul a vision of Ananias coming to him prompted Ananias to fulfill the vision. He does that all the time; he prepares the way before us. Allegiance to the Lord makes possible the blessings he has planned for others. It's amazing how he works through people who are willing. He could have completed Saul's conversion without Ananias, but he chose to work through the Church. Like Ezekiel, Ananias was chosen to stand in the gap (Ezek. 22:30). He was to be a bridge. Being on the Way means becoming the Way to others.

The final aspect of Ananias's instrumentality is accountability. He actually did what he was told, and he did it with gracious love befitting his name. Think how shallow his prayers would have been subsequently if he had not been accountable. Could the reason our prayers become rote and ritual be that we have not done what we have felt clearly guided to do in previous prayers?

The warmth of love, forgiveness, and hope is in Ananias's voice when he goes to the ravager of the Way. "Brother Saul!"— I can hear the angel's chorus in that. Ananias's attitude had changed, and he believed the Lord that this one who had been against the Church was to be one of them in the new covenant of acceptance and affirmation.

The Sauls of our life rise up before us. The cost of accountability is made clear. I must be the Lord's bridge to the very people I have placed in the tight compartments of my righteous indignation. Anybody appear in your mind's eye? That's the Way of the Lord!

When Ananias came to helpless, blind Saul, there was no resistance left in him. He was ready to receive Ananias, whom the Lord had made ready. Caution and suspicion gone, Ananias followed the Lord's instructions and laid his hands on Saul. Barriers were down and the Lord mediated his power and healing. Saul already was convinced that Jesus was alive. Now his question on the road, "Who are you?" was answered by Ananias, who must have led him into the depths of a profound understanding. The white scales which had formed on his eyes fell off. He received not only the sight of his eyes but of his heart and mind. He surrendered his life to Christ as his Lord and was baptized. Years later he put into words what had happened to him. "Therefore, if anyone is in Christ, he is a new creation;

the old has passed away, behold, the new has come. All this is from God, who through Christ reconciled us to himself and gave us the ministry of reconciliation" (2 Cor. 5:17–18). That's what began that day in Damascus through Ananias. Saul got on the Way!

Ananias's accountability to the Lord must have extended to helping him find acceptance with the Church at Damascus. Luke tells us, "For several days he [Saul] was with the disciples at Damascus." The preposition *with* carries incisive implications. Imagine the feelings of the disciples which had to be transformed before the fellowship could eat and pray with the feared Saul. The new creation in Saul's heart was matched with gracious openness and vulnerability in the Church. A new creation of forgiving love had been given to the Church also. That enabled Saul to dare to preach about his newfound faith in the synagogues, amazing and confounding the Jews, who had expected him to be an antagonist of the Way, not a proponent.

An aspect of the Lord's way with us is not explicitly stated by Luke, but is clarified by Saul-made-Paul when he wrote to the Galatians later in his ministry: "But when he who set me apart before I was born, and had called me through his grace, was pleased to reveal his Son to me, in order that I might preach him among the Gentiles, I did not confer with flesh and blood, nor did I go up to Jerusalem to those who were apostles before me, but I went away into Arabia, and again I returned to Damascus" (Gal. 1:15–17). Prevenient grace was followed by penetrating growth. An intellectual like Saul needed a period of reorientation for the gospel to become his own. There in the desert near the foot of historic Sinai the new law of grace was inputted into God's new Moses of the New Covenant. The drama of getting on the Way was immediately followed by preparation to perpetuate the Way in the world. Some suggest that Paul was alone for three years before he returned in power to preach. Only after that could he say, "For me to live is Christ!"

Times of preparation on the Way are often lonely and painful. But the Lord knew what he was doing. All that Saul had learned and experienced had to be reoriented around the triumphant truth of Christ. I have known times like that. Often I have been impatient, longing to get on with changing the world, but the Lord had to change me first. When I look back

to those times out of the mainstream of what I thought the
Lord was doing, I can see that I was being prepared for the
fast-moving currents which later carried me out to the high seas
of adventure and effectiveness. The Lord will not use us until
he has made us ready. Then we thank him for knowing what
he was doing.

When Paul returned to Damascus, the time was right to go
to Jerusalem and share his faith with the Apostles. In that confrontation we see clearly how the Way works among Christ's
people. Barnabas, whom we met earlier in Acts 4 as the Son
of Encouragement, is true to his name. The followers of Jesus
in Jerusalem were as frightened of Paul as those in Damascus
had been. Rumor of Paul's conversion had reached Jerusalem,
but most of the Church found it difficult to change their minds
about this one who had persecuted them so hatefully. "But
Barnabas took him and brought him to the apostles, and declared to them how on the road he had seen the Lord, who
spoke to him, and how at Damascus he had preached boldly
in the name of Jesus" (Acts 9:27).

How did Barnabas know that? He had more than hearsay, I
believe. I think the "great encourager" went to Paul to find out
for himself. While the church in Jerusalem resisted, Barnabas
was a reconciler. His response to Jesus always spelled responsibility for someone who was misunderstood or resisted. We can
only imagine what that time of fellowship between these two
great men must have been, but we do know that a bond of
love was forged to galvanize a deep friendship. Barnabas threw
opinion and caution aside and interceded for Paul with the
Jerusalem church. The Greek actually implies that he took him
by the hand and led him in among the Apostles to assert his
belief in the authenticity of Paul's conversion, convictions, and
new character. That's what our Lord wants to have happen
among us who belong to the Way! We cannot travel the Way
very far if we do not discover this essential element of being in
Christ. We are interceders, reconcilers, enablers of understanding between people who love Christ but find it difficult to tolerate
or affirm each other.

Once again the account of events in Acts becomes very personal. Between what persons do I need to be a Barnabas today?
Am I a healer of wounds or acid in the open sores of conflict?

As I write this, the Lord is putting on my heart broken rela-
tionships between people I know. If I want to continue to grow,
I cannot say "No!" Few times in history have needed Barnabases
as much as now. Think of your family, your congregation, the
wider Christian fellowship. I don't know about you, but I have
my marching orders. For that we will all need higher gifts.
Paul had experienced the higher level of the Spirit's gifts in
Barnabas. He knew from experience when he wrote later, "And
I will show you a still more excellent *way*" (1 Cor. 12:31).
Love is the Way. No matter how Spirit-gifted we become, if
love is not spelled out through our being reconcilers, we have
detoured from the Lord's way.

I remember a soccer game between Edinburgh and Glasgow
in which two self-appointed bleacher coaches on both sides of
me were shouting instructions to the players. One favorite player
affectionately called Geordy was the target of frenzied cheers
when he did the right thing and jeers when he goofed. In one
particularly bad move he missed the ball and tripped over several of his fellow players. The two Scots beside me shouted a
prophetic word. I'll never forget it. It applied to me and to many
Christians I know.

"Geordy, Geordy, that's not the way. You're not on the way,
you're in the way!"

It makes all the difference for now and eternity whether we
are on the Way or obstructing the Way. Getting out of the way
and getting on the Way is the difficult lesson the Church had to
learn. It's to that lesson we next turn our attention.

CHAPTER 11

Getting on the Lord's Agenda

Acts 9:32–11:18

We all have agendas. Some of them are open for others
to see; some are hidden. They list what we want, when
we want it, with whom and under what prescribed conditions.
We have them for ourselves, other people, our families, our
careers, the Church, and our environment. Agendas are necessary to help us focus our goals and move steadily and effectively toward them. When you know a person's agenda you
can discern what he thinks is important, what values dominate
his direction, or what reservations hinder his development.

Congregations also have agendas. They are a composite of
what the majority of members believe a church should be and
do. Often the agenda is written from culture and conditioning
rather than from faith and guidance by the Holy Spirit. What
we have experienced previously or found meaningful is usually
the basis of a congregation's agenda.

There is nothing more crucial for individual Christians, or
for congregations, than to ask, "What is the Lord's agenda?"
The question forces us to consider what his next steps are for
us. That requires prayer, study of the Scriptures, and faithful
seeking of his specific direction. It demands a persistent query:
"Lord, what's next? Where do you want me, or us, to be and
do tomorrow, this month, next year, five years from now?"

The early Church had a difficult time getting on the Lord's
agenda. He had made it clear prior to Pentecost and the birth
of the Church. "You shall be my witnesses in Jerusalem, and

in all Judea and Samaria and to the ends of the earth" (Acts
1:8). But the Church had been reluctant at each step to adopt
this agenda. Even as it had, it still circumscribed the agenda
with the prejudiced belief that the gospel was for the exclusive
redemption of the Hebrew people in a widening geographical
assignment. They believed the Church's agenda was limited to
the conversion of Jews in Jerusalem, Judea, Samaria, and the
uttermost parts of the earth. As we have seen, it was only with
reservation that the Samaritans were recognized as recipients
of the gospel, and the Gentile world was still excluded by centuries of ingrained prejudice. The Church's priorities were dominated by the belief that salvation was through, from, and for
the Jews.

But the next step on the Lord's agenda for the Church was
the inclusive expansion of the gospel to the Gentiles. Acts 10
and 11 carry the impelling account of how the Lord forced the
Church to scrap its agenda and adopt his. And to do that he
had to change the mind and heart of the Church's revered
leader, Simon Peter. Long before, the Lord had told Peter that
he would build his Church on the faith the Spirit had given him
(Matt. 16:13–20). Now it was time to spell out the implications.
The breakthrough had to happen in Peter before the Lord could
use him to convince the Church. That would not be easy.
Peter was a strong-willed person with tightly arranged presuppositions. Change and growth had never come quickly for him.
The Lord knew that from each step he had enabled him to
make. But he also knew this about Peter: once he understood
what the Lord wanted him to do, he could be trusted to do it
with passion and pertinacity. That's the focus of Luke's next
scene in the Acts of the Holy Spirit.

Simon Peter is back in the limelight for the author's story
of how the Church was liberated from being a sect of Judaism
to becoming an unbound, inclusive fellowship without barriers—the Lord's agent of reconciliation for all men, Jews and
Gentiles alike.

Simon Peter's ministry had brought him to Joppa on the
Mediterranean coast. The Lord had used him powerfully in
healing Aeneas in Lydda on the way, and in raising Dorcas
from death there in Joppa. The grace of the Lord Jesus was at

work in him and must have been softening his rigid Hebraism, for he was willing to stay with Simon, a believer who was a tanner. Association with anyone who worked with dead animals was strictly forbidden for an orthodox Jew. A tanner had to live fifty cubits outside a village because of his ritual uncleanness, so clearly delineated in Numbers. But this tanner also loved Christ, and Peter's prejudices were coming unglued.

One day at noon, Peter went up on the flat rooftop of Simon's house to pray. Two things, one on his mind and the other in his stomach, converged to prepare him for what was about to happen to his agenda. I believe the Gentile question was on his mind. Was the gospel for all people? Then, as Peter prayed, he became hungry. While he waited for the food to be prepared, he fell into a trance and saw a vivid portrait of a great sheet being let down on the earth by four corners. What was in the sheet revolted this ritually impeccable Hebrew. It contained all kinds of animals, reptiles and birds, some of which were strictly forbidden for Hebrew consumption in Leviticus 11 and Deuteronomy 14.

Peter was therefore shocked when the voice of the Lord said to him, "Rise, Peter, kill and eat" (Acts 10:13). Imagine the internal confusion that caused! Peter's response was immediate and obstinate. "No, Lord, I have never eaten anything that is common or unclean." What he meant was, I have never eaten anything outside the regulation of the law, and I will not do it now. The voice's thrice-repeated admonition was direct and unambiguous: "What God has cleansed, you must not call common." The Lord was crossing Peter's preconditioning and prejudices, and the Apostle found it difficult to understand. His legalistic piety went beyond the Lord's!

But the Lord was not altering the valid food laws which had sustained the health of Israel. He was up to something more profound than that. The Lord had in mind not the foods Peter should eat but the people he should love. That vision was to dawn on Peter gradually as he grappled with the parabolic meaning of his experience in the light of what was about to happen to his agenda.

As he pondered the perplexing implications of what he had seen and heard, three messengers came to the tanner's house.

They had come to lead Peter to a person who would be the key
to unlock what the Lord was saying to him and into an encounter
which would change the destiny of the Church.

Again Luke astounds us with the perfect timing of the Lord.
Just prior to his reorienting vision to Peter at Joppa, he appeared thirty miles north in Caesarea to a Roman centurion by
the name of Cornelius. We are told four significant things about
him. He was a leader in the famed Italian Cohort, made up of
soldiers from Rome and noted for valor and gallantry. He was
in Caesarea with his whole household, which means he was
either retired or ranked highly enough to be awarded the company of his family and servants. He was deeply respected by the
Jews. The reason for this was that he was a proselyte to Hebrew
monotheism and was distinguished for his almsgiving charity
and prayerful piety. It was during a time of prayer that he was
told to send for one called Simon Peter lodging at a tanner's
house in Joppa. As the drama unfolds, we begin to understand
why. What was to happen to him would clarify Peter's dream,
but it would also give the Church the vision of the Lord's agenda.

Peter's emerging emancipation from legalism is indicated by
his willingness to eat with the Gentile messengers and lodge
them overnight. The next morning, together with six other believers, Peter and the messengers set out on the journey to
Caesarea. The miles along the sea gave Peter time to think—
and pray. I imagine he reflected that there must be some relationship between what the Lord was trying to say to him and
the fact that he had instructed Cornelius to request his presence.
Was Cornelius, a Gentile, like the forbidden animals in the
sheet? Were both made clean by the Lord? Peter was unsure.
But his gracious, accepting vulnerability when he arrived at
Cornelius's home indicates that he suspected the Lord was up
to a very special strategy in his own life.

Cornelius had called his family and friends together to wait
for Peter. Luke tells us that the centurion's whole household
shared the reverence and search for God of this strong, exem-
plary man. Not only a great leader of men but also of his own
family and servants, he wanted them all to share Peter's arrival.

When Peter entered his house, Cornelius's gratitude for his
willingness to come, coupled with his reverence for the famed
leader of the Church, compelled him to fall at his feet and

honor him. Peter's response to this is equally moving. "Stand up; I too am a man" (Acts 10:26). He had come to witness about the one who alone was worthy of worship. The prayerful contemplation on the road had obviously clarified his purpose in being there.

He got right to the point. "You yourselves know how unlawful it is for a Jew to associate with or visit anyone of another nation, but God has shown me that I should not call any man common or unclean." Clearly, he had interpreted and understood the vision. Caeserea and Gentile Cornelius had previously not been on his agenda. Observe the clarified obedience to the Lord's agenda: "So when I was sent for, I came without objection." Now note how Peter's being on the Lord's agenda is communicated in his freedom to discern Cornelius's agenda. He did not burst into the room and begin preaching. He graciously asked why the Roman had wanted him to come. A sure sign that we are on the Lord's agenda is our willingness to listen to people in order to communicate in contextual empathy. "I ask you then why you sent for me." The messengers had told him that! But Peter wanted to hear it from Cornelius himself. That communicated esteem and affirmation. Cornelius responded by recounting the appearance of the Lord, and he expressed his honest willingness to hear all that the Lord had commanded Peter to say.

Luke tells us that Peter opened his mouth and began to speak. He had opened his heart and mind to the Lord's new priority before he opened his mouth. Therefore, what he said was prophetic and profound and it indicated a radical change in Peter. Feel the Lord's love pour through the inclusive words he spoke: "Truly I perceive that God shows no partiality, but in every nation any one who fears him and does what is right is acceptable to him" (10:34). The word *perceive* translates the verb *katalambanō*, meaning "to take hold of, to grasp with the mind." Combined with *truly* (of a truth), the verb form and tense means that the truth had been dawning on him. There in Cornelius's house, in the presence of these spiritually receptive Gentiles, Peter knew it was true: God did not play favorites with the Jews, and salvation was available to anyone "who fears the Lord and does what is right." He did not mean that reverence and right actions assure salvation, but rather

that salvation was offered whether a person was a Jew or not.
Up to this time, Peter, along with the whole Church, had
believed that one must become a Jew before being able to
experience the grace of God in Christ. That's a radical change
of agendas!

Peter's new agenda noticeably affected his whole presentation of the gospel to Cornelius and his household. He preached
Christ: that God sent him as a gift of love; that he went about
doing good, healing and liberating people; that the response of
God's people was to crucify him; that God's response to the
worst men could do was to raise Christ from the dead; that he
is judge of all men; and that forgiveness is offered to *everyone*
who believes in him. But two things stand out in the record of
what Peter presented. One is a powerful parenthesis: "He is
Lord of all." The other is an inclusive offer of hope: "*Every one
who believes in him shall receive forgiveness of sins through
his name*" (Acts 10:43, emphasis mine). We sense the new
day dawning in Peter. Fresh insight was flooding his mind, clarifying the Lord's universal ministry and the availability of remission of sins for all people. The Apostle was obviously as
moved by what he was saying as were those who heard him.

Then Peter was gloriously interrupted. The Holy Spirit confirmed his message. Those who listened experienced the power
of the Spirit in them and among them. He gave each of them
the assurance of his presence, the conviction that the gospel
was true, the faith to appropriate the grace offered through the
Cross, and the fire of dynamic praise. The result was a burst
of adoration and exultation. The gift of faith enabled acceptance, and the gift of tongues expressed the joy. Glad and
ecstatic utterance of praise filled the room. Their own learned
language was inadequate; God gave them utterance "too deep
for words" to magnify him for what he had done. The gift was
not induced or manipulated by Peter, who was the most surprised of all. Here was tangible proof of God's new agenda.

But Peter was not alone in his delighted amazement. The six
fellow believers he had brought with him from Joppa also
heard these Gentiles with loosened tongues giving utterance to
the fact that the new life in Christ had been given to them.
Along with Peter, they were the Church alive to receive and
baptize the new believers into the Body of Christ.

I am invigorated by the irregularity of the infilling of the
Spirit this passage reveals. The Gentiles received the Holy Spirit
before they were baptized. The Apostle had not laid his hands
on them, as was the customary practice. Nor did they receive
the Holy Spirit after baptism as was the case with Philip's Samaritan converts. The Holy Spirit could not be packaged in
carefully defined theological procedures. Jesus had anticipated
that when he told Nicodemus: "the wind blows where it will"
(John 3:8). The Lord's agenda is definite about objectives, but
it is always open concerning how he will fulfill them. He shows
us not only what we are to do, but gives us the assurance of
what he will do for and through us with his unexpected interventions. We can be sure of the first and will be surprised by
the second. That is so we will trust him and not what we have
known of him before.

But that's exactly what the church in Jerusalem found difficult to accept. The leaders of the church had a closed agenda,
and it did not include the conversion of Gentiles. One faction
in particular, the circumcision party, found it impossible to
stretch its prejudices to accept the fact that Peter had eaten
with Gentiles. How amazing! Its dispute with Peter was not that
the Gentiles had received the Holy Spirit, but that Peter had
fraternized with non-Hebrews.

Fortunately, the circumcision party's agenda did not represent the whole church in Jerusalem. The Apostles and other
believers in the mother church gave Peter a hearing. Acts 11:
1–18 summarizes Peter's defense, backed up by the presence
of the six witnesses he had taken to Caesarea with him. He
had thought ahead. In ancient times, seven witnesses were required to validate a fact of an occurrence. Peter and the six
made their testimony of what had happened. The Apostle was
under fire, but a greater fire, the fire of the Holy Spirit, burned
within him as he recounted what had happened to the Gentiles.
The climax of his message to the Church brought an awesome
silence: "If then God gave the same gift to them as he gave to
us when we believed in the Lord Jesus Christ, who was I that
I could withstand God?"

It was an ultimate question. The future of the Church as a
world-wide movement of the Lord to reach all people, regardless of race, hung in the balance. But the same Spirit who had

blessed the Church through its infant years and now had fallen
upon the Gentiles, was there. He galvanized the Church around
a momentous decision. You and I are blessed recipients of
what they concluded. Giving glory to God for what he had done,
they adopted a new agenda, saying, "Then to the Gentiles also
God has granted repentance into life."

Our review of this axial passage has led me to some very
pivotal perceptions about getting on the Lord's agenda for my
own life and the Church.

First, our agenda must be consistent with the Lord's revealed
agenda for his people. He has been very clear about what he
wants us to be and do. There are essential verities which he will
not contradict. He has called us to be saints—holy, set-apart people, belonging to him. Our ultimate purpose is to know, love,
and obey him.

But he has loved us to make us lovers of people. There is no
confusion about his essential agenda that we are to love him
by loving others and the world he died to redeem. We are called
into ministry, ordained by the Spirit to be witnesses. People, all
races and types of persons, are priority on his agenda. What
people have been, are, or do does not exclude them from his
grace or from our involved concern. We are to go into *all* the
world, and how we react to people is the test of how we have
responded to the Lord himself. Our personal ministry can never
be based on inclination to "our kind of people," or dislikes conditioned by our background. Whatever else we do with our time,
energy, or resources, if our passion is not people—loving them,
introducing them to the adventure of new life, sustaining them
in growing, and caring about their spiritual and social needs—
we are not on the Lord's agenda! Nor are the congregations of
which we are a part. That ultimate clarification of our agenda
based on the life, message, Cross, and commission of our Lord
in Scripture eliminates a lot of the ruminating we do about
knowing the will of God. It becomes the narrow door through
which many of our activities and expenditures will not fit.

That presses me to the second conclusion this passage has
made painfully clear: our agenda must be based on our present
experience of the Lord, not the Lord of our previous experience.

Though Peter lived in a new covenant of grace, he was
ordering his agenda on the old covenant of law. That's why the

Lord had to break into his preconceptions to communicate his plans. Peter was trying to force the Lord to live in the strait jacket of Hebrew exclusionism and favoritism. Everything he had been taught and had experienced as a Hebrew was contradicted by the vision the Lord gave him.

We all have an immense capacity for formulating theories about what God is able to do on the basis of what our experience of him has been. Peter's words, "Lord, I have never . . . !" articulate our dependence on what we have experienced. The Lord's response is, "Never say never!" Never allow what has been to determine the limits of what will be. Never expect the Lord to perform within the confines of previous performance. His persistent word is, "Behold, I am doing a new thing" (Isa. 43:19). Never tell the Lord you will do only what you have done before.

Yet, I think of all the times we say, "Never!"—"I will never move, change my feelings, alter my directions, accept certain people." The very things about which we say "never" become the very things the Lord puts on our agenda. Flexibility is the fine mark of faith and freedom.

The Lord is confronting all of us with a sheet let down from heaven. What's in yours? Every time we say that's just not our bag, the Lord opens the bag and gives us a new phase of his agenda.

Alexander Whyte challenged his St. George's West Congregation in Edinburgh to do just that on a Sunday evening when he preached on this text over sixty years ago. "If you would take a four-cornered napkin when you go home, and a Sabbath-night pen and ink, and write the names of nations, and the churches, and the denominations, and the congregations, and the ministers, and the public men, and the private citizens, and the neighbors, and the fellow-worshippers—all the people you dislike, and despise, and do not, and cannot, and will not, love. Heap up their names into your unclean napkin, and then look up and say, 'Not so, Lord, I neither can speak well, nor think well, nor hope well, of these people. I cannot do it, and I will not try.' If you acted out and spoke out all the evil things that are in your heart in some such way as that, you would thus get such a sight of yourselves that you would never forget it. And, for your reward—and there is no better reward—like Peter, you would one day come to be able to say, 'Of truth I perceive that

God is no respecter of persons. But in every nation, and church, and denomination, and party of men . . . God has them that fear him, and that work righteousness, and that are accepted of him.' And then it would go up for a memorial before God, the complete change and the noble alteration that had come to your mind and to your heart."*

I took Whyte's advice. My sheet was filled with people and situations which self-righteously I had relegated to "Never, Lord!" My "never-never land" was overpopulated with people. In most cases, I had either broken or resisted a relationship because of what I had felt was justified indignation, based on my understanding of the Lord's will and judgment at the time. Then I asked the Lord to show me which of these were on his new agenda for me. I was amazed in subsequent weeks how my new readiness made remedial, reconciling encounters possible.

So often I hear people say, "The one thing I will never do is—" or "That's the last thing I'd be willing to do!" Usually that is the first thing we are asked to do! The point is that we adventurers in Christ must constantly evaluate whether the God of our experience, a God of our own memory's making, is the Living God who is pressing on to the new growth in us and the Church.

John Wesley's New Year's prayer in his Covenant Service at the midnight hour of an old year is an excellent creed for those of use who enjoy the false comfort of "never-never land." This prayer could put us to working on the Lord's agenda:

"I am no longer my own, but Thine. Put me to whatever Thou wilt. Rank me with whomever Thou wilt. Put me to doing; put me to suffering. Let me be employed for Thee; or laid aside for Thee; exalted for Thee or brought low for Thee. Let me be full; let me be empty. Let me have all things; let me have nothing. I freely and heartily yield all things to Thy pleasure and disposal. And now O glorious and blessed God, Father, Son and Holy Spirit, Thou are mine and I am Thine. So be it. And the covenant which we have made on earth, let it be ratified in heaven. Amen."

---

* Alexander Whyte, *Whyte's Bible Characters,* 2 vols. (Grand Rapids: Zondervan, 1953), 2:164–65.

Once the Lord's agenda is clear, how do we stay on it? The final thing I discovered in this passage is that getting and staying on the Lord's agenda is motivated by faith and not feeling. There will be times our willingness lags and we would like to evade responsibility. That's just why the Lord's agenda is so crucial. It sustains us in the midst of emotional ambiguity.

Recently I saw an advertisement for a Biomate Computer. You can buy it for $10, postpaid. It promises to chart your life cycles for you and tell you about yourself. All you do is set it to your birthdate, flick the dials each day, look at the charts and cycle curves, and you will know when to buy, when to sell, when to act fast, when to stall, when to exercise or rest, even when to stay home in bed. The Biomate promises to show you your emotional, intellectual, and physical cycle.

I read on in wonder at the hyperbole. The advertisement promised to show a purchaser his good and bad days in advance for months—even years—and how he was likely to "shape up" on a given day according to his biorhythm. Claim was made that the Omi Railway of Japan has compiled an accident-free record using the biorhythm method and that athletic teams win or lose according to whether they are on the "high period" of all their cycles. Studies of historical characters, according to the manufacturers, indicate that the bad decisions of history have been made on "critical days" or mid-cycle periods. They even go so far as to assert that Custer's disastrous last stand occurred on a day when his emotional and mental cycles were at low points—days when his judgment and decision-making ability were likely to have been below par.

It's a good thing Peter was not equipped with a Biomate on the rooftop in Joppa! The hard sell of the ad vividly portrays life without the Holy Spirit. Good days and bad days, emotional highs and lows, intellectual creativity and disability, cannot be calculated by a machine. The Holy Spirit is the source of our motivation. He will guide and direct all our days. What the Lord's agenda envisions, he will empower. When we are open, he will give us what we need. We can move on steadily toward our goal.

Luke has led us through the most critical transition the early Church faced. It's alarming to realize that contemporary Christians, and today's Church, are still wrestling with the same issues. This passage speaks loudly to our time because it leaves us all with questions which will not rest unanswered:

To what extent have I gotten on the Lord's agenda?

What do I need to do to alter my priorities according to that agenda?

Who or what am I resisting because of prejudice or pre-conditioning that may not be from the Lord?

What would my life look like if I were to seek to live daringly by his timing and not just my own inclinations and feelings?

In answer to those questions I want to challenge you to write out what you prayerfully discern is God's agenda for you. Then compare it with what's happening in your life. Any difference?

CHAPTER 12

How God Prepares Us
for What He Has Prepared

Acts 11:19–30

Two things grip my attention in the second half of Acts
11. Luke does not directly interrelate them, but an inspiring implication is there. Saul is called out of his preparatory
seclusion at Tarsus to join Barnabas in teaching and preaching
in Antioch; and it was there that the disciples of Jesus were for
the first time called Christians. The two facts are inseparably
interlocked. What had happened to Saul since he was sent to
Tarsus made possible what happened at Antioch. The Lord had
prepared him for what he had prepared!

Calculations of the chronology of the history of the Church,
coupled with Paul's own account in Galatians, indicate that he
was seemingly shelved in Tarsus for about ten years, a long time
for such a dynamic man to wait, study, and pray. But Paul was
too hot to handle in Jerusalem, and the Apostles had had to get
him out of the city. His powerful teaching of Christ had so enraged his fellow Hellenistic Jews that they were seeking to kill
him. The Church, fearing for his life, secretly brought him to
Caesarea and sent him north to his home city of Tarsus.

In Galatians 2:1, Paul says that after fourteen years he went
back to Jerusalem. That was after his first visit after his conversion, his second visit to bring a missionary offering, and his
first missionary journey. According to my arithmetic, that means
he spent a long period in Tarsus between his encounter with
Christ and his active ministry which started with Barnabas at
Antioch. We have no record of what Paul did during these long

years, but the account of his subsequent ministry and the clarity
of his message in his letters to the Church later reveal plainly
what the Lord did in him during that time. In the quiet inactivity
of that dynamic decade the Lord was reshaping a living man
into his own image. Paul's intellect was reoriented around the
triumphant truth that Jesus was the Christ, the expected Messiah
and Lord of all. His emotions were refashioned around the person of Christ. His will was refined to do the Lord's will.

We wonder if he became impatient during this long time of
waiting. There must certainly have been times of painful disappointment that he could not move out with vigor to proclaim
his Lord. But it was not yet the Lord's timing. He had to wait
and wonder.

Victor Hugo once said, "There is one thing stronger than all
the armies in the world: an idea whose hour had come." I would
add: a man gripped by an idea whose time has come. During
the period in Tarsus, the Lord was getting Paul ready for the
world and the world ready for him. We can only contemplate
how much sooner the Lord could have used Paul if the Church
had not been so reluctant to adopt the Savior's agenda. Again
we are startled by the Lord's commitment to work in and through
his people, the Church.

We've all known a Tarsus-time of waiting. Perhaps we are
in one of them right now, wondering where the action is; God
does provide ordained periods of preparation. In something Paul
later wrote to the Thessalonians we find a key to unlock the
meaning of the potential power of those times: "For this is the
will of God for you, your sanctification" (1 Thess. 4:3). Sanctification is the Lord's process of making us holy; that's the root
of the word. To be holy is to belong to the Lord, be made like
him, and be liberated to do his will. Once we give our lives to
Christ, he begins the crucial process of renovation. Paul emerged
from Tarsus with convictions that had become his character.
"For me to live is Christ!" (Phil. 1:21). "I am determined to
know nothing save Jesus Christ and him crucified" (1 Cor. 2:2).
I am convinced that it was during the long years of waiting that
Paul's theology of Christ was worked through. What he wrote to
the Ephesians years later flowed from the headwaters of the
Tarsus experience.

Paul, an apostle of Christ Jesus by the will of God, To the saints who are also faithful in Christ Jesus:

Grace to you and peace from God our Father and the Lord Jesus Christ.

Blessed be the God and Father of our Lord Jesus Christ, who has blessed us in Christ with every spiritual blessing in the heavenly places, even as he chose us in him before the foundation of the world, that we should be holy and blameless before him. He destined us in love to be his sons through Jesus Christ, according to the purpose of his will, to the praise of his glorious grace which he freely bestowed on us in the Beloved. In him we have redemption through his blood, the forgiveness of our trespasses according to the riches of his grace which he lavished upon us. For he has made known to us in all wisdom and insight the mystery of his will, according to his purpose which he set forth in Christ as a plan for the fulness of time, to unite all things in him, things in heaven and things on earth. In him, according to the purpose of him who accomplishes all things, according to the counsel of his will, we who first hoped in Christ have been destined and appointed to live for the praise of his Glory. In him you also, who have heard the word of truth, the gospel of your salvation, and have believed in him, were sealed with the promised Holy Spirit, which is the guarantee of our inheritance until we acquire possession of it, to the praise of his glory (Eph. 1:1–14).

Christ had become Paul's message, hope, and life. The years of preparation had made him ready. Now it was time, and what a twist! Some of the very people who had been scattered from Jerusalem years before because of Paul's persecution of the Church were to be used in preparing for him a city in which to begin his ministry in full force. At Antioch, around the eastern tip of the Mediterranean from Tarsus, some dispersed disciples of the Lord from Cyprus and Cyrene preached the gospel to the Greeks. Luke tells us in Acts 11:21 that "the hand of the Lord was with them," meaning that the power of the Spirit was at work convicting and confirming. The result was that a great number of them believed. In keeping with its new agenda, the church in Jerusalem sent Barnabas to Antioch to affirm and validate the gift which the Lord had given to the Gentiles in Antioch. The Lord was behind it all! Who but Barnabas, the great encourager, could have communicated delight and affirma-

tion more powerfully? And who else but Barnabas would have
been open to the Lord to think of Paul as the only person who
could match the challenge and opportunity of a city like Antioch? The Lord does not make mistakes!

"So Barnabas went to Tarsus to look for Saul; and when he
had found him, he brought him to Antioch" (11:25–26). The
Greek implies that Barnabas really had to search for Paul, indicating that Paul's sojourn in his home city had really been a
time of inactivity for prayer and contemplation.

I relish my mind's-eye reconstruction of the meeting of these
two men. Barnabas was breathless with news of what the Lord
had been doing with the Church. His excitement was apparent as
he recounted his recent experiences in Antioch and the current
evidence of the Lord's blessing among the Gentiles. Then his
greatness of character is revealed. I imagine he said to Paul,
"My friend, we can't meet the challenge without you. No one in
the Church knows the Gentile world as you do. There's no one
with your learning and education in both Hebrew and Greek
thought! Paul, we need you; the Lord needs you; he sent me to
find you!" Now feel with Paul what he felt when he heard that.
The waiting was over; it was time. And he was ready! He was a
Christ-filled, Christ-captivated, Christ-motivated man. The
preparation had been worth it!

How I wish I could have been a part of the exuberant conversation between these two as they made their way along the
road to Antioch. There are few conversations in Scripture that
I enjoy recapturing more than that one: Barnabas filled with
joyous anticipation about what was ahead, Paul overflowing
with insight and wisdom from years of contemplating the ancient Scriptures in the light of his new Lord. I am sure that as
they approached Antioch their conversation focused on the
Lord's strategy for reaching that city with the gospel. They must
have bubbled over with uncontainable enthusiasm about what
was ahead of them. We wonder if Paul felt the heartwarming
conviction: "Lord, thank you for what you have put me through.
Forgive me for ever doubting! Now I can see your perfect will
being worked out. Lord, I'm ready. You have prepared me for
what you have prepared. Let's get on with it!"

Syrian Antioch was a formidable place to begin a ministry. It was third only to Rome and Alexandria in prominence at the time. Known as one of the "eyes" of Asia, it was the residence of the Roman prefect and the seat of political power for that area of the Roman Empire. The culture of this metropolitan city at the mouth of the Orontes River was Greek. Strategically located fifteen miles from the Mediterranean Sea, Antioch had become very cosmopolitan. But something else had made the very name of the city synonymous with rampant immorality. In this "sin city," chariot racing, gambling, and debauchery took priority in the persistent pursuit of pleasure. And controlling the ambience was the worship of Daphne, whose temple five miles out of the city housed prostitute priestesses. Apollo's famous pursuit of Daphne in the laurel groves around what became the site of the temple was reenacted night and day by the "worshipers" and the ritual prostitutes. The phrase "the morals of Daphne" became descriptive throughout the world of immorality at this time.

It was in that kind of city that Paul and Barnabas began the adventure of their ministry together. What a team those two were! Each complemented the other: Barnabas with his sensitive, empathic graciousness; Paul with his incisive, razor-sharp intellect and highly polished, articulate presentation of Christ. And there together, the Lord used the two of them to win and instruct a great multitude of converts to the Lord. There must have been something especially dynamic in the way they preached and taught the gospel. Vitality, vibrancy, and urgency must have been in the clear trumpet call with which they pierced the religious and moral ambiguity of the city. Alerted to something fresh, undeniable, and liberating, the new converts to Christ astounded the city. Their beliefs and style of life demanded a designation, some title to set apart the followers of Christ. A nickname was coined, and it has held fast through the centuries. At Antioch, in the midst of the false gods of pride, political power, and pleasure, the disciples were for the first time called Christians.

There is only one explanation: Paul's preaching! The preparation in Tarsus was bearing its first fruit. I am convinced that there were several identifiable things which earned Christians their new title. What began as a slang designation with the suffix *-ian,* meaning "belonging to the party of," or "a partisan of," was prompted by the centrality of Christ in the quality of life and message of the church in Antioch.

Paul's seclusion had solidified his message. He was rooted and grounded in Christ as the only hope of the world. To be "in Christ" meant everything to him. Christ was leader and Lord, Master and King. Paul talked Christ, lived Christ, and preached Christ. The Living Lord was more real to him than the air he breathed: his companionship was convincing, his witness was undeniable. Paul's clarity about Christ made the faith a personal relationship which satisfied the empty longings of the converts in Antioch.

The result was that the Church in Antioch exemplified a Christ-centered life that had to be given a name. I am moved by the fact that Greeks gave these converts a name that was identified with a Hebrew term, *Messiah,* and that had a Latin suffix. How appropriate for the name of those who belonged to the Lord of all life and the ruler of all races! They must have talked so much about Christ that there could have been no other adequate name for them. But more than that, they loved each other with a quality of love that they identified as coming from the Lord himself. They walked in Christ, were guided by Christ, and feared neither life nor death because of Christ. Being called a Christian was more than a religious category; it was a description of a relational conviction.

And yet, I believe that there must have been something more that prompted the title of Christian. People are basically self-centered and oriented to their own interests. I can't help feeling that there was a jesting, almost mocking flavor to the nickname the Greeks gave the followers of Christ, whose lifestyle must have been a smarting contradiction to the licentious immorality of Antioch. Perhaps there was even a bit of rage in the city's descriptive name. The title "Christian" meant something then. Surely it was costly and demanding for converted temple prostitutes, as well as those who had worshiped at the temple, to begin to grow in Christ. Soldiers, scholars, businessmen, and Jews from the Hebrew colony all made up the church. What a mixture of humanity and religious backgrounds! Their lives must have become impellingly different under Paul's leadership, but then he had been prepared to lead people like these, at a time and place like Antioch.

One last aspect of the life of the Church at Antioch demands attention. It is specifically mentioned by Luke. A prophet named Agabus from the church in Jerusalem prophesied a famine. There would be great need among the followers of Christ in Judea. The response of the church at Antioch was to take up a collection for their needs. This indicated not only the gracious self-giving of the indwelling Christ but a unity among his people, regardless of race or geography. Christ's people had loyalty to each other. That was something new—citizens of Antioch caring about citizens of Judea, all because they belonged first to Christ and then to each other. If they had been willing to do that, certainly that same generosity had been exemplified to people in Antioch. No wonder they were called Christians! Paul must have preached more than concepts of Christ. He gave them an example of how to share Christ's love. That's the only satisfactory explanation of the power in the Antioch church after one year's preaching and teaching.

But behind it all was a decade of prayer, study, and obedience. Paul had paid the price of power.

And so must we. The Church in America needs to rediscover the centrality of Jesus Christ. The plateaus of preparation are to be used for new bursts of effectiveness for him. We need pastors and church officers whose first priority is Christ and time alone, and then together, with him. We need church members who are Christ-filled, oriented, and empowered.

That idea says a couple of things to me. We can't give away what we do not have. Whenever we pass through "dry periods" or feel shelved from active duty for a time, we are to accept what is happening as an ordained interval of preparation and we can be confident that the Lord has not bypassed us. If we trust him and listen to what he wants to say, as well as learn from what he allows us to go through—be sure of this—he will use us more effectively than ever before. Sickness, times of inactivity, or other changes of circumstances which alter our usual schedule and involvements can be used by the Lord to prepare us for what he has prepared. "Lord, teach me; show me your way; help me to grow in knowledge of and love for you!" That's the humble prayer for the hiatus. Then we can begin to see things from his priorities and planning. Nothing is wasted for God. What we go through, what we face in life's excruciating disappointments, or what we are forced to learn when we get quiet enough to listen are all preparation for future ministry with people.

There is only one thing to do when we are sent off to our Tarsus: focus on Christ! He is all we need. But is he enough for you?

That's the question a friend of mine was forced to ask at an ineffective time in his ministry. Things seemed to be at a standstill. Nothing was working out for him. Work, family, the Church —all were unresponsive and estranged. His energetic leadership seemingly was unappreciated by the people he wanted desperately to lead. Over the years he had transferred his security from Christ to his own plans and programs. Now nothing was going the way he wanted. That drove him back to prayer and long periods of penetrating fellowship with the Lord. "Am I enough for you?" the Lord asked. "If you only had me, would you be satisfied?" The long period lasted until my pastor friend could say "Yes!" Then the power returned and with it greater effectiveness for Christ than he has ever known.

> Judge not the Lord by feeble sense
> But trust Him for his grace;
> Behind a frowning providence
> He hides a shining face.*

In the ebb and flow between preparation and participation with the Lord, the issue is trust. If we trust him, he will use the preparation to get to us so that subsequently he can get to people through us and our participation. The Lord is never in a hurry. When he's finished with us at Tarsus, there will be an Antioch, and it's worth waiting for. The people we live with, or work among, will be blessed. The power of Christ through us will help them to assume the name of Christians!

---

* William Cowper, "God Moves in a Mysterious Way," 1774.

CHAPTER 13

When the Answer Keeps Knocking

Acts 12

Prayer is not just to get God to do something, but to help us realize what he has done already. It is not an argument to convince God of what we need, but a conversation in which he shows us our need to recognize what he has *previously* done and is *presently* doing. It enables us to enjoy what he has entrusted to us.

Prayer is focusing on the gifts of God. Of all gifts he gives us, the most precious, and at times the most perplexing, are the people in our lives. Intercessory prayer for people is not for the purpose of getting God to change his mind about them, but for us to discover his mind for our relationship with them. Talking to God in prayer not only puts us in touch with him but puts us in touch with people. When we share our concerns about people with the Lord in prayer, he shows us how to share ourselves with those people.

When most of us think about prayer for people's needs, our minds leap to something we want God to do or change. We immediately see the yawning gap between what they are and should be, what they have and what they need, what they have done and ought to do. We envision prayer as the bridge between what is and ought to be. We have learned that there are abundant resources of God for people if we will pray. That is good. But I want to focus on the power of prayer for appreciation as well as anticipation. There is a profound level of prayer that goes beyond remission for what is past or requests for what we long to be for the people we love. In-depth prayer for people liberates us to enjoy them right now, where they are, as they are. William Law was right: "There is nothing which makes us love a man so much as praying for him." And prayer-born love frees us to recognize that the person is himself God's greatest answer to prayer.

That's what the early Church had a difficult time comprehending in their prayers for Peter. They could not apprehend what God had appropriated.

The beloved leader of the Church had been imprisoned by King Herod Agrippa I, probably in the Temple of Antonia. The king had learned that persecution of the Christians strengthened his relationship with the Jews. His execution of the Apostle James had won him the favor of the turbulent people whose approval he desperately needed. Peter was next. But while Agrippa pondered the most expeditious method of executing Peter, the Church prayed. The followers of the Way knew "the Way of the Lord" for crises like that. Nothing was too great for their Christ! But did they still believe that? This passage of Acts makes us wonder.

Luke impresses us with the humanly impossible situation through the context of the prayers of the Church to their Lord for Peter. We are told that Herod had seized him and put him in prison with no fewer than four squads to guard him. That means sixteen soldiers divided into four watches, each of three hours' duration. "The very night when Herod was about to bring him out [for execution, the Greek implies], Peter was sleeping between two soldiers, bound with two chains, and sentries before the door were guarding the prison" (Acts 12:6). Here is the picture of a soldier on each side of the sleeping saint, probably as many as four sentries at the door of the cell, and soldiers from the squads strategically positioned—an imposing sight of human power and precaution. Herod was taking no chances.

Neither was the Church! They prayed for a greater power to intercede to help Peter. But Luke does not tell us how or for what they prayed. Did they pray that Peter would be strong even to death? Perhaps they prayed that he would be able to witness to the guards. Some may have prayed for a miraculous release. But did they really believe it would happen? That question is forced upon us by the amazing fact that when the Lord answered their prayers, they could not fully appreciate what had happened.

In response to the Church's intercession, the Lord interceded. He sent an angel to Peter who liberated him from his chains, got him past the first and second guards, and opened the iron gate of the prison leading out to the city. As the incarnate answer to prayers, Peter headed directly for John Mark's house, at which the Lord's people had gathered in the memory-filled Upper Room to pray. A stone wall separated the house and gardens from the street. A heavy wooden gate provided the only way inside. Peter paused at the gate to knock. A maid named Rhoda was delegated by the intercessory fellowship to see who was interrupting their prayers. She recognized Peter's voice when he implored her to open the gate, but she was so befuddled by the personified answer to their prayers that she could not open the gate. She ran back to the Upper Room to tell the praying disciples that Peter was at their gate! Now grapple with the unbelieving response. They said to her, "You are mad." When she persisted, they expressed incredulity another way: "It is his angel!" That response implies human nature's capacity to expect the worst. The disciples actually entertained the dreadful possibility that Peter had been executed and his ghost had come to them. Or perhaps, in keeping with the idea held at this time that each person had a guardian angel, they concluded that Peter's angel was not busy doing what they had prayed for, but was there to comfort them about an excruciating eventuality. Whatever the case, they did not believe it was Peter. The Church was so engrossed in praying for Peter that they could not accept Peter!

"But Peter continued knocking" (Acts 12:16). There's a text to "drive the coulter deep, to wake my living man from sleep." The answer to the Church's prayers kept waiting for a response. We have to be amazed when we contemplate the insensitivity of the Church. But then the truth hits us where we hurt. Who is our Peter for whom we have prayed, and what lack of faith keeps him or her waiting and knocking at the gate? Many of us would rather go on praying than open the gate and accept God's personalized answer. What if Peter had not kept on knocking? It was dangerous for him to stand out in the street; he could have been arrested again. What would the Church have done then? Would they have dared to go back to prayer for a second miracle when they had not accepted the first? Surely they would, for we do it all the time. Perhaps that's why our prayers

are so empty and habitually unexpectant! This passage of Acts
tells us a lot about the prayer life of the early Church and more
than we may want to know about our own. In my own life the
Lord has used this passage to expose not only what I have done
with the gift of prayer, but also what I do with the gifts which
come from praying.

The first thing I learned is that my prayers are often limited
to my preconceptions of what I think God will do. I am forced
to wonder what it would take to convince me that with God all
things are possible. I am like the early Church. So much had
happened to those followers of Jesus in that Upper Room. There
in John Mark's home they had received the Last Supper, had
realized the presence of the resurrected Lord, and had been
rejuvenated by the power of Pentecost. Miraculous answers to
prayer had attended the early years of the Church's growth. As
we noted in a previous chapter, they had prayed for boldness
and the room had been shaken with power. But the years had
wilted their expectancy. The account of their reaction to Peter's
reappearance clearly indicates that they either had not dared to
pray for his release; or if they had dared to pray that, they
had anticipated that it might not happen. Why else would they
be surprised and incredulous? But are we any different? I'm not,
too much of the time. Do you share the problem? Are your
prayers limited to the careful confines of what you think God
can do?

The core cause of the unadventuresome prayers of the Church,
perhaps, is that they believed more about the formidable power
of man than they believed about the unlimited power of God.
The prison and the guards—who could escape that? And look
at James; he didn't escape. The pall of his execution hung
heavily on the Church. The same thing would probably happen
to Peter. Why pray for release? They lost the two-dimensional
formula for great praying: daring requests and unreserved re-
linquishment. They had the latter, but forgot the first. They
trusted Peter to God and prayed for him, but did not ask for
his miraculous release. The comforting thing about that, however, is that even their halting, doubting prayers were mightier
than Herod.

Many of us are afraid of bold prayers because we do not
want to be embarrassed by an answer which is less than or dif-

ferent from what we asked. We feel we must protect God's reputation by never getting out on a limb with requests which may not be granted. Our faith is so frail that we feel we cannot afford a disappointment which would snap the thin thread of our hope that he is real, that he hears and answers prayer. The combination of unreserved petition and unrestrained trust in the Lord's timing and wisdom makes for dynamic praying. He alone knows what's best for us, the Church, and our times. His answers are "Yes," "No," or "Later"; but a loving providence guides all three! All we need to do is think of some of the things for which we prayed that we now see would not have been maximum for us if they had been granted. With that confidence we can pray with freedom and joy, knowing that the Lord will answer according to his overarching benevolence. That conclusion leads to a second thing I discovered from this passage.

There are times when we are so occupied in praying for an answer that we can't recognize it when it comes. That was the problem with the Church's prayers for Peter. The Lord interrupted their prayer time for Peter with the Apostle himself. They weren't ready for that!

We seem to find comfortable security in persistent, preoccupied praying about a problem. The familiar feeling of distress over a difficulty or a need becomes more satisfying than the answer. This is especially true when the answer demands that we incarnate the prayer we have prayed and become part of God's answer for a person. Often the prayers complain more about people than they confess our trust in God. We complain to God about what needs to be changed or corrected in a person. But then we find it demands too much when we are asked to affirm the changes that occur.

That's what happened to a group of people who were concerned about their pastor. They decided to pray, "Lord, revive him or remove him!" Quite sure that it would be the latter, they could not encourage the first alternative when it began to take place. They found greater pleasure in the problem than assurance in the answer.

A father I know prayed ceaselessly about his son. The young man's emotional problems were of grave concern to him. Then one day, he shared the problem with a friend. The response was not what he expected. "Unless you are willing to spend time with your son, all the praying will miss the mark! You are the answer to your own prayers. He needs *you!*" But the father did not recognize the answer and kept on praying for his son to change.

There are times we cannot gain full vision from our prayers because we have not accepted the portion of the answer which is staring us in the face. The complete unfolding of an answer to prayers for people awaits recognition of the portion of the answer which has been given. A woman told me about a friend who was having difficulty handling life's relationships, and we prayed together about her friend. Recently, I saw her and asked how her friend was doing. When I probed a bit, I learned of real evidence of a change. But the woman had not seen her friend's first efforts to be different as the beginning of God's answer. I asked her if she had affirmed this initial attempt to reach out. She hadn't. She said that she had completely missed what a change this represented in her friend. Think how often this is repeated in family life. Parents pray for their children but let negativism about them completely dominate their attitude about the result. No wonder the child becomes discouraged in his efforts to respond to the nudgings of the Spirit to become the very person his parents prayed he would become. This paradox is no less true of children's prayers for their parents or brothers and sisters. Andrew Murray said, "To be thankful for what I have received and for what my Lord has prepared is the surest way to receive more." Perhaps our unresponsiveness to the answers accounts for why so little is happening as a result of our prayers for people.

But this passage has taught me something even more crucial. The Church was so intent in prayer for Peter that they did not *enjoy* Peter as the answer to their prayers. I can feel with Peter what he must have felt as he made his way through the dark streets of Jerusalem from the prison to John Mark's house. Excitement must have grown within him as he realized that his release was the Lord's answer to the prayers of the Church. What joy and delight must have surged through him as he hurried through the night! Perhaps he pictured what it would be like to burst into the Upper Room and have the fellowship break into an enthusiastic welcome and then prayers of praise. Perhaps he was even being a bit playful as he knocked on the gate, waiting to savor every moment of the realization of the Lord's answer.

What great disappointment he must have felt when the Church found it so difficult to accept his living appearance as the answer to their prayers. After first arguing with Rhoda, when they finally did open the gate, they found it difficult to enter into the triumph of Peter's homecoming.

Luke often tells us a great deal by what he does not tell us. In every other evidence of the Lord's gracious intercession he records the Church's doxology of praise and adoration. There is no mention of delight and exultation in the Church's response to Peter's liberation. Most of all, there is no expression of enjoyment of Peter himself. The Church had not discovered that the purpose of prayer for a person is to break us open to relish the wonder of that person for himself.

That presses me to ask myself, "How many of the people I pray for know how much I enjoy them? Has prayer for people released me to accept the awesome gift of each personality?" I am just learning what this means. Increasingly, prayers for people have become times of penetrating insight into the uniqueness and value of those people. When I linger in prayer and understand that conversation with God about people is not only telling God about them but also allowing God to tell me what I need to know about those very people, my prayers come alive. As I listen intently with an open mind and heart, I feel their struggle for identity, meaning, and fulfillment. I hear their hopes pulsating through their hurts. I see the real person trying to break free to love and care.

Recently I have discovered a way to pray for people that has paid off in subsequent encounters with them. In prayer, I try to use all my faculties to observe and hear the Lord pray for the person about whom I am praying. I picture our Lord praying with that person as the center of his concern. Then I listen to the loving intercession. My response is usually amazement. I learn things I never knew and gain insight which years of observation could never reveal.

I got that idea from something Robert Murry McCheyne once said. The insight came to me from what he found in prayer for himself. "If I could hear Christ praying for me in the next room, I would not fear a million enemies. Yet distance makes no difference. He is praying for me." I tried that. It filled me with new courage and hope about my own personal needs. Then I thought, "Why not try the same thing for other people? Why not listen to Jesus praying for them?" Then Romans 8:26 came to mind. "We do not know what and how we ought to pray, but the Spirit himself intercedes on our behalf with sighs too deep for words" (Berkeley). Our Lord cannot only pray for our needs, but teach us how to pray for others! The exciting thing is that then we can pray with new confidence because we know how to pray for the very things we have heard and felt the Lord praying for. There's the mysterious secret: First pray to know how to pray, and then pray for the things the Lord is more ready to give than we are to ask. I have never done that without receiving a fresh burst of delight and affirmation for the person about whom I have heard him pray.

To intercede means "to pass between." Christ is our eternal intercessor. From whom could we better learn to intercede according to the will of God? I have constantly rediscovered new warmth and graciousness for the people as I have passed between them and the resourceful, limitless Lord. The result is profound gratitude not only for the Lord, but for the person I am bringing before him.

Robert Louis Stevenson said, "I will think more of your prayers when I see more of your praises." Praise and prayer go together. If prayers for people do not lead to new praise to God for them and what he is doing in them, our prayers will become an evasion. The whole issue is: Do people feel our praise to God for them? Paul constantly thanked God for the people to whom he wrote his Epistles. "I thank my God through Jesus Christ for all of you" (Rom. 1:8). "I give thanks to God always for you . . ." (1 Cor. 1:4). "I do not cease to give thanks for you, remembering you in my prayers . . ." (Eph. 1:17). "I thank my God in all my remembrance of you, always in every prayer of mine for you all making my prayer with joy, thankful for your partnership in the gospel from the first day until now" (Phil. 1:3–5). The same praise to God for people communicates esteem and appreciation in Paul's letters to the Thessalonians, to Timothy, and to Philemon. Has anyone ever read that in a letter from us or heard us say it to them?

All this centers on a powerful, convicting truth: People themselves are God's answer to our prayers about them. If that ever were communicated to them as a result of our prayers, a lot of the things we agonize about in prayer for them would be on the way to healing.

The answer keeps knocking. Peter's at the gate of the wall around our hearts that we've built up over the years for protection, privacy, individuality, separateness. But there's an opening and a gate. And people are knocking. Prayer sensitizes our ears to hear the knocking. Overtures of affection, pleas for help, cries of loneliness, eloquent silences which shout for attention, tender touches lest we forget the person exists, or angry outbursts leaping like flames from the cauldron of frustration within —all knocks at the gate!

"But Peter continued knocking"—I can't leave that until I have put in the place of Peter's name all the names and then the faces of the people knocking at my gate. Who are they for you? "And when they opened the gate, then they saw him and were amazed." It's always that way: when we open the gateway of our hearts, we *see* the person for whom we have prayed. To see is to behold, to admire, to honor. Elizabeth Barrett Browning in *Aurora Leigh* said, "God answers sharp and sudden on some prayers,/And thrusts the thing we have prayed for in our face." That's what happens when our prayers for some change or adjustment in a person's life are answered, not only in the particular thing for which we prayed, but when, in response to the Lord's love, we are thrust face to face and heart to heart with the person. And that's what we all want most of all, isn't it? In answer to our problem-oriented prayers, the Lord gives a person-centered answer. The answer keeps knocking until we accept the person himself as God's gracious gift.

CHAPTER 14

How to Become a Free Person

Acts 13:1–47

We hear a lot these days about "bottom line," a term
that originated in the business world. Bottom line is the
undeniable focus of the final figures on a financial statement,
the conclusive result of income and outgo, expenses and profit.
A good businessman's penetrating question about any venture is
"Okay, what's on bottom line?"

But the term has developed broader implications. Now we
use it to encompass the tangible results of any presentation or
program. Bottom line is the tabulation of the effects of our
efforts. It stands as the calculable, measurable outcome of an
investment of time or energy, as well as of money.

Bottom line of the gospel is freedom. The final accounting of
our experience of the love and forgiveness of our Lord is whether
or not we have been set free to live the abundant life. God has
made the ultimate investment by coming into the world in Jesus
Christ to live for us, die for our sins, and be raised up to be
with us forever. In the spiritual economy of God, that investment
of himself is bottom-lined to the extent our experience of his
love has liberated us from fear, guilt, the past, and self-negation,
to love him, ourselves, and others.

But many of us are not free. We are incarcerated in prisons
of our own making and the making of others. We are haunted
by the hurts of the past; we feel we must somehow be good
enough to deserve acceptance from God and others; we are
afraid to be and express our true selves; we long for approval and

affirmation, and we constantly adjust our lives to ensure their flow; we ache for love and yet habitually do the things which make us unlovable.

Four people come into focus in my mind's eye. All have a deficit at bottom line. Though each of them is a Christian, when it comes to being life-affirming, loving, and lovable, the value of the gospel is almost washed out or counterbalanced by self-negation, debilitating memories, and inadequacy. One is a high school senior who does not like herself. Her family and friends have not helped reshape her self-image. Past hurts in trying to reach out to her peers have met with rejection. Now she is immobilized by fear. What would it mean for her to become free in Christ? The next person is a young man just out of graduate school. His relationship with his father has been demeaning, and his faith in Christ has not been able to free him from the anger and hostility that he feels inside about what his father did to him. What would Christian freedom be for him? The third person is a compulsive people-pleaser. From childhood she learned that love must be earned. She feels she must constantly do something for her husband, children, and friends so that she will be worthy of their approval. She can never relax; her life is a constant stream of effort to assure a desired reaction from people. What would this person look like and how would she handle life's relationships if she were set free by our Lord? The final person is a master manipulator. His own insecure relationship with Christ forces him to work people like puppets. His job gives him great power, which he uses with equivocation and dissimulation to get people to perform. At home he is not very different. His wife and kids are rewarded when they do what he wants, when he wants it. When his patriarchal authority does not work, privileges are dangled like bait or material retaliation is threatened. How could a deeper experience of Christ free this manipulator to dare to motivate by love?

It is with these people in mind, and hosts of others like them, that I want to talk about bottom-line freedom. Perhaps you are like one of them or know someone who is, or maybe, in your own way, you desire to discover a new freedom. The purpose of this chapter is to meet these very pressing, practical needs for our emancipation through Christ.

How do you become a free person? I hear that question from

people everywhere. Living in a free land does not ensure personal freedom. Nor does attending church. Being religious never made anyone free. We all know too many church members who are up-tight, unloving, and chained to compulsive patterns and personality quirks. Often we could be counted among them.

We are like the religious Jews to whom Paul preached in Antioch of Pisidia. He gave them, and now provides for us, a clear answer to the question of how to become a free person. Freedom in Christ was the bottom line of his magnificent sermon in the synagogue, recorded in Acts 13. Everything led up to a triumphant conclusion in verses 38 and 39: "Let it be known to you therefore, brethren, that through this man [Christ] forgiveness of sins is proclaimed to you, and by him every one that believes is freed from everything from which you could not be freed by the law of Moses."

There's a clear formula of freedom. It declares what God has done, what we can receive, and what happens as a result. Catch the dynamic progression: the faithfulness of God, the forgiveness offered in Jesus Christ, the faith that grasps the gift, and the freedom which follows.

Paul had come a long distance to proclaim the faithfulness of God there in the Antioch synagogue. What happened to him along the way gave a ring of reality to his message. Months before he and Barnabas, along with Mark, had left another Antioch in Syria and sailed to Cyprus on their first missionary journey. From Cyprus they sailed to Attalia, a seaport in the district of Pamphylia on the northern coast of the Mediterranean. Then they made their way a few miles to Perga. There two painful things happened to Paul that made his trust in the faithfulness of God a fresh experience of his life. John Mark defected the mission and the Apostle contracted a physical disease. Most scholars suggest that it must have been the malaria so prevalent in the lowlands around Perga. I suppose that is what sent him northbound over the treacherous Taurus Mountains to recover at Antioch, elevated at 3,600 feet. His own reflection on this in his letter to the Galatian churches, of which Antioch was one, gives us some insight: "You know that it was because of a bodily ailment that I preached the gospel to you at first!" (Gal. 4:13). Study of the virulent form of malaria known in this area at that time reveals that it caused headaches manifested in pain "like a red-hot bar thrust through the forehead," or a chisel cutting into the temple.* Paul was a sick man with a "thorn in his flesh" (2 Cor. 12:7) when he reached Antioch, but he would not turn back! The bold adventurer of Christ knew he was being healed and so pressed on to preach the good news of the gospel. Knowing the circumstances under which Paul preached his message about the faithfulness of God in the synagogue at Antioch gives us perspective on the kind of Christian freedom he proclaimed. It had an "in spite of" quality that precludes our ever saying, "That's fine for you, Paul, but you never knew the debilitating difficulties that keep me from freedom!"

Paul was one of the freest men who ever lived. We find the root of his remarkable freedom in his convictions about Christ. Retracing history, Paul shows his listeners in the synagogue what God had done in Christ to set his people free. He reminds them that the same Yahweh who called his people out of Egypt, gave them the promised land, and blessed the kingdom of Israel under David was the Lord God who had come in the long expected Messiah, Jesus. With careful, scholarly detail he recounts the truth both of what God offered in the Messiah and how his people rejected the gift. His message rises in a crescendo as he reminds the people of the crucifixion and the victory of the resurrection. His rhetoric is tuned to full force when he says, "Let it be known, therefore, brethren, that through this man . . ." Behold the man! Christ was the full fruition of the faithfulness of God.

There is no lasting freedom apart from Christ. Paul later wrote the Galatians, "For freedom Christ has set us free!" Christ alone was the emancipation for him.

How do you become a free person? You must begin with a relationship with Christ or your freedom will have no real beginning or lasting power. All the things which keep us from being free people can be liberated by him alone. Christ made that clear in his own message. "If you continue in my word, you are truly my disciples, and you will know the truth and the truth will make you free." The incredulous priests and Pharisees responded, "We are descendants of Abraham, and we have never

* William Barclay, *The Acts of the Apostles* (Edinburgh: St. Andrew's Press, 1962), p. 110.

been in bondage to anyone. How is it that you say, 'You will be made free'?" Then Jesus gave the key to freedom. "Truly, truly, I say to you, every one who commits sin is a slave to sin. The slave does not continue in the house for ever; the son continues for ever. So if the Son makes you free, you will be free indeed" (John 8:34–36). The Son of God alone can set a person free from sin and guilt. The truth about him and an experience of his love is the basis of freedom. But how does this happen?

Paul presses on to make the process clear. "Through this man forgiveness of sins is proclaimed to you" (Acts 13:38). Forgiveness and freedom are inseparably linked. The faithfulness of God provided the Cross and Resurrection as the foundation of our freedom. Only a forgiven person is free.

We know that from experience. The memory of past failures is like sand in the gears of our effectiveness. We are in the present what we have been in the past. The careful computer of memory records all the things we have done or have had done to us. We cannot wipe them out with redoubled efforts at goodness or self-justification. All that we have done to ourselves and others haunts us until we are forgiven. But the forgiveness must be radical and deep by One who has authority to forgive. Only an incarnate God upon the Cross can do that. "Forgive them, for they know not what they do" (Luke 23:34). But we knew, Lord! And the voice of love that paid the price for our sins responds, "Neither do I condemn you; go, and sin no more" (John 8:11). Can it be true? All that we have said and done, forgiven? Yes, even before we ask. It is love's priority and power to forgive.

The psalmist found this. "For thou, O Lord, art good and forgiving,/abounding in steadfast love to all who call on thee./ Give ear, O Lord, to my prayer;/hearken to my cry of supplication" (Ps. 86:5–6).

But do I realize the unrelinquishing love of our Lord in my own life as a fact of my own experience? The syndrome of failure, forgiveness, and repeated failure was finally broken in my life when I realized that I was forgiven even before I sinned and that there was nothing that I could do to make God stop loving me; that his forgiveness was given before I asked for it and my often reluctant request was grasping for a reality which had been finished for me on Calvary. The Cross did not change

God's attitude toward me; it revealed his unchanging nature. That finally melted my compulsive, repetitive pattern and gave me a first experience of freedom. But there was no deep personal freedom until I forgave myself. The reason I kept on doing the things which caused me guilt was because I could not be as gracious to myself as God had been. Arrogant pride! I was playing God over my own life. I was shocked when a friend helped me see this. The bars of my own "guilted cage" kept me locked in and unfree. Then one night in prayer I felt the Lord very near and powerful. "Will you love Lloyd as much as I do?" he asked. "Forgive him! I have."

The full force of that experience did not become a realized experience until I learned how to forgive others. Next to our memories of our own failures, the thing that keeps most of us from being free people is our unwillingness to forgive others. The surest sign that we have received the forgiveness of God is our willingness to forgive people, past and present. C. S. Lewis was right: "Everyone says forgiveness is a lovely thing, until they have something to forgive." The Lord's prayer mocks our reluctance to forgive: "And forgive our sins—for we have forgiven those who sinned against us" (Luke 11:4, *The Living Bible*). There is an undeniable equation there: we cannot fully experience true forgiveness of God if we will not forgive. And our retort is, "I'll forgive, but I can't forget!" How silly! That's just another way of saying, "I can't forgive." Pride again! Stack that up against a God who says, "I will remember their sin no more" (Jer. 31:34). Our freedom is dependent on the gift from God of a poor memory of others' failures.

Most of us need deep, remedial surgery on our memories of other people's sins, especially where they have hurt or frustrated us. Often it takes a loving friend to help us relive the pain, actually express our feelings, and then give forgiveness. But only the divine nature of the indwelling Holy Spirit can give us the power for true forgiveness. He alone can enable us to "be kind to one another, tenderhearted, forgiving one another, as God in Christ forgave you" (Eph. 4:32).

Now Paul gives us the secret of that power. "And by him [Christ] every one that believes is freed from everything from which you could not be freed by the law of Moses" (Acts 13:39). Freedom is not only the fruit of forgiveness, it is rooted in faith. This verse from Paul's sermon is the core of his theology and the basis of the psychology of Christian freedom. Here is the justification by faith alone which Paul spells out repeatedly in his Epistles. It is the good news of freedom for self-righteous, religious people.

Some background will help. The Law was given through Moses for the ordering of the life of the people of God. It was intended to guide the people of Israel in a right relationship with God and with one another, but it was never intended to be a basis of righteousness before God. Only an abandoned trust in his grace and mercy could do that. But instead of trusting in the goodness of God, the people trusted in their own goodness by trying to earn their status before God by impeccably keeping the Law. The result was that self-justification, making oneself right with God through human effort, actually became a god below God. They worshiped the Law and their own capacity to please God more than God himself. They were not free. They negotiated their own piety to the extent that they did not need God! It was the unforgivable sin. They denied any failure or inadequacy. By denial of sin there was nothing to be forgiven. Dependence on God and trust in his forgiveness and salvation through the Cross was unnecessary for them. Who needs a Savior when he believes he can save himself? But that effort to save ourselves is the ultimate demise of freedom. God came in Christ to liberate us from this compulsion. And faith, as a response to life, is the only thing God wants. By faith, the inner condition of our insufficiency is overwhelmed by the victorious adequacy of Christ to save us, now and forever.

Faith alone, Paul asserted, could make a person acceptable before God. Our efforts will not make us good enough. In this monumental statement in the synagogue at Antioch, the Apostle used two of his favorite words: *pisteuō* ("believe"), closely related to *pistis* ("faith"), and *dikaioō* ("to set right with God on the basis of faith"). In Romans we feel the full impact: "The righteousness of God is revealed through faith for faith; as it is written, 'He who through faith is righteous shall live' " (Rom. 1:17). "But now the righteousness of God has been manifested apart from the law, although the law and the prophets bear witness to it, the righteousness of God through faith in Jesus Christ for all who believe. For there is no distinction; since all have sinned and fall short of the glory of God, they are justified by his grace as a gift, through the redemption which is in Christ Jesus" (Rom. 3:21–24). Luther put it clearly: "Faith is a living, daring confidence in God's grace. It is so sure and certain that a man could stake his life on it a thousand times." Bottom line for Luther was indeed *"sola fide."* The just shall live for faith alone!

What does that have to do with freedom? Everything! When, through the gift of faith, we claim our righteousness with God, we know with assurance that we are loved and that nothing can change that. The insecurity of having to be adequate is gone. We are free to be ourselves, love ourselves, and give ourselves away to others. When we know that God is pleased with us out of sheer grace we could never deserve, we do not have to try to win his pleasure. The outcome is joy and an unstudied capacity to do those things which are indeed pleasing to him— not as a requirement, but as a result. The test of freedom is not just what we are free to do, but what we are free not to have to do.

This has amazing implications for our relationships with the people of our lives: ours with them and theirs with us. We are free from the necessity of earning the love of people and requiring that they justify our love for them. Standards and bartered approval are no longer required. When I think of people with whom I am free to be myself, I find without exception that they are people who are so secure in God's unmerited favor that they exude acceptance of me. I feel affirmed and liberated in their presence. The secret is that they feel good about themselves! This has helped me to realize that the times I imprison people with judgment, guilt, and feelings of inadequacy are when I feel badly about myself. The only cure of that is fresh grace. We all have a conditioning capacity of establishing rules and regulations for a relationship. "I will love you if and when—" we say or imply. The cause is usually our own insecure relationship with our Lord. When we are not free in that, there is slim chance that the people around us will be free. Paul Sherer said, "We find freedom when we find God; we lose it when we lose him." But the essence of our freedom is that God will never lose us. When that assurance is the ever-recurring experience of our faith, we will be free. We need to do as G. K. Chesterton suggests: "Let your religion be less a theory and more a love affair!"

> I find, I walk, I love; but O the whole
> Of love is but my answer, Lord, to Thee!
> For Thou wert long beforehand with my soul;
> Always Thou lovedst me.*

Freedom covers all dimensions of time. We are free to take a backward look and receive forgiveness for ourselves and others.We can take an inward look to see those things which fester in us and make us insecure, and then accept the healing righteousness of God. We can take an outward look to people and dare to shower them with the overflow of our Christ-oriented self-delight and acceptance. We can take a forward look, knowing that the future is not an enemy, and meet each challenge, knowing that power is available. Realized forgiveness is but a prayer away. That's bottom line for a blessed life!

Paul's stirring message of freedom in Christ won him a hearing from the whole city of Antioch. The Jews who had been profoundly moved by him in the synagogue now were deeply disturbed by the response of the city's Gentiles. That response filled them with jealousy, but it also confirmed the guidance of God in Paul's life. With prophetic clarity he articulated his direction: "It was necessary that the word of God should be spoken first to you. Since you thrust it from you, and judge yourselves unworthy of eternal life, behold, we turn to the Gentiles" (Acts 13:46).

That marked an end of an era and the beginning of a new age. The Gentile frontier was unmistakably open, and pioneer Paul was eager to break the trail. He pressed on with freedom because he knew the Lord went before him to prepare the way. Luke sounds the note of prevenience when he shows that those who believed had been prepared to respond: "And when the Gentiles heard this, they were glad and glorified the word of God; and as many as were ordained to eternal life believed. And

---

* "I sought the Lord, and afterward I knew," Anon.

the word of the Lord spread throughout all the region" (Acts 13:48–49).

But life on the new frontier was never devoid of two conflicting realities for Paul: the hospitality of the Gentiles and the hostility of the Jews. The Gentiles were responsive and the Jews persistently dogged his tracks, disturbing his ministry and dissuading his converts. But freedom in Christ provided joy in the midst of difficulty and persecution.

Bottom line of the gospel is freedom expressed in joy, for us as well as Paul. The nature of that joy is what I want to consider next.

CHAPTER 15

Joy When You Don't Feel Like It

Acts 13:48–14:7

This past year has been the most difficult year of my life. My wife has been through five major surgeries, radiation treatment, and chemotherapy. I am thankful that I now know she is going to make it. During the same year, I suffered the loss of several key staff teammates whose moves were very guided for them, but a source of pressure and uncertainty in my work. Problems which I could have tackled with gusto under normal circumstances seemed to loom in all directions. Discouragement lurked around every corner, trying to capture my feelings. Prayer was no longer a contemplative luxury, but the only way to survive. My own intercessions were multiplied by the prayers of others. Friendships were deepened as I was forced to allow people to assure me with words I had preached for years. No day went by without a conversation, letter, or phone call giving me love and hope.

The greatest discovery that I have made in the midst of all the difficulties is that I can have joy when I don't feel like it—artesian joy. When I had every reason to feel beaten, I felt joy. As the prayers were being answered, the Holy Spirit infused a seemingly limitless flow of joy. In spite of everything, he gave me the conviction of being loved and the certainty that nothing could separate me from him. It was not happiness, gush, or jolliness but a constant flow of the Spirit through me. At no time did he give me the easy confidence that everything would work out as I wanted it on my timetable, but that he was in

176

charge and would give me and my family enough courage for each day: grace. Joy is always the result of that. I found that the more I recaptured the Lord's limitless love, the more joy I felt. The gift and the Giver were one. What I had told others thousands of times I now knew for myself: joy is a fruit, a manifestation of the indwelling Holy Spirit.

That's Luke's startling account of the joy of the early Christians. He sandwiches an amazing statement between two experiences of difficulty, rejection, and persecution. The ministry of Paul and his company in Antioch of Pisidia ended in a mass movement against them. The success of the gospel among the Gentiles was more than the Jewish leaders could tolerate. They incited leading men and women of the city against them and drove them away from the city.

It was the same story at Iconium, a few miles away. The bold proclamation of the good news of grace, confirmed by signs and wonders, brought both great response and hostility. An attempted stoning made them flee the city. But between these sad tales of the two cities, Luke attests to the joy of the Apostles when they had every reason not to feel joyful: "And the disciples were filled with joy and with the Holy Spirit" (Acts 13:52).

Joy is the outward expression of the rhythms of grace from the drumbeat of the Master. When his Spirit beats indefatigably and persistently within, there is calm, trust, and hope. We know that sickness, circumstances, people, or whatever might happen cannot defeat us.

We can't help marveling at Paul and his friends. In both Antioch and Iconium they poured out their lives for people. They preached, taught, and ministered with love. Success always spelled renewed rage from the Jews. The temptation to give up would have engulfed them if it were not for the power of the Holy Spirit. Difficulties were not a sign of defeat, but a call on to the next place to share love.

Luke tells us that when the Christian adventurers left Antioch they "shook off the dust from their feet" against the people who opposed them, and went on. At first this looks like vitriolic anger. Not so! The Lord himself had given the instruction, "And if any place will not receive you and they refuse to hear you, when you leave, shake off the dust that is on your feet for a testimony against them" (Mark 6:11). The practice was rooted in an old custom of the Jews: when returning to Palestine from a neighboring nation, they shook the dust of foreign defilement off their feet. For Jesus, the practice meant something much more than condemnation. It was a sign that, having done all we can, we should get on with the urgent opportunities at hand. The results are never ours to tabulate. That's the mood I feel in Paul and his followers. They had done all they could. The world was waiting for the gospel. Antioch was in the Lord's hands. The preaching of the gospel had taken root, and the city would never hear the end of it! No wonder the winsome evangelists were filled with joy and the Holy Spirit. Confident trust burst forth in joy.

But there's a deeper reason for this evident joy. It was not just the presence of the Holy Spirit, but what he did in them to produce the fruit of the Spirit in joy. Based on the whole witness of the New Testament, we can surmise the source of the joy engendered by the Holy Spirit.

Jesus had said that the Holy Spirit would bring to our remembrance all that he said and did. The convincing content of joy is that the Lord himself is synonymous with joy. The Old Testament prophets predicted that he would bring joy. At his nativity the angels proclaimed, "Behold, I bring you good news of a great joy which will come to all the people" (Luke 2:10). His life brought joy to people who believed in him wherever he went. Joy was the exclamation point of his message. "These things have I spoken to you that my joy may be in you, and that your joy may be full" (John 15:11). "So you have sorrow now, but I will see you again and your hearts will rejoice and no one will take your joy from you. Hitherto, you have asked nothing in my name. Ask, and you will receive, that your joy may be full" (John 16:22, 24). The Lord's final prayer on the night before he was crucified was that the disciples "may have my joy fulfilled in themselves" (John 17:13). The resurrection victory brought joy. Christ had won and so could his followers. If death could be defeated, all things were possible.

The Holy Spirit never allowed the early Christians to forget that. He kept the drumbeat constant: "In this world you will have tribulation, but be of good cheer, I have overcome the world!" (John 16:33). Joy became the inseparable companion of difficulty. What Paul later wrote the Colossians from Rome, he knew for himself and his friends in the midst of rejection and physical persecution in both Antioch and Iconium: "May you be strengthened with all power, according to his glorious might for all endurance and patience with joy" (Col. 1:9–11). The Holy Spirit had taught him that! To be full of the Holy Spirit is to be constantly reminded of Jesus, his message, his victorious resurrection, and his power.

But there was another reason for the joy of Paul and his band. Jesus had hinted at it in his parable of the lost coin. Remember? When the woman finds the lost coin, she calls together her friends and neighbors saying, "Rejoice with me, for I have found the coin which I had lost." Jesus interprets the meaning, "Just so, I tell you, there is joy before the angels of God over one sinner who repents" (Luke 15:9–10). The joy of the Christians between Antioch and Iconium was the joy of heaven in their hearts. What they had done brought joy to God; he returned the gift. They had been a part of the miraculous transformation of hundreds of people who had given their lives to Christ. There is no greater joy. To know that we have enabled people to live abundantly now, and triumphantly forever, is joy that no frustration or circumstances can diminish. It was being part of a movement like that that gave Paul joy. Joy is not only an outer expression of the inner work of grace in our own hearts; it's the expression of delight over being part of the transformation of the world. If we are not involved in personal caring to help others know Christ, our own personal care will sink us. To miss that joy is to miss everything.

I know that's true. At the darkest times during this past year, my life was brightened by my work with people. Each time I needed a lift the most, the Lord would give me someone in trouble and in need of him. Sharing his love in the context of the victory over despair he was giving me personally seemed to help others. Each time a new person gave his life to Christ and started the adventure, I was filled with almost uncontainable joy. The result was that I could return to the excruciating realities of my own situation with renewed conviction that our Lord could do all things.

There's a further reason Paul and his friends were filled with joy and the Holy Spirit. Their fellowship was joy. They had each other. I like to imagine what they said to each other after each traumatic difficulty. I can feel the encouragement that they gave each other as they bound up each other's wounds. Don't miss the warmth of "I couldn't have made it without you!" expressions of mutual affirmation. Joy is the only adequate word to describe the fellowship of the early Church. More than fighting a common enemy, they shared a common cause nourished by an undiminishable conviction.

We all need the joy of the fellowship. We were never meant to make it alone. Our Lord uses the difficult times to break us open to a receptive dependence on our brothers and sisters in the faith. We need them to remind us of our real purpose and of our only source of power. Most of all, we need someone to understand what we're going through and to pray for us and with us. Martin Luther was right: "Christians are a blissful people, who can rejoice at heart and sing praises, stomp and leap for joy. That is well pleasing to God and doeth our heart good when we trust God and find in him our pride and blissfulness."

I have found that same thing with my congregation in Hollywood. When I look out over my people assembled for worship, I feel wave after wave of love. We are bearing each other's burdens. Openness about my own needs has not only made a vital contact of mutuality, but has affirmed that we all need grace—the pastor most of all. My joy is a result of that! It was the Lord's people who helped me know that the word of the Lord was for Lloyd: "Count it all joy, my brethren, when you meet various trials, for we know that testing of your faith produces steadfastness" (James 1:2).

If we wait for the right feelings we will never experience joy. In fact, it's usually when we feel like it the least, because of our surroundings, circumstances, or life's eventualities, that joy captures our feelings—the ecstasy of eternity. Regardless of what's happening around us, we know we are loved, forgiven, cherished—amazing grace, peace that's inexplicable. And, thanks to the Holy Spirit, it's a joy that won't quit!

CHAPTER 16

The Ultimate Manipulation

Acts 14

I was invited to preach recently at a church which had an impelling neon sign on the roof. The bright letters spelled out "JESUS ONLY!" I thought a lot about that as I waited for the service to begin. My homiletical mind darted to different ways I could finish the sentence: Jesus only saves; Jesus only sustains; Jesus only strengthens; Jesus only secures. Not a bad claim for a church! I was anxious to meet the pastor and come to know the people so as to see what congruity there was between the sign and the quality of life in the congregation. I was not surprised to find that the church faced the same problems of finances, attendance, and inactivity which cripple most congregations. The sign had been erected years before, I was told. It was put there to declare to the world that this was one church which would depend on Christ alone. But now, by the people's own admission, the words should have read "JESUS AND!"

The people believed in Christ, but as for many contemporary Christians, he was but one of the many sources of their security, meaning, and purpose. Their lives contradicted the sign. Family, jobs, possessions, people, achievements of the past, hopes for the future, our nation—all ranked closely with Jesus in the raw pressures of life. But then my critical analysis was softened as I got to know the people. They really wanted the sign to be true. As for me and my house—and church—so do I. But is it?

I was empathetically one with the people in a quest to make it so! To do that, Jesus would have to become more than one of our many gods.

Syncretism has been around for a long time. It's the spiritual sickness of having more than one god. That never troubled the Greeks very much. They had a pantheon of gods, and there was always room for one more. The people of Israel constantly were tempted to add the fertility or war gods of pagan nations to Yahweh for good measure. Elijah almost lost his sanity and life over that enfeebling dilution. His words are strangely penetrating even today for Christians in the Church. "How long will you go limping with two different opinions? If the Lord is God follow him; but if Baal be god follow him" (1 Kings 18:21). It finally comes down to that choice, doesn't it? The Lord will accept anything in us except a place in our constellation of diminutive gods. The ultimate manipulation of Christ is the idolatry of people and things on an equal status with him.

This was exactly what Paul and Barnabas faced in Lystra. Before coming there, they had survived hostility, hatred, persecution, and near-death because of the gospel. They had experienced every possible response to Christ from Jew and Gentile alike—except one. At Lystra they faced the subtle evasion of the message through idolizing of the messengers. I want to focus our exposition of the last lap of the first missionary journey into the district of Lycaonia recorded in Acts 14 on the Lystra experience because of the inherent implications it has for us today.

Lystra was about six hours' journey southwest from Iconium where Paul and Barnabas had lived out their joy in the midst of resistance and persecution. In most places the Gentiles heard them gladly. At Lystra they heard them all too gladly.

I came across a reference in Ovid, the Roman poet, which helped me understand Lystra's ready response to the Apostles. In Metamorphosis VIII Ovid tells of an ancient myth which made the people quick to receive these missionary peripatetics. The legend goes that Zeus and Hermes had come to that region disguised as mortals. No one accepted or welcomed them except one couple, Philemon and Baucis. A flood of judgment was sent in retaliation, and all were drowned except this old couple. They were made guardians of a spectacular temple outside of Lystra and were turned into great, magnificent trees when they died. Familiar with this folk-legend, the people of Lystra were taking no chances. They welcomed Paul and Barnabas and gave them access to their city. They watched them carefully. Could this be Zeus and Hermes returned a second time?

Obviously the two Apostles did not realize that they were being sized up for deification. They immediately went about their usual activities of preaching and teaching Christ. We are sure they proclaimed Christ at the beginning of their ministry because of the manifestation of faith in a man who was crippled from birth. Only Christ enables the kind of faith Paul observed in the man's face as he preached: "He listened to Paul speaking; and Paul, looking intently at him and seeing that he had faith to be made well, said in a loud voice, 'Stand upright on your feet!' And he sprang up and walked" (Acts 14:9–10). The cripple was healed.

That did it! Now the people were convinced that Zeus and Hermes had returned. But they had been so intent on fitting Paul and Barnabas into the personified categories of their previously established deities that they had not heard what they had said about Christ and his salvation. They were so excited that their bilingual tongues lapsed from Greek into their native Lycaonian. What began as a whispered rumor in a crowd now reached a fervor. "The gods have come down to us in the likeness of men!" they shouted. Barnabas, massive and strong of stature, they identified as Zeus, the head of the ancient Greek pantheon; and Paul, because of his gift of speech, they called Hermes, the god distinguished for eloquence and rhetoric. The celebrative excitement of the crowd grew as they devised ways of welcoming their "gods." Just outside the city gate stood the temple memorializing the previously inhospitable reception of these very gods. The people would spare nothing this time! Oxen were prepared for sacrifice; garlands of flowers were draped over the sacrificial oxen and on the visiting deities, and spread everywhere in honor of their coming.

It finally dawned on Paul and Barnabas what was happening. The people had not heard the gospel they preached. Instead, the two of them were about to be deified in the Greek pantheon! Horror gripped them. What could they do? How could they make the people understand that they had come to Lystra not to be made great but to preach a great Christ; not to become two of many gods, but to proclaim the living God? The Apostles tore their garments, not a very godlike thing to do. But that was a radical Hebrew way of expressing consternation over a sacrilege. The high priest had done this with angered rage over Jesus. Now, in a strange twist, here were two followers of Jesus rending their clothes in a desperate attempt to acknowledge Christ as Lord, and not be counterfeit gods themselves. Something had to be done and said to help the people understand that they were men just like themselves, in need of the true God as much as they were.

We think of the many great politicians, monarchs, generals, and preachers who have failed at just that point. History's pages are filled with accounts of gifted leaders who have manipulated the populace to follow them as deified answers to people's need to be led. Most of them have ended up being manipulated by the mob.

Paul refused to be one of Lystra's gods. "Men, why are you doing this?" he asked. "We also are men, of like nature with you, and bring you good news, that you should turn from these vain things to a living God . . ." (14:15). He wanted the people to know that he had the same weaknesses, inadequacies, and appetites they had. He had tried his own variety of "vain things" to justify himself before gods of his own making. Here is an incisive word for the Christian communicator and witness. The establishment of our humanity and what God has done with the raw material of our natures makes our message impelling and believable. We are not to impress people with piety, but present our impressive Christ who has dealt with our spiritual poverty.

Paul shows his skill at communication. He begins where the people are, with what they believe. His purpose is to proclaim one God who is Lord, creator, and source of all. He begins with the known realities of the heaven, earth, and sea; the seasons, rains, and harvest; the benevolent providence of food and gladness. From these taken-for-granted blessings, he shows them the source in the Lord God of all creation.

But still the people did not listen. Paul's eloquence, and not what he said, refortified their determination to honor him as one of their gods. (The most effective way of evading truth is to deal with it rather than having it deal with us.) They cheered Paul as Hermes and refused to come to grips with the true God he proclaimed.

That's manipulative inclusion at its best—and worst! They did not really want to learn what their new god said; they wanted him on their own terms. By their accolades they kept him from going on to present the truth that the Lord God, about whom he spoke, was the only true God who had humbly come "in the likeness of man" to live and die for their salvation. Paul never got around to that, because the people were too determined to keep him within the confines of their religious presuppositions. Sentimentalism kept them from salvation!

I am prompted to make a comparison of Christians in the Church in America with the people of Lystra. Most of us have come to Christ with rigidly set securities. We accept him as Savior out of our need for further security, assurance of his love for daily pressures now and promise of eternal life for the future. Like the people of Lystra, we keep our other gods. Idolatry of Christ as a historical figure makes us fanatic about the celebration of his birth and death. But idolatry is always adoration at a distance. It's the ultimate manipulation. We get what we want and need, but avoid the penetrating transformation of our lives. We whittle Christ down to our size and fit him into the portfolios holding our accumulation of gods. We deal with him to keep him from dealing with us.

There is no more clever way of capturing and domesticating a truth than accepting it and rehoning it to fit our preciously held ideas and convictions. We do that with Christ all the time. We all have needs for strength and power to do and be what we have determined. We all long for wisdom and insight, personality prowess and attractiveness, effectiveness and influence. Christ can provide that. So we accept him and his love to enable us to get on with our predetermined goals. By our worship and adoration, we avoid the radical reorientation of our natures and the direction of our lives.

When Jesus was born there was no room at the inn. But today, we not only have room in an inn, but a penthouse suite away from reality. Jesus is a V.I.P. to be honored, but not believed in or followed. In America, he is a custom but not the true Christ; a captured hero of a casual civil religion, but not

the Lord of our lives. We have never really grappled with
the question they asked at his birth, "What shall we do with the
child that is born?" Or during his ministry, "Who is this? What
can we do with this Jesus who claims to be the Christ? What are
we to do? For this man performs many signs. If we let him go
on thus, everyone will believe in him!" Or Pilate's mocking
question to the Jews in the mob at the time of the trial, "Then
what shall I do with the man whom you call the King of the
Jews?" (Mark 15:12). And after the Crucifixion and Resurrection the question was not silenced. Now it was focused on the
people in whom the living Christ reigned: "What shall we do
with these men?" Lystra answered that question most cleverly
of all. And as in Lystra, our times have answered with equal
evasion and equivocation. Take him in! Accept him as the
greatest *man* who ever lived! Revere him as the most penetrating psychologist who ever analyzed life. Mark the calendar B.C.
and A.D. Plan your customs around his birth, death, and resurrection. Speak of the gentle Jesus, meek and mild. Paint por-
traits of him, write the libraries full of line and verse about him.
Sing for him; preach about him. We will have done everything
we can with human skill and duration—except one—made him
the absolute Lord of our lives!

We have almost been successful at making Christ fit our
specifications. We have tried to do what people around the
Savior attempted during his earthly ministry. The disciples
and the leaders of Israel all tried it. But he would not be manipulated. Nor will he be now! He wants nothing less than that
we become new creatures in him. He must become the only
Lord of our lives, the only guide of our activities. Then the
labyrinth of secondary, falsely deified diminutive gods can be
put into perspective. No longer a pantheon of the gods of our
security system, they can be expressions of our dependence on
him. Then people, positions, possessions, and plans can be the
focus of our loyalty—not to them, but to Christ. Isaac Watts
says what we all long to mean.

> When I survey the wondrous cross
>   On which the Prince of Glory died,
> My richest gain I count but loss,
>   And pour contempt on all my pride.

Were the whole realm of nature mine,
That were an offering far too small;
Love so amazing, so divine,
Demands my soul, my life, my all.*

But there's another aspect of the Lystra story that exposes our effort to manipulate the truth. We put the communicator on a pedestal and evade the communication. We have a seemingly limitless capacity to give the honor that belongs to Christ to the people who seek to introduce us to him. Pastors, parents, friends, and teachers who have brought us the good news are often made the source of our security. We elevate them to supersainthood and miss for ourselves the dynamic that has made them admirable. We make matinee idols out of Christian leaders and forget that the greatest honor we can pay them is to become what we admire in them. There is no finer affirmation than to live the faith they have exemplified. The reason there are so many prima donnas in the pulpit is that we have given the messenger more honor than the message. We need someone to be for us what we are not willing to dare to be ourselves.

Paul learned what every Christian leader is eventually forced to discover: there is no rage like a rejected manipulator's. If he cannot fit Christ or his spokesman into a comfortable compartment for his own ends, he will turn in angry retribution.

I talked to a church officer of a congregation whose pastor had resigned under conflict. I asked the man what happened. "The man did not fit. He preached a Christ that rocked our foundations. Everything that we hold dear in society and the church seemed in question. He did not help us to live our lives; he made us question all our values. The people could not take it. Besides that, he told us about his own needs. How can a person who has needs help us with our needs?" I could hardly believe what I heard. The man did not realize the self-incrimination he had delivered. Neither Jesus nor Paul could have pastored that church. They would not "fit" either.

Notice how quickly the crowd at Lystra changed. It's embarrassing to plan a sacrifice and an exaltive celebration and have the guest of honor, a visiting "god" at that, refuse the throne

*Isaac Watts, "When I survey the wondrous cross," 1707.

of deification. When the Jews came from Antioch to disturb
Paul's ministry, the Lystra manipulators were manipulated themselves. The excitement over Paul-made-Hermes turned to bitter
hatred. When he would not do what they wanted, they did to
him what people have done for centuries to the gods of their
own making who will not perform to specification.

Look at the result of the initial preaching of the gospel at
Lystra: the pantheon of pagan gods still intact; the preachers
of the gospel captured as two more gods, and the people unenlightened. The people were still in charge. Idolatry works.
But it usually has a tragic end.

Paul was bitterly stoned by the mob at Lystra under the
careful instigation and instructions of the angry Jews. They left
him on a garbage heap outside the city thinking he was dead.

Luke has kept a serendipity for us. He says, "But when the
disciples gathered about him, he rose up and entered the city."
What disciples? Did they come from other communities to assist
Paul and Barnabas and to offset the hostile influence of the
Jews who tracked his steps? Perhaps. But further study reveals
that the preaching of the gospel in Lystra had more results
than the idolatry of the mob. Lois and Eunice were converted
during Paul's visit. His beloved Timothy, then about fourteen,
grandson of Lois and son of Eunice, must have made his first
commitment to Christ during the stormy days of preaching the
gospel at Lystra. We wonder if he was in that circle of believers who gathered around Paul to pray. We do know that
their prayers were answered. Paul was not dead! The Lord
healed the gouges and blows of the stones. He had promised
Paul that he would never be without two strengthening realities:
the Holy Spirit and the fellowship of the Church. What do any
of us need more than that? The surprises of God are readily
available when our ultimate trust is in him and nothing else!

Now Paul could get back to what he had started at Lystra.
He faced the people with the truth they previously had refused
to consider. Once again Paul was the message he proclaimed.
Let your imagination run freely to consider what it must have
been like to have the same man they had left for dead come
striding back into the city to preach the gospel. No wonder
many believed. And he would be back to encourage and enable
them. A strong, vital church would be waiting for him when

he returned on the second missionary journey. He had stood his ground against the most beguiling temptation, the temptation of being manipulated.

We can feel the spring in his step, the lilt in his voice, and the determination on his face as he and Barnabas finish the first missionary journey in Derbe, go back through the cities where they had preached and then cross the sea to Antioch in Syria to share the good news! "And when they arrived, they gathered the church together and declared all that God had done with them, and now he had opened a door of faith to the Gentiles" (Acts 14:27).

We are forced to wonder what would happen to and through us if the "Jesus Only" faith of Paul were ours and, as he did, we could use all that we have and are to bring glory to Christ and not to ourselves.

CHAPTER 17

No Strings

Acts 15:1–16:5

One of the best ways to understand a situation is to live empathetically in the skin of one of the principal participants. When we feel, think, and identify with him, we see the problem or opportunity from a personal perspective. What we would have missed with observation and analysis from an uninvolved distance becomes very real. Often the most creative way to do that is to select, not the hero of the story, but the antagonist. The issue becomes sharply clear.

That's what I want to do with Acts 15. I want us to consider what it might have been like to be a Pharisee who accepted Christ as the Messiah. There were many of them in the early Church. They founded what was called the "Pharisees' Party," a formidable power block in the emerging new Israel, the Church.

Capture the stability of the Pharisee's training and Hebraism, his immersion in Mosaic Law and tradition, his pride in being part of the chosen people of God. Live in his shoes as we relive the steps of his rigorous education, and joyous participation in Israel's customs. Feel the loving arms of parents and family as he is circumcised on the eighth day; catch the awe and wonder he felt sitting at the feet of the elder Pharisees studying the Scripture; identify with the pride he felt when he became a son of the Law at his bar mitzvah. Become one with him as he grew to full manhood and earned the revered status of a Pharisee, and consider how he must have burst with satisfaction

as he put on the dignified robes of a leader of Israel. Training
had made the Pharisee a vigilant protector of the Law which
had guided his people in persecution, bondage, and debilitating
occupation by foreign nations. Circumcision was the outward
sign of the covenant for every male Jew. It became a symbol
and sign of being part of God's special people. The original
intention was that no Jew would ever become self-righteous;
but always remember that he was who he was and had the distinction he had because he was Yahweh's chosen person.

Now our identification takes on profound complexities. Stay
on in the mind and heart of a Pharisee as his neat world of
rules and regulations, rites and rituals, is challenged by the life
and message of the people who claim that Jesus of Nazareth
is the Messiah. Relive the turbulent civil war within as he
traces the Scriptures and is increasingly convinced that the followers of the Way are right, and then confront the hostility
and anger imbued within him by his fellow Pharisees about
the Christians. Contemplate what it would take for the learned
Pharisee to grapple with the reality of confessing that Jesus is
the Christ at the cost of ridicule and ostracization. Pour your
future advancement down the drain! Anguish over the wrenching of family ties as you are rejected by parents and relatives
and eventually considered as one who is dead because of your
newfound faith.

It was not easy for a Pharisee to become a believer. It cost
him everything. But look who he received in return—Jesus,
the Messiah! For the Pharisee, a completed Jew, the Lord was
the incarnate culmination of everything he had studied and
learned. No need to do away with his heritage; now he was a
fulfilled Hebrew among the still-expectant Hebrews. There was
no need to denounce his background. In fact, he held it more
tenaciously than ever, so much so that he believed that every
Jew should find what he had found as a reality of his heritage.

But if Jesus was the Messiah of the Jews, what did he think
about non-Hebrews who also became convinced of his Lordship? Now the Christian Pharisee had a problem. Conditioning
and cultural pride flowed in his bloodstream. His people had
paid a high price to maintain their uniqueness. He was not willing to give away the centuries of particularism that had made
Israel a great people for the Lord to people who did not con-

form. If Jesus was the Hebrew Messiah, anyone wanting his salvation would have to become a Hebrew first! How else could he know the full meaning and purpose of God? The Pharisee Christians banded together to make sure no one slipped by Mount Sinai on the way to Calvary! The Law of Moses must be maintained as the preliminary preparation to the new life in Christ.

Often the disciples of the movement are more fanatic than the leaders. The Judaizers became the vigilantes of the Pharisee party in the Church. They had one conviction and one indomitable zeal: a person must become a Hebrew before becoming a Christian; and no Gentile could be admitted to the Church without circumcision before baptism.

Now the issue becomes complex. Cornelius had been admitted under Peter's persuasive oratory and undeniable assertion of the blessing of God. It was one thing to open the door a crack to admit a proselyte of Judaism into the Church, but what would the members say about the wholesaling of the gospel by Paul and Barnabas? News of the result of the first missionary journey had reached Jerusalem. In almost equal proportion to the expansion of the Church among Gentiles who were being baptized Christians without circumcision and obedience to the Law and tradition of Moses was the growth of the Pharisee party and the Judaizing zealots. Paul and Barnabas had to be stopped in their tracks!

This bit of role-playing in the skin of a Christian Pharisee helps us to comprehend the conflict which was heated to a boiling point in Acts 15. These converted Pharisees and their followers were not bad people; their problem was that they stood with one foot in Moses' Law and one foot in Christ's love. Now the ground was separating beneath them. They would have to leap one way or the other, but not without a frantic effort to hold back the earthquake and the resulting theological fault. Having tried to maintain "both-and," they were ending up with an "either-or" which contradicted the Messiah himself and his unqualified love for all men.

At this point some readers may be impatient with what this passage has to say to us today. One man in a group studying this passage asked, "What in the world does this squabble about circumcision have to do with our world today? Why don't we just skip over that petty issue and get on with something that will help us live out our Christian lives today!" The man could not see that the message about exclusivism had great meaning for him and his church. What he was about to learn was that the Church has never been free of the Judaizing spirit, and that equivocal acceptance of people troubles most of us all the time. I asked the man a couple of questions: "Do you ever hold back your approval until people become what you want? Can you think of any instance when the Church was more culturally conditioned than Christ-centered? What secondary things do we require of new Christians to satisfy our standards which may not be essential to Christ, or for them?" With that, one of the other members of the group broke in, "And can't we learn about how to deal with conflict the way the early Church dealt with this issue?" Suddenly, the man was back with us. We focused on Luke's account with new vigor. At the end of the meeting, he said, "I'm more of a Judaizing Pharisee than I thought!" And so am I. Perhaps so are you!

The point is that unqualified love is not easy for any of us— either to give or to receive. Perhaps that's the reason there are so many qualifications placed on the love we express to others. Their performance or perfection, according to our preconceptions, becomes the basis of how much of ourselves we will give them as a reward. Qualified love is the means of control, a motive for people's response, and a method of retaliation. We all feel it from others most of the time and measure it out ourselves. The reason is that, like the Judaizers, we have our own convictions about life which we hold as dearly as we do Christ. The security system of our previously held values, which we talked about in the last chapter, usually gets in the way of loving unqualifiably. The Judaizers had Moses, the Law, and circumcision; we have patterns, practices, and prejudices. The hidden source of our attitude toward others who must measure up is kept inside of us: we love ourselves with qualified acceptance; we reserve our self-affirmation until we have climbed up to some vague image of achievement or worth. We seldom, if ever, reach it, and instead continue in miserly, meager self-appreciation.

We have difficulty experiencing what the Judaizers refused to learn. The gospel is a sharp sword which cuts through the thicket of qualified love. It is the good news which proclaims that God loves us as we are and enables us to become what he intends us to be. He is not the protector of a previous dispensation but the source of a new disposition. *Christ is God's love with no strings!* He came to his people when they did not deserve his love; he gave himself away to people who misunderstood and misused him; he died for sins people refused to confess; and he was raised up in final affirmation that not even the rejection expressed in his cruel death could defeat his unqualified love. In a world of "only-if," bartered affection, he called a new breed of "love-regardless" people and sent them into the world to express his indefatigable love for all people, of all nations, as they were, where they were, in spite of what they had been or could ever become. Just as in his own ministry Jesus had loved Jew, Samaritan, and Gentile alike, so too he had unshackled Paul and Barnabas from exclusive Hebraism to proclaim grace in Christ and faith as the only necessary response. We will miss the impact of that unless the account of the Church's dispute over circumcision puts us squarely in the Pharisees' party to contemplate what we require of people before we accept them. We may have more rigid requirements than the Lord! His love has no strings!

The Judaizers who came to attack Paul and Barnabas when they returned to Syrian Antioch had strong strings attached to the gospel. As the carefully instructed emissaries of the Pharisees' party of the church in Jerusalem, they came to level off the enthusiasm about the results of the first missionary journey among the Gentiles. They were shocked by the unqualified acceptance of the non-Hebrews without their first having been required to become Jews. They came down hard on the obligations, not only of the Commandments and the protracted rules and regulations which traditions had made sacred, but on circumcision as the outward identification of a Jew with the old covenant. There could be no admittance, encouragement, or nurture given to these new Gentile converts until they had fulfilled that requirement! Paul and Barnabas took on the Judaizers in heated debate and then headed for the Church's headquarters in Jerusalem to get the issues settled once and for all.

The summit meeting at Jerusalem would determine the future of the Church. Not only was the expansion of the gospel among the Gentiles at stake, but the quality of the Church's fellowship as an expression of unqualified love. Loaded for battle, the believers of the Pharisees' party leveled their aim on Paul's ministry to the Gentiles: "It is necessary to circumcise them, and to change them to keep the law of Moses" (Acts 15:5). Paul took the blast and returned his best shots. Fortified by the marvelous accounts of what had happened to the Gentiles whom God had loved without reservation and given the gift of faith, he held his ground against requiring circumcision of them. When the Apostles and elders gathered for prayer and discussion of the issue, they sought the guidance of the Holy Spirit.

Peter had been through this same problem over the conversion of Cornelius, as we discussed earlier. Now his seasoned judgment on the matter ended further debate and led to a Holy Spirit–inspired decision. Peter said, "Brethren, you know that in the early days God made choice among you, that by my mouth the Gentiles should hear the word of the gospel and believe" (15:7). God's direction had been clear before: why question in the darkness of conflict what had been revealed in the light? With force of conviction, he called them to remember that only God can judge the heart. That was something new which they had known in the Church in contrast to the judgmental Judaism in which many of them had been raised. "And God who knows the heart bore witness to them, giving them the Holy Spirit just as he did to us; and he made no distinction between us and them, but cleansed their hearts by faith" (15:8–9).

Peter's theology had been written in experience, with the Lord guiding each realization. He had not worked out an ideology for penetration into the non-Hebrew world; his observation of what God was doing among the Gentiles clarified what he should do. The implication for the Church was to be careful about correcting God or demanding from people what he had not required. "Now therefore, why do you make trial of God by putting a yoke upon the neck of the disciples which neither our fathers nor we have been able to bear? But we believe that we shall be saved through the grace of the Lord Jesus, just as they will" (15:10–11).

That's the real key to unlock the power of unqualified love.

It is by grace alone that any of us has experienced forgiveness and hope in Christ. Peter wanted the Church to remember that the level ground of grace was the only sure footing beneath all Christians, Hebrew and Gentile alike. No one in the Church had an edge. Faith was the open door through which they all had to pass. And that was not their achievement, but God's gift.

The Lord won the day in Jerusalem. Unqualified love and acceptance was expressed to the Gentile converts. Circumcision would not be required. In order to nail down the decision once and for all, a letter was written to the churches clarifying the orders from headquarters. It rapped the knuckles of the Judaizers and asserted the new attitude of acceptance which the Church would have to the non-Hebrew world. Circumcision would not be a qualification, but a few necessary things to grow in Christ were mentioned. The letter counseled the converts to abstain from what was sacrificed to idols, from what was strangled, and from unchastity. Even in this advice we feel the mood of concern rather than judgmental qualification. It was a new day in the Church!

The Holy Spirit was the source of the power of this unqualified love. The letter which was sent out carried the depths of the prayer and guidance of the Holy Spirit that had been given. "For it seemed good to the Holy Spirit and to us to lay upon you no greater burden than these things" (15:28).

The Church had moved from standards to sensitivity. The Holy Spirit–guided decision and subsequent communication to the Church expressed more concern for the Gentile converts than for the preservation of tradition not essential to salvation or new life. Motivated by love, the church leaders counseled the new believers on the things which were necessary for advancement in Christ rather than admittance to the Church.

We are moved to make an inventory of the secondary cultural traditions which we require of people before we will accept them in Christian fellowship. The realization that our own brand of Christian experience or church organization can become more important to us than Christ makes us a bit more tender in our judgment of the Judaizers in the Pharisees' party. Our customs may become more crucial than the truth they were established to maintain. Religious exclusivism is often based on the distortion of a gift. Whatever becomes part of the security system we bring into the Christian life will often be expressed in qualified response to others.

Pentecostals, Scots Presbyterians, Swedish Lutherans, Roman Catholics, and countless others share this problem. Whether it is speaking in tongues, clarity of theology, traditions of the Reformation, or historically developed liturgical practices, we all run the danger of listening for our own language or of putting people through the paces of our heritage before we accept them as brothers and sisters with unqualified love. Many powerful movements in Christian history began with an emphasis which was liberating but later incarcerated potential participants. The Oxford group movement's insistence on its brand of "sharing" or "honesty"; or the free churches' esoteric insistence on the identifiable mark of a "second blessing" are good examples. The emphasis was excellent, but when it became more important than Christ, it became exclusive.

The personal implications of all this are unsettling. We all have value systems which we try to baptize into sanctified importance. Education, background, habits of dress, codes of ethics, and standards of living often become a legacy that we bring into the Christian life and use to Judaize people. We evade responsible caring by relegating judgment—all in the name of Christ!

It is in our personal relationships that we find unqualified love most difficult. We give ourselves and our acceptance "if and when" we have received what we want and people do what we want them to do. The breeding ground of this kind of qualified love is in the family. The church often reflects it more than it does the gospel, and the pattern becomes a habit.

But we are in good company, as Luke shows us in his account of Paul and Barnabas's preparation for the second missionary journey. Paul had fought and won one of history's most crucial battles over the Gentile converts. He was not able, however, to apply the same truth to his relationship with John Mark. You will remember that the young missionary had defected at Pamphylia in the face of sickness, persecution, and hardship. Magnanimous Barnabas wanted to give him a second chance. Paul would have none of it! Mark had failed and "Paul thought best not to take with him one who had withdrawn from them

at Pamphylia, and had not gone on with them to the work"
(15:38). Sharp contention resulted between Paul and Barnabas, and the two giants of the faith separated, each going his
own way to spread the gospel.

Luke is very honest with us. Paul's love for Mark was qualified. But the most disturbing thing was that they parted unrec-
onciled about the issues.

That does not give us scriptural justification for the divi-
sions and schisms of Christian history; it only explains them.
We all have a stopping point beyond which we will not proceed in the expression of love.

But before we become too severe with Paul over his attitude
toward Mark, we need to distinguish between the decision he
made and the way he communicated it. Mark had not measured up, and Paul, a man of high standards, found that difficult to accept. In his judgment, it was not best for him, the
ministry, and Mark himself for Mark to go along. That the
conflict split Paul and Barnabas is the saddest result. Nowhere
in Luke's account does it say that the two prayed and that it
seemed good to them and the Holy Spirit for Mark to remain
behind or for the two of them to multiply their ministry by
doubling their efforts in two directions. That's the unstated but
evident failure of two of the greatest men who ever lived.

This passage helps us to realize that we never reach greater
heights in learning or discipleship than we can express to one
person in a painful conflict. This dark paragraph on the pages
of Acts does not give us freedom to run roughshod over people
because Paul and Barnabas didn't make it. Read the subsequent life of Paul and repeatedly you will find references to his
remedial efforts to affirm Mark and make up for the qualified
love he expressed that day at Antioch.

I can imagine how Paul felt as he sailed off without his beloved Barnabas. Silas tried to fill the emptiness, and soon Paul
enlisted Timothy at Lystra to join his missionary band. An
aspect of the preparation of this younger brother for ministry
provides a further dimension of our understanding of unqualified love. Timothy's mother, Eunice, was a Jew, and his father
was a Greek. Though his matriarchal lineage made him an acceptable Jew, he had never been circumcised. Paul circumcised
him so that he would have no impediment in his ministry with

the Jews whom they would meet and seek to convert in their travels. We wonder why this was necessary after the long battle over circumcision in Jerusalem. Here's the other side of Christian victory: Paul had won but he did not want to flaunt his victory. By having Timothy circumcised, he showed that a Christian is free to fulfill regulations unnecessary to him in order to win people for whom they are crucial. More than a simplistic "in Rome do as the Romans do," this is love unqualified by Paul's own preference. He wanted nothing to stand in the way of effective ministry. The great communicator knew that identification was an essential part of effective witness.

Now we are confronted with another, even deeper dimension of what it means to love people without strings. Not only do we relinquish anything which will cause our judgmentalism of others, but we are also to remove anything which will cause them to judge us and miss our message. Habits, quirks of behavior, irrelevant beliefs and associations which cripple us in getting through to people must go! No strings can be attached to people or to the extent to which we will go to reach them with unqualified love.

CHAPTER 18

The Serendipitous Life

Acts 16:6–10

On a grim, foggy winter's day in 1754 at Strawberry Hill, Twickenham, England, Horace Walpole read a Persian fairy tale which brought springtime joy into his life. To share the liberating truth he had just discovered, he wrote a letter to his old friend Horace Mann, who was serving as an envoy to Florence, Italy. In the letter he told about the "thrilling approach to life" the folk tale had given him and how it had helped him recapture an expectant excitement about his daily work.

The tale was about three princes of Ceylon, who had set out in search of great treasures. Though they did not find the treasure for which they searched, they were constantly surprised by more magnificent treasures they had not anticipated. While looking for one thing, they found unexpected delights along the way. They grew in the realization that the true secret of an adventuresome life is in our awareness of unexpected happenings in usual circumstances.

The ancient name of the island of Ceylon is Serendip, which accounts for the title of the fascinating, impelling story of unanticipated discoveries—"The Three Princes of Serendip." From this Walpole coined the word *serendipity*. It explained a reality which he had known through his studies and work: his most significant and valued experiences had happened to him while he was least expecting them, and the serendipity was always more precious than the thing sought for.

Seren-dip-ity. The parts of the word unlock its meaning: the dip of the serene into life. A serendipity occurs when the serene dips or breaks into the secular *(saeculāris)*, this age and time. It is the breakthrough of the Holy Spirit into our usual circumstances, the surprise that occurs to us when we are seeking to know and do his will.

A serendipitous life is distinguished by surprisability. An eighth beatitude might be, "Blessed are those who are surprisable, for the unexpected always happens." When we lose our capacity to be surprisable we settle into life's ruts of responsibilities and demands with the terrible conviction that we must do everything ourselves. We expect very little and are not disappointed; we aim at nothing and we hit it. One thing I know about God: he delights to surprise us with serendipities we never expected.

A serendipitous life is expressed in spontaneity. It is the capacity of grasping the unexpected, the freedom to respond to the unplanned. A tragic thing happens to us when we outplan God and resist his interventions because they were not on our carefully calculated agendas.

An openness to these unscheduled gifts results in a supernatural sagacity. The Holy Spirit infuses penetrating insight, sound judgment, and keen perception. These are intellectual serendipities of wisdom. A life is marked by serendipitous wisdom when we suddenly see an answer and a direction we had not anticipated. We are invaded by insight from beyond. It's the grand realization, "Well! I had never thought of that!"

Sensitivity to life and people is the result. We know what Elizabeth Barrett Browning meant: "Earth's crammed with heaven,/And every common bush afire with God;/But only he who sees, takes off his shoes."* We come alive to unlimited possibilities! Every person and situation is a gift crammed with God. We discover that the process is as important as the product and that people are the valued discoveries of the process. People themselves, as unique gifts, become God's serendipities.

The crowning joy of a serendipitous life is security. We come to expect great things from God and are free therefore to dare great things for him. Eventually we come to expect the sur-

---

* *Aurora Leigh,* bk. vii.

prises and know that God will always be on time with his
gracious, liberating infusion of power and direction. When we
get to the place where our lives are completely under his control and our decisions are guided by expectant prayer, then we
become profoundly secure in the reliability of his providence.
We can repeatedly say with Jacob, "The Lord is in this place
and I knew it not!" But in fellowship with the ubiquitous Holy
Spirit, our ever-present Friend in our every situation, we can
say, "The Lord is in this place, and we know it!"

Acts 16:6–11 is Luke's description of the serendipitous life.
Three very different noblemen of the Kingdom of God set out
from Lystra on the next laps of the second missionary journey—
Paul, Silas, and the newly recruited Timothy. They went in
search of the treasure of the Kingdom's new converts to Christ
in Pamphylia and regions beyond.

In this dynamic account of the guidance of God, we discover
a very valuable secret: a truly serendipitous life is life in the
stream of the Holy Spirit. Like the princes of Serendip, the three
adventurers in Christ headed out in search of new frontiers to
conquer and were surprised by an unexpected blessing they
could never have planned or anticipated.

Paul wanted to go to the Roman province of Asia (not to
be confused with what we think of today as Asia but the ad-
joining province west of Pamphylia extending over to the eastern coast of the Aegean Sea). He felt that this was the next
focus of the Spirit's strategy. However, the Holy Spirit said no.
Luke's language describing the closed door on the province of
Asia is very specific: "Having been forbidden by the Holy Spirit
to speak the word to Asia . . ." (Acts 16:6). The Greek word
is *kōluthentes,* the aorist past participle of *kōluō,* "to hinder,"
and it expresses antecedent action; that is, prior to entering
Asia, the Holy Spirit made it clear that Asia was not priority.
How this was expressed we do not know. Some have suggested
that sickness prevented Paul's going. Others have conjectured
that resistance from the Jews made the journey untenable. Still
others have supposed direct, forbidding guidance from the Holy
Spirit. Whether the Holy Spirit said no in inner feeling or outer
frustrations, the result was the same; Paul was a Spirit-sensitized
man who could read the signposts erected for his direction. I
prefer to believe that this prayer-saturated saint was so open to

guidance that the Spirit could implant convictions of direction. The Lord had something greater in mind than the sought-for treasure in Asia.

With the door of Asia slammed shut by the Holy Spirit, the three princes of the King headed north to preach throughout Phrygian and Galatian territory. Unanticipated surprises occurred all along the way. People found new life in the Savior and new churches were born. Paul's letter to the Galatians helps us appreciate the extent of this phase of the mission. But the greatest serendipity God had prepared was still ahead.

Further north, the adventuresome band approached the border of Mysia. When they came opposite Mysia, they wanted to go northeast to the wilderness area of Bithynia. Luke tells us that the Spirit of Jesus did not allow them. Here the Greek verb is a present active form. That means that, whereas the first prohibition was prior, this one was simultaneous. Paul and his companions wanted to go in one direction. The Lord wanted them to go in just the opposite direction. Another door closed, they headed east to Troas on the Aegean coast.

The supreme serendipity of the Lord was to be expressed there, given to Paul in a dream. A man from Macedonia across the sea appeared in his dream with the compelling supplication, "Come over and help us." When the Apostle awoke, he knew the uncertain wandering was over. Here was a clear direction. He and his friends would go over to Macedonia to preach the gospel there.

The Acts account becomes first person at this point. This is the first of the "we" passages, indicating that it was at Troas that Luke himself joined Paul and his band. Some questions arise about Luke's influence on Paul's serendipitous dream. Was Luke from Macedonia? Was he the personification in the dream? Or had Paul, Luke, and the others talked to a Macedonian about the territory's need for the gospel on the day before the guiding dream occurred?

We do not know. What we do know is that the term Luke uses to describe the nature of the Lord's guidance indicates that perhaps reason and revelation had coalesced to make the direction indubitably clear. "And when he [Paul] had seen the vision, immediately we sought to go on to Macedonia, *concluding* that God had called us to preach the gospel there" (16:10, emphasis mine). The word for "conclude" is *sunbibazontes,* the present active participle of *sunbibazō,* "to go together, to coalesce, bind or knit together, to make things agree and arrive at a conclusion." That strongly suggests that the vision substantiated a prior possibility. Perhaps Luke and Paul had discussed what God was saying to each of them. He had brought them together in this seaport. Questions like these must have been asked: "Lord what are you trying to tell us? Why the closed doors? What next? Where do you want us to go according to your infinite wisdom and infallible strategy? Macedonia?"

The dream removed all doubts. The focus of the Church was radically altered and immeasurably released to change the world. Europe and eventually the world mission of the Church resulted from the serendipity at Troas. G. Campbell Morgan affirms: "It is better to go to Troas with God than anywhere else without him."* Because Paul went to Troas with God, he could now bring God's good news to Europe. In search of one treasure, he discovered an infinitely greater one along the way!

This penetrating paragraph of Acts has deepened our understanding of the serendipitous life in the Spirit. We have learned things which never occurred to Walpole when he first coined the word.

First of all, the truly serendipitous life is discovered in the stream of the Holy Spirit. Paul was a man who had been caught up in the fast-moving currents of the Spirit's movement in history. Immersion in the Spirit's presence gave him guidance and enabled him to make right decisions. Guidance is not something we go to God to get; it is the inner assurance which comes from being carried along the riverbed, through the rocks and rapids of dangerous alternatives. Psalm 46 is a promise realized in post-Pentecost power. "There is a river, the streams whereof shall make glad the city of God, the holy place of the tabernacles of the most high" (v. 4, KJV). To me, that means that God's presence among his people will be like a flowing river. The "most high" knows the past, present and future, beyond time and space; yet he has chosen to flow in the affairs of man to guide and direct their decisions according to his infinite wisdom.

---

* *The Acts of the Apostles,* p. 377.

This same image is found in Isaiah's prophecy which we now see fulfilled in Christ and experienced through his Spirit.

> Behold, I am doing a new thing;
>   now it springs forth, do you not perceive it?
> I will make a way in the wilderness and
>   rivers in the desert (43:19–20).

Now catch the undeniable relationship of the river and the outpouring of the Spirit in Isaiah 44:3: "For I will pour water on the thirsty land,/and streams on the dry ground;/I will pour my Spirit upon your descendants,/and my blessing on your offspring." John caught the vision of the river of God's Spirit: ". . . He showed me a pure river of the water of life, bright as crystal, flowing from the throne of God and of the Lamb" (Rev. 22:1).

Paul and his missionary friends were being carried by the river of the Holy Spirit. They had stepped into the fast-moving currents of the guidance of the Lord. They were not so much seeking guidance as in a flow of guidance. Each decision was not an occasion to reintroduce themselves to the Spirit; rather, they were swept along, given instructions and directions before and in the midst of each phase of the evolving mission. There was constancy and consistency.

The second thing this passage has retaught me is that in the flow of the Spirit, the Lord's no becomes part of his ultimate yes! As we are carried along in the stream of the Spirit we can depend on both our reason and our inner feelings. We belong to our Lord. If we have surrendered all of life to him we can dare to trust our negative as well as positive thoughts and feelings. There are possibilities which are not maximum for us if we are to be available for what God has planned. It was not the Lord's timing for Paul to go into Asia at that time, although later it would be right for him to go to Ephesus on the coast of that province. The Lycus valley of the region would never be touched by Paul personally. Colossae, Laodicea and the other cities of the area would be reached later by his disciple Epaphras and would be entrusted by the Lord to the faithful pastoral care of the Apostle John. Both Revelation and the pastoral epistles of John give us evidence that the Lord took care of that area in his own way and according to his own strategy. Master strategist and planner, he had more than the Apostle Paul to deploy. He gave his no to Paul about going into Asia at that time because he wanted to get him on to Macedonia. Retrospectively, we can see that he was right.

We all know times when we feel blocked and certain directions seem to be wrong. The temptation is to get out of the flow of the river and move up some little stream of our own choosing. Sometimes, when we do, lack of the Spirit's guidance results in depleted energies and the ineffectiveness of our efforts. Often, it takes the Lord a long time to get us back in the mainstream, out of the eddies of our own self-determinism. Paul could have gotten stuck in Asia, never to be heard of again, unless the power of the currents of the Holy Spirit had torn loose his tenacious efforts to get out of the flow of power or rechannel the riverbed the Spirit was cutting through the wilderness ahead of him.

I remember the seasoned instruction of a Canadian guide who told me how to keep my directions clear and not get lost while canoeing in the wilds. "Stay in the main river. Let it carry you south. Don't get off into side streams that only appear to be the way to go, or you'll never make it!" Sound advice for life in the Spirit!

I am alarmed by all the good, attractive things I have almost done in my life. Looking back, they would have been disastrous for the ultimate things God wanted me to do. In times like that, the drumbeat of the Master becomes quiet and then stops altogether. Awesome inner silence! In its deafening quiet I have heard the undeniable no! When I resolve not to do what seemed so right by my own standards of judgment, the drumbeat begins again, quickening its beat and pace as I turn in a new direction.

But going in the direction that is guided always involves risk. That's the third thing this passage has revealed. Paul and his band pressed on, taking the risk that the Holy Spirit knew what he was doing with them. They did not make camp and refuse to proceed when at any point they were forbidden by the Spirit to go into Asia or Mysia; they risked moving in new directions each time the road they were on was disqualified by the intervening Lord. That got them on to Troas and to an assurance of what they were to do.

I must confess that I don't enjoy ambiguity. There are times I wish the Lord would write out the instructions and send them by some angelic messenger so that I would know what I am to do and say for every moment of the rest of my life. But the Lord knows me too well to do that! He knows that I would put my trust in the instructions and not in daily, momentary communication with him. He gives me the long-range goals, to be sure. I am not in doubt about the central purpose of my life to proclaim the gospel, communicate love to individuals, and be part of the adventure of the Church. But for the daily decisions about priorities and programs, he gives only as much as I need to know in order to do his will in each situation. The risk is in daring to believe that he will be faithful to give me all I need to know, say, and do in the momentary challenge or opportunity. That way I can learn from both the failures and successes. When I offer the Holy Spirit a ready and eager mind, an alert and aware sensitivity, and live in consistent communication, he does give me discernment. The author of Proverbs knew: "Trust in the Lord with all your heart,/and do not rely on your own insight./In all your ways acknowledge him,/and he will make straight your paths" (3:5).

And along the path, there will be surprises we never anticipated. Our assurance is that God knows what he is doing; he can get through to us with his plan; our willingness makes possible his wonders; and he will use our obedience as occasions of productivity we never imagined possible. That's the excitement of a serendipitous life.

CHAPTER 19

Turning the World Right Side Up

Acts 16:11–17:34

There's an old Celtic benediction which ends with the words, "And may the wind always be at your back." When Paul and his adventuresome missionary band set sail for Macedonia with a clear and decisive call from the Lord, Luke tells us they made a "direct voyage." He uses a Greek nautical term for sailing in front of the wind, of having a following sea press a vessel on through the sea. That must have been a liberating affirmation for Paul. The wind, and more than that, the Holy Spirit, was pushing them on to the next phase of the strategy for expanding the Church.

We feel that same power filling the sails of the Apostles all through the Macedonian ministry and beyond into Greece. The Lord was not only out front beckoning them on, beside them as companion, within them as gift-giving Spirit, but also behind them with driving power. Surely that's the reason that Acts 16:11–17:34 portrays an aspect of Paul's life in Christ which was both his glory and the reason his ministry brought such disturbance wherever he went. This quality is one which desperately needs to be rediscovered by Christians and the Church in our time.

The key verse expressing this quality was spoken by an incited mob in Thessalonica. It dramatizes the dynamics of the Apostle's life and explains the difficulty he had not only in Thessalonica, but in Philippi and Athens as well. As a matter of fact, the statement could well be a charter and challenge of the thrust of the amazing New Testament Church. No communicator was ever given a finer compliment. The enraged mob cried, "These people who have turned the world upside down have come here also" (Acts 17:6). Moffatt translates it, "These upsetters of the whole world have come here too." In Philippi Paul and his people were accused of disturbing the city, and in Athens his teaching brought consternation. What was it that caused such a strong reaction? Whatever it was, we need to recover it again today.

I believe that the reason for the triumph and resultant trouble of Paul's ministry is that he uncompromisingly preached the essential truth of the gospel: Christ the Messiah—the crucified, resurrected, living Lord of all life. He could not be dissuaded by side issues or distracted by beguiling philosophies. He proclaimed the essentials of new life in Christ, a response of repentance and faith, and the necessity of absolute allegiance and obedience. Cutting a swath through the economic, religious, philosophic presuppositions and loyalties of the time, his message earned him the title of an upsetter of the whole world. Indeed, he was that. So was the Master before him. And so must we be.

There is a difference between being simplistic and being profoundly simple. It's one thing to be simplistic because we have not examined alternatives to a truth we hold; it's quite another to be sublimely simple because we have studied and sifted through the alternatives and have come to a settled conviction of a truth which clarifies and conditions all others. Simplification is the result of penetrating thought and experience, not a substitute for them. It enables us to cut through complexities with unadorned incisiveness and clarity.

Paul, one of the most brilliant and highly educated men who ever lived, was simple because he was an essentialist. As a scholar he had worked his way through all of the philosophies which captured the minds of his time. As a honed Pharisee, he had an impeccable education in religion. As a man, he had tried all of the facsimiles for meaning and purpose and found them wanting. His experience of Christ had brought integrating unity to his mind and heart. His gifts as an intellectual had been captured to think through the implications of Christ as the only Savior and Lord. His sensitive spirit had been invaded by the unifying power of the indwelling Lord. Emotional healing and health resulted. His will was marshaled to seek and do the will of his Lord. The result was that he wanted every person to know, experience, and respond to the living Christ. He had no other plan or purpose. That alone was essential for existence.

Christ was the essence of life. Through him and the power of his resurrection men and women could live abundantly, then and forever. Paul's dedication to essentiality would not bend, blend, adjust, or water down his basic message.

And that's what got him into trouble. His message seldom dealt with the cultural or social complexities of the cities in which he preached. But wherever he went, the clear proclamation of the essential gospel cut deeply into social sickness, religious pride, and cultural intellectualism. He did not go about with a self-image of being an upsetter of the world; he preached Christ. The implications of that reorienting dynamic brought confrontation with economic, ecclesiastical, and political injustice which resulted in disturbance throughout his ministry and eventually cost him his life.

Paul would never have thought of himself as a radical, yet he was one of the most remedially radical men of history. He was not a self-appointed revolutionary; yet creative revolution resulted in his train. Long before the term *radical* took on ultraliberal political overtones, it meant just the opposite. Actually the word means "of the root," pertaining to the original, fundamental, underived essence. Paul was radical in his determination to get to the root of man's need and God's gift of Christ. He plunged through all the layers of distorted thinking and distracting loyalties to the core of man's emptiness and then proclaimed the fullness of the gospel. That action brought a conservative revolution—a reordering of priorities, presuppositions, and purposes to conserve the essence of life as God ordained it to be lived.

Paul's Lord was the original conservative revolutionist. He called for a radical, to-the-root change and an absolutely new beginning. He demanded repentance, faith, and obedience to him. The reorienting revolution began in fellowship with him and emerged in character and conviction. Then in response to him, his people were challenged to evaluate everything in life and society. The result has always been literally upsetting as people's lives, and their whole world, are turned upside down. The conserving revolution has been going on ever since. For example, the Reformers had no intention of developing a new or separate church. They wanted to return to Christ, the essentials of his message, and the model of the New Testament Church. The Scriptures were the mandate of their radical Christianity, which brought revolution in the indulgence-ridden, inquisition-frightened, and politically corrupt Roman church. New denominations were not the purpose of the Reformers. Second- and third-generation organizers of the truth institutionalized into structures and intellectualized into confessions what had begun as an effort to get back to basics.

There is a conserving revolution taking place in our time. Many of us are part of it. We are to be the essentialists of our age. It's time again to get back to essentials; to dare to be simple but not simplistic; to order our lives and our churches around Christ and the Scriptures; to allow his lordship to unsettle anything in us or our society which contradicts the gospel. In fact, if what was said of Paul and his men is not being said about us and the churches of which we are a part, there's something wrong. When has anyone said of us, "The people who have turned the world upside down have come here also"?

In the context of that disturbing question, I want to look at Luke's account of what happened in the three cities we are considering in this passage.

What happened in Philippi brought indigenous evidence of Paul's growing reputation as an upsetter of the world. Philippi was a Roman colony. It was occupied by veteran Roman soldiers sent there to colonize in reward for years of faithful service to Caesar. Over the years the city had become a little Rome. Roman dress, language, and customs dominated the life of this European city located on the Egnatian Way, the Roman highway which connected the Aegean Sea with the Adriatic. It was an outpost of Rome, and its citizens were given the rights of Roman citizens—autonomous government, and the same dignity as if they lived in Rome itself. Philippi, as a result, became a leading city with considerable political pride.

Apparently there were few Jews there, because when Paul

began his ministry by the riverbank at what was designated as a Hebrew place of prayer, he spoke only to women. It took ten Hebrew males to establish a synagogue. The anti-Semitic charge subsequently brought against Paul indicates that Jews were probably not welcome in Philippi.

Paul initiated his preaching of the gospel in Philippi in a very benign way. He proclaimed Christ to the Hebrew women, and Lydia and her whole family became the first fruits of his labors. He could have gone on like that for a long time without running into trouble, but something happened to a slave girl of soothsaying powers. She followed Paul and his missionary friends wherever they went, saying, "These men are servants of the Most High God, who proclaim to you the way of salvation" (Acts 16:17). Quite a compliment!

Yet Paul was annoyed. He knew the difference between the Holy Spirit's gift of prophecy and the demonic possession which resulted in fortune-telling. He could easily have accepted the affirmation of Satan to enable the work of Christ, but as an essentialist he would have none of it! Actually the woman was deranged, but people with soothsaying gifts were given great honor in those days, since it was believed that they had lost their wits and that the mind of the gods had been placed within them. Luke's text means literally that the young woman had "a spirit, a python" *(echousan pneum puthona).* The superstition derived from the belief that the god Apollo was embodied in a snake at Delphi, also called Pytho. From that idea, the name *pytho* was used for anyone in whom the gods were believed to have implanted unique capacities of soothsaying or ventriloquism. The truth about this woman, however, was that she was demon-possessed, and Paul, like his Lord Jesus, was being confronted by the beguiling benediction of Satan on his ministry. He saw the woman for the pitiful plaything for profit her masters had made her, a person in need of exorcism and the healing power of the Lord Jesus. To the spirit distorting her he said, "I charge you in the name of Jesus Christ to come out of her."

Now Paul was in trouble. He had not come to Philippi to clean up the practice of material gain from human sickness; he simply did what he had to do out of obedience to Christ. Retribution resulted. The owners of the slave girl brought Paul and Silas before the magistrates, charging that they were disturbing the

city, when actually it was these pimps for profit using the de-
mented woman who were disrupting the colony of Rome! We
wonder what "front money" they paid the magistrates to buy
their favor, for the punishment of Paul and his followers did
not fit the "crime." They had them severely beaten and placed
in stocks in an inner prison.

In the midst of the persecution and imprisonment Paul returned to essentials. Christ was his faithful Lord. He would intervene. All would be well and used for the glory of God. He and
Silas sang hymns at midnight in affirmation of their faith. The
Lord's answer was an earthquake which not only released Paul
and Silas and brought about the conversion of the jailer, but gave
birth to a strong church there in Philippi which would never
forget Paul or the Lord he proclaimed.

The gospel had disturbed a city because Paul would not change
his message or accept the accolades of the demons to use Satan's
power to do the Lord's work. Philippi needed to be disturbed.
And so does Los Angeles, or New York, or New Orleans, or
your city. Preach Christ, live life in him obediently, refuse a
league with satanically induced social problems, and you will
have a revolution—be sure of that! The only difference today is
that you may find some good church people a part of the em-
bedded society which produces the city's sickness. Then our essentialism will bring us into conflict with more than the magistrates!

In Thessalonica, where Paul earned the title of an upsetter of
the world, he confronted not economic interests, but religious
pride. Thessalonica was the capital of Macedonia and a "free
city" with its own constitution and magistrates, known as poli-
tarchs. It was a flourishing commercial city with an excellent
port, and the main street was part of the Egnatian Way. What
was to happen to the people there was crucial for the establishment of the Church in Macedonia.

Luke's summary of Paul's ministry in Thessalonica captures
the vital elements: the Apostle's clear proclamation of the essence of the gospel and the revolution it causes among religious
people. Unlike Philippi, Thessalonica had a strong synagogue
and a large population of Jews. We are told that Paul focused
his ministry among them proclaiming Christ as the fulfillment
of the Scriptures. Note that he did not theorize or philosophize
about his ideas. He exposited the Hebrew Scriptures using three

methods: argument, explanation, and proof (Acts 17:2–3). He
wanted to make clear the fundamentals of Jesus as Messiah, his
death for the sins of the world, and his resurrection victory as
the only hope. He stated flatly, "This Jesus, whom I proclaim to
you, is the Christ."

The essentialist was rewarded for his clarity. The gift of faith
was given to some of the Jews, a great many of the devout Greeks
who had become inquirers on the fringe of the synagogue's life,
and not a few of the leading women of the city. It was the last
two categories that got Paul into trouble again. Remember Paul
did not go to Thessalonica to cause a revolution in the synagogue.
He simply exposited the Scriptures and proclaimed Christ as
Savior. That is sure to bring unsettling results in any religious
institution!

The Jews were jealous. They had enjoyed the prestige and
profit of the proselytes they had brought to Judaism. They neither
wanted to accept Paul's teaching nor lose the influence they
had gained among the Greeks who did.

What can a religious person do with his jealousy of another
person who has superior depth and spiritual power? Direct confrontation on the real issues never works. The only thing to do
is demean the self-worth of the person causing the jealousy.
The leaders of the synagogue could not say, "Look here, our real
problem is that our pride has given birth to jealousy and sees
a clarity and power in Paul we don't have. He has been able to
do for these people what we could not do!"

Because they could not say that, they took the only recourse
open to them. They gathered the rabble of the city, fired them
into a frenzy of hatred, and sent them to do their dirty work for
them. It was the inflamed mob, carefully tutored by the Jewish
leaders, who cried out the accusation which was really an affirmation. Paul and Silas had alarmed the city with truth which they
knew would be distorted. Indeed, Paul had turned the world
upside down. Actually, his gospel was the only hope of setting
it right side up!

Again Paul's radical teaching of Christ had exposed the dis-
tortions and sickness of a city. The resulting riot was caused not
by the gospel but the vested interests which were upset by it.
Paul barely escaped with his life. But as in Philippi, the dynamic
seed of the gospel had been planted. A great church resulted

and grew strong, later to receive two of Paul's most powerful letters.

Some new disciples guided Paul's journey by sea to Athens. Silas and Luke remained behind to continue the work in Thessalonica. Alone in Athens, Paul continued his indefatigable mission to preach Christ. In this garden of culture, religion, and philosophy, he kept to his essential message. Daily in the agora, the marketplace in the shadow of the magnificent Acropolis, and in the synagogue, his message was the same: "He preached Jesus and the resurrection" (Acts 17:18).

Now opposition was to come from a very different source. Here the issue would be not economic or religious, but philosophical. Athens had statues for all the gods of their pantheon. Two philosophical schools, however, dominated the city. The devotees of one, the Epicurean, asserted that happiness and pleasure were the principal aims of life. Everything happened by chance; the gods were remote and did not care, so worry and concern made little difference. Eat, drink, enjoy. The Stoics were just the opposite. Everything for them was fated by the gods, and life had to be lived according to nature without emotional intensity or involvement. The purpose of life was to accept nature and find one's place in it. The Stoics were pantheistic, seeing their gods as all and in all.

No wonder the Athenians were upset by Paul's preaching of Christ and the Resurrection. They listened to him and leveled a very serious charge against an intellectual, calling him a "babbler." The word means seed-picker, a term used for birds which flit about picking at seeds, or persons who go about scavenging scraps of food. In some cases, it actually meant a philosopher who belonged to no recognized school of thought, but had picked bits and pieces of thought from many different systems of philosophy. The more serious charge against Paul, however, was that he proclaimed foreign deities. His accusers were wrong on both accounts. He was anything but a seed-picker gathering up bits of thought. He had one Lord and one central conviction. As for foreign deities, he proclaimed one God and sovereign of all creation.

The result was that Paul soon had to defend his beliefs before the Areopagus, a kind of philosophical review board which investigated ideas and intellectual persuasions. Eager for argu-

ment and debate, the intellectuals of Athens enjoyed disputation
of ideas, but always from the safe distance of philosophical
contemplation. Luke analyzes the temper of the city: "Now all
the Athenians and the foreigners who lived there spent their
time in nothing except telling or hearing something new"
(Acts 17:21).

Paul's essentialism about Christ and the Resurrection had
brought a response, however sophisticated. We are told that the
philosophers "took hold of him and brought him to the Areopagus" (17:19). The verb is strong, though it does not imply
an arrest. They "laid hold" of Paul with determination, not as
violent as the rough provincial magistrates of Philippi or as
frenzied as the agitated mob of Thessalonica, but with imperious
insistence nonetheless. Paul had upset Athens with his "new"
teaching, and the philosophers wanted to see what it was he was
saying that was causing so much disturbance.

Before the august Areopagus, Paul is a master communicator
as he presents the essential message of the gospel. With his
unique audience in mind, he begins where they are. He takes a
known to present an unknown to them. "Men of Athens, I perceive that in every way you are very religious. For as I passed
along, and observed the objects of your worship, I found also
an altar with this inscription, 'To an unknown god.' What therefore you worship as unknown, this I proclaim to you" (17:22–
23). With that he has the philosophers' attention and he is off
with a flourish of impelling rhetoric carefully honed for his
listeners.

Paul begins with God as creator, the source of all life—not
the anthropomorphic creation of man's speculation, but the
creator of man, whom he designed to know him and love him.
Next Paul proclaims that this God has guided all history and is
the one on whom all life depends. He is not the object of man's
groping search, but man is the subject of his grace. The drumbeat of the Spirit quickens its beat as Paul moves into the in-
carnation and the forgiveness offered by "a man whom he
[God] has appointed." Christ is implied, but the Apostle was
kept from proclaiming Christ explicitly because of a further
statement he made about him—"And of this he has given assurance to all men by raising him from the dead" (17:31).

That did it! The idea of the Resurrection brought a heated

response. Some mocked Paul, others dismissed him with polite rejection, "We will hear you again about this." We can be sure they had no intention of hearing him again! The Resurrection demanded faith. Any God who raised the dead would require more than philosophical reflection. And the one who was raised? They stopped Paul before he could talk about him. The Spirit who was guiding Paul's words was closing in on them and they wanted nothing of it. They were being pressed beyond the realm of ideas into a confrontation with the living God!

We wonder how Paul would have finished his lecture, which had very subtly become a witness. I am convinced that he would have told the philosophers what repentance and acceptance of Christ could mean to them. But that would have meant a moral inventory, confession, and a decision. Paul did not stop short of the whole truth; the intimation of his intention made the intellectuals stop him short of the one truth which could have enabled them to live forever. How very sad!

Resistance to the gospel has many distorted forms. In reality, Athens was no different from Philippi or Thessalonica. In all three cities the preeminence of Christ and the power of the Resurrection were rejected. The bland toleration of Athens was no better than the barbarism of the Macedonian frontier.

But Luke has a way of giving a final twist to his vivid accounts. All was not lost in Athens. "But some men joined him [Paul] and believed, among them Dionysius the Areopagite and a woman named Damaris and others with them"—no little victory. Dionysius was one of the twelve judges of the Areopagus. The historian Eusebius claims that later he became a bishop of the Church at Athens and became a martyr for his faith. Damaris was an aristocratic woman of Athens. The "others with them" suggests more than the words would imply to a casual reader. A group of people became a strong church. Paul had not failed.

His own analysis of his ministry at Athens in 1 Corinthians 2:1–5 underlines his determination to get to the Cross and Christ crucified more quickly and straightforwardly. The point, however, is that, though Paul felt defeated in Athens, the Holy Spirit was not defeated. But note that the Spirit allowed Paul to go through the experience of feeling that he had failed. He was pressing the Apostle into an even deeper commitment

which he later expressed with new determination. "When I came
to you, brethren, I did not come proclaiming to you the testimony
of God in lofty words or wisdom [as he had in Athens]. For I
decided to know nothing among you except Jesus Christ and
him crucified" (1 Cor. 2:1–2).

I know how Paul felt and have been forced to learn what
he discovered. Recently when I spoke at a college, I had little
response from the students. I flew home, depressed by a sense of
failure. Where had I missed? My conclusion was that I had tried
to expose my learning rather than share what I had learned
about the triumphant adequacy of Christ. The experience was a
recall to be an essentialist. The Lord allowed me to live with
that for days until his purpose for me was deeply ingrained.
Only after that was accomplished did the Spirit allow me the
comfort of a flood of letters from students who had indeed found
Christ and hope in my speech. I was left with a combination
of thanksgiving and a new commitment. It was as if the Lord
were saying, "I used what little you gave me to work with; what
happened is only a portion of what can happen in the future if
you will trust me."

We are called to be upsetters, people who turn the world
upside down. To live Christ, share Christ, help people to know
him, and shape our whole lifestyle around him—that is our
only purpose. The world is already upside down in confusion
and desperation without him. When he turns our own world
right side up, he then calls us to do the same with the world
around us. That will require that we become Christian essentialists with one message and a singular hope. And we will never
be without the Lord's help to do it. That's what the defeated
Paul learned in Corinth and what we press on to discover for
ourselves in the next chapter.

CHAPTER 20

A Reliable Guide for Confident Living

Acts 18:1–23

Recently, a man said to me, "I can take anything if I know it will end. There's no limit to the short-range difficulties I can face. What gets me is when I get into a problem that won't quit. Just when I think it's over and I can relax a bit, I get hit by a new wave of frustration. I don't know how long I can hold out unless I can see that I'm going to get to the end of the thing!"

My friend was in trouble living out his faith on his job. He experienced resistance from his employees and reserve from his supervisors. He felt he was cornered. About the time he thought he had worked out a solution, he received a new blow.

We all feel that way at times. Most of us can empathize, if not with the application of our convictions to our work, certainly in our relationships, challenges, and difficulties in other areas. We can endure brief vicissitudes; it's when they drag on endlessly that we are tempted to give up hope.

Another friend expressed the same feelings about a prolonged illness. "Just when I think I have licked this thing, I have a new setback. Then the demons of despair move in for a frontal attack. I become more sure of the relentless sickness than of God's resources of healing. I don't want to give up, but I'm tempted!"

I believe that's the way the Apostle Paul felt when he reached Corinth. He had been driven out of Macedonia and blandly tolerated in Athens. The persistent hostility of the Jews con-

219

fronted him wherever he went. Would it never stop? Exhausted
in body, mind, and spirit, Paul was a prime candidate for despair.

The ambience of Corinth didn't help. Sensualism, materialism,
and vice confronted him as he finished the fifty-mile walk from
Athens and entered the cosmopolitan city. On the Acroconinthus,
towering above the city, the temple of Aphrodite reputedly
had one thousand consecrated prostitutes. No wonder the term
corinthianize has become another word for fornication around
the world. This boom town was the capital of the province of
Achaia and the chief commercial city of Greece. Voluptuous
prosperity was mated with frivolous, "thinging-it" sexuality.

As Paul walked through the marketplace he could see the
Arabian balsam, Phoenician dates, Babylonian ivory, Egyptian
papyrus, Cilician goats' hair, Lycaonian wool, and Phrygian
slaves everywhere for sale in this Vanity Fair of the Roman
Empire. What would this pagan city hold for the preaching
of the "Life"? The Apostle wondered if he had courage to begin
again. If he did, what would be the response? His heart was
heavy with memories of Philippi's beating and imprisonment,
the Jews' disruption of his success in Beroea; the anger of the
mob in Thessalonica; the polite, smug complacency of the
Athenians. A pall of depression hung over him.

Here was a sick, discouraged, troubled man. Later he described his condition in a letter he wrote back to the church
at Corinth: "I was with you in weakness and in fear, and in
much trembling" (1 Cor. 2:3).

Paul's worst expectations about Corinth were soon confirmed.
Exhaustion and depression mingled and gave illegitimate birth
to negativism. When he went to the synagogue to proclaim
Christ, he was met with the opposition he had expected. The
Jews reviled him. If he had been rested and refortified, his
angry response might have been different. But with the impatience and pique we all know when we have run out of steam,
Paul responded, "Your blood be upon your heads!"—a vitriolic,
eloquent way of saying, "To hell with you!" Now defensive pus
seeps from his repeatedly descabbed wounds—"I am innocent"
and next a justified, but painful break with his people and the
synagogue—"From now on I will go to the Gentiles" (Acts
18:6). Hurt and hopeless, he implied, "I have tried to share good
news with you, and you have shut the door in my face over and

over again. Now I'm going to work with people who want to listen."

There had been signs of God's providence and intervening care in Corinth, but Paul was so low he was impervious to them. The Lord had given him friends like Aquila and Priscilla, who had been driven out of Rome by Claudius and had come to live in Corinth. They were fellow tentmakers and believers in Christ as Lord. Their hospitality to Paul had helped, but not enough. Crispus, the ruler of the synagogue which had rejected the Apostle, had become a believer. What more did the troubled Tarsusian want? Some men have preached for years with less response. But, like Elijah of old, this adventurer for the Lord had had enough. He had fought for the Lord and was tired out. The saints of God are most vulnerable when they do their best and evil is still seemingly undefeated. Elijah broke down when he defeated the priests of Baal on Mount Carmel only to find that Jezebel had seemingly achieved a final victory in her tireless efforts to get rid of him. He turned on his heel and ran for his life, feeling that he was finished. But God had only begun. The way of grace of God nursed the prophet back to health, and hope brought him to a new level of experience of the mystery of the Spirit's resourcefulness. From that point on, he knew that his task was to allow God to work through him rather than trying to work for God. I am convinced that something like that happened to Paul.

The context of the passage about Corinth and the content of the Lord's message to the discouraged man of Tarsus helps us to understand his feelings. For the first time, fear dominated his emotions. Like a wounded boxer, he could not make himself get up for one more punching. More than that, he had lost his imaginative expectation of what God could do in Corinth. But how the Lord ministered to him and what he said to him in a vision made a new man of him. The words of comfort become our prescription for perplexity. They should be typed out and placed on our desks or workbenches, set beside our beds, written in our notebooks, and memorized in our heads and hearts as leaven for liberation from doubt. If you feel the unrelenting persistence of evil, if you see the forces of complexity endlessly sending new troops into the battle to defeat you, if you have come to that terrible place of feeling that your finest hour will surely be followed by one of your lowest—here is a trumpet blast to exorcise your hopelessness. What the Lord said to Paul in Corinth is for the healing of our souls and for a new picture of what he can do for our realm of responsibility. But the words of rejuvenation are not given glibly; they are reserved for those who have fought the battle and have begun to wonder if it's worth it to continue. That takes in about all of us at times, doesn't it?

Here's the balm for our sores, tonic for our blood, vision for our minds. The Lord appeared to discouraged Paul and said, "Do not be afraid, but speak and do not be silent; for I am with you, and no man shall attack you to harm you; for I have many people in this city." The same Lord says the same thing to you and me. Moffatt translates the Greek, "Have no fear, speak on and no one shall attack or injure you; I have many people in this city" (18:9–10). The message was clear: "Stop being afraid; speak on no matter how discouraged you are or how filled with doubt or the feeling of ineffectiveness; trust me! I am with you. . . . Proof of that is the people I will give you whom I have elected to be mine, some of whom know it and others who soon will." That's an assurance to lift our mood from the attitude that "if anything can go wrong, it will!" to the conviction that "if anything can go right, the Lord will make it possible!" What a change!

The first thing the Lord wanted to heal in Paul and to exorcise from us is fear. He wants to lift us out of the syndrome of fearing success because of the failure that may follow, a major problem for Paul, who knew that as surely as his ministry was successful there would be conflict with the Jews. It had happened that way wherever he went. I think he got to the place where he was certain that a response from believers would invariably be followed by retaliation from the religionists. His success always came at a very high price to him personally. He had been beaten, imprisoned, and rejected. Now he was afraid. He had forgotten that trouble was but the shadow of the wings of the Almighty. He could have used Francis Thompson's discovery: "Is my gloom, after all,/Shades of His hand, outstretched caressingly?" ("The Hound of Heaven").

Paul lost sight of the fact that there was only one man to fear in Corinth: the person who lived in the skin of Saul of

Tarsus. That was the inner man the Lord was concerned about. Horizontal tensions were pulling him apart until the vertical Truth pulled him together, saying, "Don't be afraid!"

Someone said, "There are only two days a week in which I will not worry: one is today; the other is tomorrow." Paul finally learned that when he discovered that the Lord will not allow any more difficulty than will bring a person to deeper faith in him. Later he wrote to his friends in Corinth: "So far you have faced no trial beyond what man can bear. God keeps faith, and he will not allow you to be tested above your powers, but when the test comes he will at the same time provide a way out, by enabling you to sustain it" (1 Cor. 10:13, NEB). Paul had experienced this himself there in Corinth.

Love extinguishes the fires of fear. Paul felt newly loved by the Lord. Fear grips us when we lose our grasp on grace. It is like mist or clouds which can only be dissipated by sunshine or wind. The warmth of the love of the Son of God and the wind of the Spirit does both.

I think it was during this vision that the Lord also communicated what Paul recorded sometime later: "He said to me, 'My grace is sufficient for you, for my power is made perfect in weakness.' I will all the more gladly boast of my weaknesses, that the power of Christ may rest upon me. For the sake of Christ, then, I am content with weaknesses. . . . For when I am weak, then I am strong" (2 Cor. 12:9–10).

The brilliant communicator of grace had become weak enough to experience for himself a fresh flow of what he had preached to others. Love filled the riverbed which had become stagnant with the polluted waters of fear. He not only felt loved in a new way through the Master's personal intervention; he also felt new love for the people he feared. We cannot long nurse fear about people we love. I personally feel Paul was able to praise God for the weakness which had brought him to a new experience of grace. William Law put it this way: "For it is certain that whatever seeming calamity happens to you, if you thank and praise God for it, you turn it into a blessing." As I write this I am encouraged to thank God for the very things that cause me fear. I feel very differently now. Perhaps you may be prompted to do the same thing before going on in this chapter. Another Apostle—John—gives us the hope which experience had carved into his character. "There is no fear in love, but perfect love casts out fear" (1 John 4:18). Even now I can feel that healing. Do you?

The second ingredient of the Lord's prescription was to encourage Paul to speak and not be silent. He was given confidence to continue. The discouraged man was to learn that weakness was to be a blessing for forceful proclamation. Silence would imprison his fear; boldness would liberate it. His own fear and trepidation was not a curse but a condition of dynamic communication. He would have to depend on the Lord and not his own eloquence. His uncertainty about his own gifts would not only make him receptive to the gift of the Spirit, but would forge a bond of identification with his hearers.

I have learned this repeatedly in my own life. When my strength is depleted, when my rhetoric is unpolished by human talent, when I am weary, the Lord has a much better tool for empathetic, sensitive communication. The barriers are down. When I know I can do nothing by myself, my poverty becomes a channel of his power. More than that, often when I feel I have been least efficient, people have been helped most effectively. It's taken me a long time to learn that the lower my resistances are and the less self-consciousness I have, the more the Word of God comes through. There is less of the club of judgment and more of a cross of grace. In a time like that I need to hear what I am saying more than the listeners; the result is that they hear what I may have blocked from them before.

What about you? Are you feeling weak or fearful right now? Thank God! Now's the time to speak and not be silent. It's a blessed time of productivity—a gift from the Lord. Embrace the troubled moment; make it a friend. Whatever you do, the glory will go to Christ and not to you. That's where it belonged all along!

But we cannot, dare not, speak or move out courageously without the next assurance the Lord gave Paul: "For I am with you—" The New Testament's crises could be punctuated with these words that promise the Presence. They had articulated the final promise to the frightened disciples in Jerusalem at a time of unprecedented uncertainty: "Lo, I am with you always" (Matt. 28:20). And the Lord had always been faithful to his promise in repeated evidence and confidence-instilling breakthroughs that never failed to happen when the expanding Church needed them the most. The Rock of Ages was always in the tumultuous sea with lighthouse words for the storm. "Come unto me, all ye that labor and are heavy laden, and I will give you rest" (Matt. 11:28, KJV). When we are so low that we can't reach up to touch bottom, it's time to put our feet on the Rock of Ages.

David Livingstone learned that afresh one night in Africa. "I read again that Jesus said, 'Lo, I am with you always.' It's the word of a gentleman and that's the end of it. I will not cross the river by night furtively as I had intended."

> When the dark waves around us roll,
> And we look in vain for human aid,
> Speak, Lord, to my trembling soul,
> "It is I, be not afraid."

The assurance of the Lord's presence is the only way Paul could face Corinth. He could not be in Corinth without being "in Christ." Nor can we, in a contemporary Corinth focused in our city, job, family, church, or challenge, without the confidence of "Lo, I am with you."

That's the story of the courageous Christians I know about. When the going is rough and they say, "Well, what's going to go wrong next?" then is the time that the voice too deep for words thunders, "Lo, I am with you." In this difficult life, seeing "the goodness of the Lord in the land of the living" is often clouded. But what David discovered is all the more ours on this side of Calvary and Pentecost. "Many are the afflictions of the righteous; but the Lord delivers him out of them all" (Ps. 34:19). *The Living Bible* puts it, "The good man does not escape all troubles—he has them too. But the Lord helps him in each and every one." I believe that. I have passed through the most trying year of my life as a result of sickness suffered by my wife. We both now can say with Paul about this current Corinth or any to come: "For this slight momentary affliction is preparing for us an eternal weight of glory beyond all comparison" (2 Cor. 4:17).

The promise of the Lord's presence is followed quickly in Paul's vision with protecting providence. The Lord assures Paul of help against harm: "No one will attack you to harm you."

That had not always been true: he had known persecution. Nor
would it be true in the future: there were physical vicissitudes
ahead. The point is that at the moment when Paul could take
no more, the Lord interceded for his protection. At future times,
when he was stronger, when what happened would engender
deeper faith, and when physical persecution could be used as a
witness of his trust and confidence, the Lord would allow it.

But it is important for us to remember that the Lord's presence
is not a warranty of unlimited protection. We cannot blissfully
believe that if we trust him life will be a bed of roses. But be
sure of this: he will be with us! The Lord allows only what we
can take. The liberating assurance is that nothing can separate
us from him. With the knowledge that he can use all things
for his glory, and with the realization that even death cannot
defeat us, we can live courageously in the perspective of peace.

The final aspect of the Lord's message to Paul changed his
attitude about Corinth and his ministry there. The Lord would
give him fellowship to face frustrations. Paul was not alone in
Corinth. The Lord said, "I have many people in this city." The
grammatical construction of the Greek uses the dative of personal interest to communicate added meaning. Some knew they
were chosen and called; others would soon, if Paul would hold
on.* What a refreshing picture it was for Paul to know that
Corinth was not a foreboding city of hostile people but a city
filled with potential converts who would join him in a great
church. I think the Lord wanted to impress two things on the
frightened Apostle's mind: that Corinth had people who were
already alive in the New Life and also those who were ready
to respond if he loved on. The Lord was saying, "Hang on, Paul!
I am at work."

The Savior wanted thanksgiving from Paul for what his grace
had provided already—for the gifts of Priscilla and Aquila; of
converted Titus who lived next to the synagogue; of Crispus,
who had accepted Christ at the great cost of being expelled as
head of the synagogue. All these had been given to the Apostle
to withstand the challenge of Corinth. And what about Silas and

---

* I found A. T. Robertson helpful in his exposition of this passage in
Word Pictures of the New Testament, 3 vols. (Nashville: Broadman
Press, 1943), 3:299.

Timothy, who came with good news of the faithful disciples who were strong in spite of everything against them in Macedonia?

But the prevenient grace of the Lord was to go before Paul. The Spirit enabled Gallio, the proconsul of Achaia, to protect Paul when the hostile Jews brought him to trial before the tribunal. Under the influence of the Lord's protective care, Gallio threw the case out of court, saying, "If it were a matter of wrongdoing or vicious crime, I should have reason to bear with you, O Jews; but since it is a matter of questions about words and names and your own law, see to it yourselves; I refuse to be a judge of these things." Then he drove them from the tribunal, refusing to be a patsy for their prejudices. The Jews did not dare to trouble Paul any further in Corinth.

Paul remained in Corinth eighteen months, preaching and teaching Christ unhindered. He could not have done that without the Lord's recruitment of those he had chosen and elected to believe. They joined the Apostle in a different outlook on Corinth—instead of anxiety, anticipation; not mere endurance, but expectation. Everywhere Paul went, in everyone he met, he was looking for the Lord's people. No one was excluded from the possibility of being or becoming a fellow Christian.

That can happen to all of us for our city, family, or place of work. We can have the eyes of the Savior. Then we will see people, not problems; we will discover people who share our vision and who long to find what we have found.

I talked to an actress who had become a Christian in her last year of graduate training in theater in a Midwest university. The warm, loving fellowship there meant a great deal to her emerging new life in Christ. When a Hollywood movie company awarded her a contract, she came to Los Angeles wondering if she could ever find the same kind of dynamic friends in Christ she had found in her university. The first months were very disappointing. She concluded that there were no Christians like her in the industry. Temptations to compromise her beliefs and her personal integrity were very disillusioning. But then someone recommended that she come to see me, and I showed her the Lord's promise to Paul—the Lord had many people in Hollywood too! We prayed that she might receive the ones who were immediately available to help her and others whom the Lord would identify. We prayed that she might find the Lord's peo-

ple at her studio, apartment building, and social groups. The
next day, the Lord gave her several signs of his providence.
She dared to be more open to talk about her faith, to "speak
and not be silent." Now she is part of a group of movie people
seeking to be faithful to Christ and supportive of each other.
The Lord changed her attitude about her city and gave her his
people.

The same thing happened to the man in a large company
I mentioned earlier. When he claimed Paul's vision as his own
for his corporation, people who shared his need for fellowship
suddenly seemed to emerge from the woodwork. Not only that,
he became aware of potential Christians all around him who
were ready to believe if given a chance. The problem had been
his negative view of his surroundings.

The other day a pastor and his wife who serve a suburban
Los Angeles congregation came in to see me. They had written
me a letter telling a sorry tale of unproductive ministry, congregational resistance, and bland toleration from the church
officers. I wrote back asking to see the discouraged couple. We
talked at length about their efforts and the lack of any excitement in the congregation about Christ and his mission. Once
again the Corinth encounter of Paul with the Lord provided
help. Could it happen again—for them in their tradition-bound,
seemingly immovable church? I believed it could. We prayed
for one church officer with whom they could begin, and for a
few couples who would share their desire to find the joy and
power of Christ. We did not pray for a revival in one Sunday,
but for the Lord's people who were ready to do business with
him seriously. We asked the Lord for the gift of a new perspective; not of a dead and dying congregation, but of a church
which had within it a few people who were ready to begin.
We surrendered the results to the Lord.

The couple left my office determined to allow Christ's love
for their people to displace their fear. The pastor was determined to pull out all the stops and tell the good news of what
Christ was doing in his own life. He was determined to speak
boldly in expositing the Scriptures and telling contemporary
stories of people who had come alive in Christ. Most of all, he
began looking for the Lord's people. And they emerged! The
honest sharing of the pastor's own delight and difficulties in liv-

ing the new life brought identification. Several people said, "Hey, you're just like me. Could we get together to share and pray about what you've been preaching?" The renewal of a parish was on the way, and it's still going on. A letter from the pastor's wife recently told me of their excitement about their congregation. God had done the impossible! Tertullian was right: with the Lord "it is certain because it is impossible."

Somewhat the same thing happened to a clergyman I met at a clergy conference. Just past middle age and feeling trapped and cornered, he envisioned the rest of his life as one of being occupied with the dreary business of "playing church" with a congregation that seemed unresponsive to the gospel. After listening intently, I said, "Listen, you don't have to do what you are doing the rest of your life! You're God's person and you'll be a Christian whether you're a clergyman or not. Why not give it three more years? Give it your best shots as if these were your last three years. Do all the things you have been afraid to try; speak out boldly as if you didn't care whether you succeeded or not; give yourself away in a vulnerable witness of what the Lord means to you; dare to ask for a band of adventurers out of the congregation to meet with you to discover and do what the Lord shows you. Remember you don't have to stay there forever or be a clergyman the rest of your life. You are free!"

The man's face brightened, he smiled, and then he began to laugh with boyish delight. There were lots of other things he could do, to be sure. He was not trapped after all! He had closed the prison door on himself, but now he was free.

The most significant thing about this man's story is that when he returned to his congregation caring so profoundly that he didn't have to care fearfully, he began to model a freedom and abandonment which sparked immediate interest. "What's happened to our pastor?" people asked. One officer remarked, "I've waited all my life to hear someone tell me that what's in the New Testament can be lived now. Our pastor is not only telling about it, he's living it. We can't manipulate him with the usual techniques any more. He's on the move and I want to join him!"

The people around us have an undeniable right, whether we are clergy or laity, to see what a Christ-liberated life is like. We may not be eloquent or have all the answers, but we should be prompting the exclamation, "Wow, that's the way I want to live!" The Lord's people, elected for an exciting life, will come forward and we will not be alone.

Paul found people in Corinth who were the Lord's gift for fellowship, the birth of the Church, protection in difficulties, and the sharing of hope. As we trace his steps through the rest of his ministry, we never again find the fear and frustration he knew before the Corinthian encounter with the Lord. He subsequently faced greater problems and more excruciating persecution, but he never forgot that stimulating vision or ceased to hear the drumbeat of the dynamic promise. Paul was free from fear.

Someone defined a pessimist as a person who thinks that the light at the end of the tunnel is a train coming the other way. For a person in Christ, the light is the Light of the World!

Paul's vision and promise from the Lord are only a prayer away from any of us. Even if we feel that our difficulties are endless and that problems are as sure as the sunrise, the promise can be given to us. If we find ourselves immobilized with fear because we have tried and found frustration more persistent than hope, then we need to be quiet like Elijah and Paul to hear the still, small voice of the indwelling Lord. He is very specific about his gifts to discouraged people. If we give him our fears, he will enable us with grace to love the people and eventualities we fear. We will be able to praise and thank him for the very things that frightened us. He will show us new ways of speaking about him from the wells of our weakness. We don't have to be strong or adequate any more. Our weakness is a gift to expose his strength. He will not allow any more than we can bear for his glory. And we will not be alone. He will give us people who need him as much as we do, and who need us. People in your city and mine are waiting. "The earth is the Lord's and the fulness thereof, the world and [all] those who dwell therein" (Ps. 24:1).

That's all I need to know!

CHAPTER 21

Religion Is Not Enough

Acts 18:24–19:7

Apollos of Alexandria is one of the most remarkable men in the Book of Acts. I've never seen a church which bears his name, though what happened to him needs to happen to most churches. There have been no historic holy orders established to emulate his experience, and yet what he experienced is our greatest need today. I can't remember ever meeting anyone who was named for him, but parental hopes for a child could well be focused in his name.

Apollos is the patron saint of those who find that religion is not enough. We meet him in the last paragraph of Acts 18 in an encounter with Priscilla and Aquila in which he discovered the missing dimension of his life. What happened to him also happened to the disciples of John the Baptist whom we meet in the first paragraph of Acts 19. Apollos and the disciples were of the same breed. Acts 18:24—19:7 must be considered as a whole to catch the full impact of what God wants to give religious people who do not know him.

I like to think that what happened to the disciples of John is what our Lord wants to happen in all our churches today. Luke tells us that when Paul laid his hands on them, the Holy Spirit came upon them and they spoke with tongues and prophesied. The effusion broke them open at a very deep level to praise God. The Lord still gives this gift, but it should not be sought after nor used as a lever of judgment on those who have not received it. I have an idea that these religious, up-tight disciples of John needed the gift to break free and glorify God with adoration and exultation. As I mentioned earlier, the gift of tongues is not the only undeniable sign that we have received the Holy Spirit. I never preach "tongues"; rather I explain the gift without admonition. If God determines to give the gift in order to liberate a person to adore him, I affirm the gift and press people on to seek the higher gifts as Paul outlined them in 1 Corinthians 12.

But the sure sign that people have received the Holy Spirit is love for God expressed in a life of praise and in a desire to communicate what they have found to other people. The gift of prophecy is the sensitive, incisive, and empathetic communication of the implications of the Lordship of Christ in the context of supernatural, Spirit-given insight and wisdom into the unique needs of the persons we want to help. When the Holy Spirit is released among the contemporary religious disciples of John in our churches today, there are the undeniable signs of love, warmth, passion to share with people who do not know the Savior, and compassion for the world and its needs.

The other day I was asked what is the thrust of my ministry. My answer came quickly, the result of years of thought and experience. "My passion is to introduce religious people to the living Lord and help them receive his power. There's no limit to what we could do to change the world, share the faith, and help people, if religious people in our churches were filled with the Holy Spirit!"

That's why understanding what happened to Apollos and the disciples of John is such a crucial aspect of our study of Acts. It crystallizes what I have been trying to say in this book: the drumbeat of the Master—the living, present Holy Spirit—replaces the religious chill of distance with the intimacy and intensity of dynamic power.

In a few sentences Luke acquaints us with Apollos as a paragon of a religious man. He gives us the impressive dimensions of Apollos's dossier and paints a vivid picture of the potential he had to offer the Lord, and then, of the power the Lord offered to him. Luke wants us to identify ourselves in the portrait.

First of all, we are told that Apollos was a Jew from Alexandria. If we knew only this, we would still know a great deal, for Alexandria was a great center of learning. It had one of the greatest libraries in antiquity and an outstanding university. The finest learning of Judaism and Hellenism flowed together in this city of scholars. The wisdom of Plato and Moses met in Alexandria. Greek, Latin and Hebrew grammar, rhetoric, philosophy, mathematics, medicine, geography, and history filled the atmosphere in which Apollos was raised and educated. As a student of Philo, he probably became skilled in the disciplines of Platonism, Aristotelianism, Stoicism and Mosaism. If anyone had a right to be intellectually secure and confident, it was Apollos.

But that's only the beginning. Luke goes on to say that Apollos was an eloquent man. The Greek word used here means learned in knowledge and the ability to express it. He was able to put his thoughts in such a way as to capture the minds and emotions of his listeners. He could marshal words and shades of meaning as a skilled conductor of a highly trained orchestra elicits the most subtle nuances of sound.

That's not all. Apollos was well versed in Scripture. Not only had he read the account of the actions of God among his people in what is now our Old Testament, but he was able to interpret them with force and meaning. He followed Philo's allegorical method of scriptural interpretation, finding in each historical account a hidden and deeper meaning. No dry, conceptualist scholar, he could open windows so that his listeners could see through to truth and receive the fresh vitality of his insight. I imagine he knew most of the Old Testament by heart and could make its characters come alive in the mind's eye of his rapt listeners. His interesting and impelling speech won him first a hearing and then a following in Ephesus as people came under the spell of his oratory.

The fourth thing Luke tells us is that Apollos was among the Jewish scholars who were interested in the "way of the Lord" and had experienced the baptism of John. I think that he was a leader of the band of faithful disciples of John living in and around Ephesus. Apollos's intellectual and spiritual sensitivity made him a ready student of John the Baptist. He could affirm John's preaching of Isaiah, "Repent ye: for the Kingdom of heaven is at hand. . . . Prepare ye the way of the Lord." The eloquent communicator was doing just that. As a spokesman of those who were determined to make way for the Messiah by repentance and purity of life he had been baptized in an outward

sign of absolute abandonment of his life to open the way of
the Lord. John had pointed to the Lamb of God and Apollos
had given Jesus of Nazareth his loyalty and allegiance. His
Old Testament studies had shown him repeated anticipation
of the Messiah and had given him power to prove that Jesus was
indeed the Messiah. The historical Savior and the message he
taught became the passion of Apollos's strong religious fervor.

Next, Luke tells us that this excellent preacher could teach
accurately the things concerning Jesus. He knew about his life,
message, death, and Resurrection. But for all his learning and
eloquence, he had only the characteristics of John without the
character of the living Christ. There was religion without release.

But Luke is not finished. Apollos was fervent in spirit, he says,
meaning that he was boiling over with emotional enthusiasm.
Clear thinking about the Messiah was fueled with intrepid
urgency; his convictions gave him a cause which could not be
deterred.

If this were not enough, Luke adds a sixth quality—courage.
In the presence of his peers, Apollos spoke boldly in the synagogue, taking a stand that was very unpopular at this time.
But truth was more important to him than popularity, and with
clever syllogisms, convincing logic, and dramatic dialectic, he
put it fearlessly before his audience.

Apollos was quite a man! To recapitulate, he had birth,
culture, education under the greatest scholars, intellectual acu-
men, insight into Scripture, right beliefs, boldness, courage, and
convincing communication techniques—everything. And what
can you give to a man who has everything? The same question
we must ask about many church people. Like Apollos, they
need the missing dimension. Religion is not enough!

All this background on Apollos is in preparation for an almost
unbelievable encounter. Look closely—at the conclusion of a
preaching engagement in the synagogue in Ephesus in which
Apollos swayed the crowd, moving it with wit and wisdom, two
very unlikely people brought creative correction to his life. Picture it; feel the emotion. Filled with the sense of success at the
way people had responded, Apollos must have felt the heady
wine of adulation. Then Priscilla and Aquila, two tentmaking
friends of the Apostle Paul, approached him to thank him for
his message. They had little in common with him intellectually

or culturally, but they shared the belief that Jesus was the Messiah. Note that they were able to affirm the young preacher as far as he had gone, complimenting him on his eloquence and knowledge of Scripture. Then they became skilled physicians of the Spirit for a spiritual infusion which must have been very painful. I imagine that they took him to the place where they were lodging so that the great leader would not be embarrassed in front of his avid followers.

There they shared the missing dimension. They told Apollos the exciting news that Jesus was alive as the living, loving, personal, and present Lord in the Holy Spirit. Jesus was not just a fact of history, but a friend of hope. No longer was the content of the Christian proclamation only the Messiahship of Jesus, but the indwelling power of the Lord. The Christian life was not just living for Christ, but Christ living in the believer in the presence of the Holy Spirit—Pentecost! Apollos had not heard of that. Like the disciples of John whom Paul met later in Ephesus, he probably had to confess, "I have never heard that there is a Holy Spirit!" What maturity and receptivity Apollos had: he was hungry to learn all that he could. His greatness was not in his previous learning, but in his willingness to learn from two humble, uneducated tentmakers.

"The teaching of Apollos concerning Jesus," says Foakes-Jackson, "so far as it went was accurate. But to all appearances the new Christian movement had escaped his notice, and it was certainly late in reaching Alexandria. Aquila and Priscilla heard him in the synagogue and at once realized the power his message would have if only he understood the true significance of what he was endeavoring to teach."*

"So far as he went—" What a cutting insight to describe the incompleteness of the Christian experience of so many of us! We get stalemated in our growth as a result of defensive satisfaction with our development. But the Spirit is not finished with us. He holds us in check until we are ready to receive what is missing.

If I could give a gift to religious people who do not know God, it would be Apollos's willingness to grow, to see his need, to be viable. He was given the gift of seeing that his ministry was self-propelled and self-focused; that people were impressed with

---

* F. J. Foakes-Jackson, *The Acts of the Apostles.*

Apollos, not the Lord he proclaimed. They were astounded by
how he said what he said, not what he said. He was fervent in
spirit, rather than filled with the Spirit. It frightens me to think
how easily Apollos could have missed the dynamic of the faith
offered to him. He could have said, "Listen, you tentmakers; who
are you to tell me how to live or preach! I have gotten along
very well up to this time without your help. Besides, look at the
excitement of my followers!" Or he could have offered them the
familiar con: "Thanks so much for bringing this to my attention.
You can be assured that I will give it some thought. Don't call
me; I'll call you." Or, echoing the response of others, he could
have argued about the facts and missed the personal truth. "How
could it be that we have not heard about what happened at
Pentecost after the Crucifixion? If it's not known in Alexandria,
it's not knowable. Give me proof."

But Apollos had been prepared by the Spirit to receive the
missing dimension. Secure in how much he knew, he was open
to discover more. He was committed to know all there was to
learn about Jesus. What he learned was that the Holy Spirit is
Christ alive; what he experienced was Christ indwelling.

The inner secret of what happened to Apollos is that what he
had been preaching became real to him and his own needs. I
suggest that he, like so many Christian preachers and writers,
had evaded his own message. When Priscilla and Aquila shared
what life in Christ was meant to be, only an indwelling Savior
could make it possible. Most of us don't need to know how bad
we are but how great God meant life to be. That vision necessitates the vitality of the Holy Spirit.

An outstanding layman said, "I was a faithful member of the
church for forty years before someone helped me to know that
I could know Christ personally and receive his living Spirit."
An unenlightened but eloquent Apollos in the pulpit of this
man's church had led him so close and yet so far. At a conference where there were lots of Priscillas and Aquilas to share with
him what he was missing, the man found the power of the Holy
Spirit. Then his challenge was to be like the tentmakers to his
own pastor. It was not easy. The clergyman was very satisfied
with his own learning and human gifts. It was only after several
years of persistent caring and loving involvement with him

and his family that the leading spokesman received the living Spirit. The congregation has not been the same since!

One of the great problems of the renewal of the Church in America today is that so many of the laity are way out ahead of their clergy in adventuresome, Spirit-guided living. We hear a lot about pastors who have difficulty pulling their people along, but much more these days about clergy whose religious responsibilities in keeping institutional Christianity going have diminished the vitality and fire of the Holy Spirit in their lives. As a clergyman, I need to live in Apollos's skin and then find myself among the disciples of John in Acts 19. Our problem in the Church today is not that we have never heard of the Holy Spirit, but that we have relegated mention of him to Whitsunday or to the repetition of the trinitarian formula. A leader in one of America's great churches told me that he had not heard a sermon on the Holy Spirit from the renowned pulpit of his church in thirty years! A whole generation in that church could honestly repeat the Scripture, "We have never heard that there is a Holy Spirit." It is possible to preach Christ, the Cross, outline the plan of salvation, and stir the people with the admonitions of Christian ethics without helping them to experience the power of the Living Christ, our Contemporary, the Holy Spirit.

The account in Acts of what happened to Apollos when he received power and to the disciples of John when Paul laid hands upon them is an undeniable benchmark for what needs to happen to both the communicators in our churches and the people who listen to them. The difference in Apollos's life after he stopped trying to be adequate in his own goodness and gifts and received the Holy Spirit is amazing. As a free person, empowered by God, he was able to build up not Apollos but the Church. Through him, the Lord reached people not with Apollos's adequacy but with the impelling power of the Spirit. The Holy Spirit drives home the gospel, gives the gift of faith to respond, enables acceptance and assurance which spills over to others, and enlists people in the adventure of the movement.

At Corinth in Achaia, Apollos "greatly helped those who through grace had believed, for he powerfully confuted the Jews in public, showing by the scriptures that the Christ was Jesus" (18:27–28). In his letter to the Corinthians Paul affirms the ministry of Apollos there in Corinth. "I planted, Apollos watered, but God gave the growth" (1 Cor. 3:6). It is obvious that Apollos became a strong, dynamic leader of the Church. He proclaimed more than homiletics about a historical Jesus; rather, he offered them the infusing, enabling power of an imbuing Savior alive with them. What Jesus had done for his followers in Judea was inseparably related to what he was doing among and within them in Achaia.

I am part of an Apollos Adventurers' group of pastors. We meet one day a month in which we seek to be Priscilla and Aquila to one another. We have all had extensive training in speech and rhetoric, pastoral leadership, and Bible teaching. Each month we come limping into the group's meeting to log in our month's activities in seeking to be Book of Acts church leaders. We usually need to be checked, corrected, convicted. More than that, we need to be loved. A meeting seldom goes by without a confession of our abject need of the Holy Spirit and his gifts for our ministries. If new life is breaking out in our churches, it can be traced back to the quality we share together of the Church in miniature.

It would be startling if we drove by a church today and noticed that its name had been changed from "Old First Church" to the "Church of Saint Apollos." There's no pastor who wouldn't want a church filled with Apolloses, unless he's never met an Aquila and Priscilla himself! And if you are looking for a new name to call yourself as a focus of your spiritual pilgrimage, try Apollos. Become like him, and you will become a part of the HOTFWRINE: The Holy Order of Those For Whom Religion Is Not Enough!

CHAPTER 22

Not in the Stars but in the Superstar

Acts 19:8–20:38

During a conference on "Prayer and the Holy Spirit" on
our church campus in Hollywood, the seven hundred people attending had been given a stirring call to prayer for the
nation and our city. Afterwards they had been dispersed into
seventy small prayer groups meeting all over the campus. Late
in the evening none of the groups seemed anxious to break up.
The power of the Holy Spirit was giving the people the boldness
to pray fearlessly.

I should not have been surprised by the wild-eyed, deeply
troubled young woman in her midtwenties who wandered helplessly into the courtyard. I was standing there with a friend—
deployed, positioned by the Spirit. The woman came straight
toward me. Compulsive sobs shook from her inner being. Months
before, someone had given her the telephone number of our
Helpline, but she had put it aside. Then that night she had
"happened" to find it and in desperation had called. The Helpline
counselor had given the woman the church address and had
encouraged her to come for help with what was obviously a
bizarre case of satanic possession.

The woman's face was aged beyond her years. She was skin
and bones, though money for food was not her problem. Sleep
had been impossible for weeks. A quest for help from self-styled
spiritualists had driven her deeper into her problem. She was
about to respond to a command to do something that everything
in her rational mind resisted.

The problem had begun very innocently, as a lark. The woman had been taught spirit-writing by an occult, and her loneliness had driven her to communicate with a "spirit pal," as she called him. She had asked for his name on a ouija board. A-l-b-e-r-t had been spelled out in response. Daily conversations were carried on for weeks, intimate questions asked, directions for life requested. Always there was a clear answer. Then her "spirit" became anything but a pal. He spelled out her sister's name: J-a-n-e. Simple, benign suggestions about her at first. Then a horrible command. M-u-r-d-e-r J-a-n-e. How and when was detailed. With trembling fingers she now spelled out the words, W-h-o a-r-e y-o-u? The answer came swiftly, moving her hands deliberately: E-v-i-l. Frantic, and almost out of her senses, the woman came for help, stuttering out her plight in great gushes of anguish.

After we had talked for some time, I took her to the sanctuary. Along the way, I found a church officer and his wife and asked them to help me. I anticipated what we were up against. The woman was under the spell and possession of evil. Prayers of exorcism would be required. I have learned never to do that alone. The young elder and his committed wife were wonderfully equal to the unusual task. The wife knelt before the disturbed woman seated in the pew, taking her hands in a loving clasp. We told her about Jesus Christ and his love for her; the power of his name to liberate people from evil. Then the elder and I laid our hands on the woman's head and prayed for her release.

I will never forget the transformation on her face after we prayed. Her eyes lost the glassy, wild look. Her body slumped in quiet peacefulness. That night she slept for the first time in weeks. The next day she returned and took part in the conference. She still has my Bible with verses underlined to direct her to the Savior and his power.

The Lord had given the first fruits of the prayers of the people. He had taken us seriously. To pray for a city means that the Lord will begin open battle with the forces of darkness.

This event forces me to realize again that we live in crucial days of conflict with Satan. I see the influence and possession of evil all over our megalopolis. Your city is probably no different. Palm readers, crystal-ball gazers, spiritualists, tea-leaf readers, future predicters, cults, occult and mystery religions are all a part of a gigantic, burgeoning industry making millions every year. Spiritual hunger must be fed by someone, but in this kind of feeding there's no nourishment of the soul. People are yearning for meaning, direction, an understanding of who they are and what the future will hold. These "black magic" purveyors are more than ready to offer an easy answer for a price.

The year 1967 was historic in the American toy industry. Ouija boards took the lead over Monopoly as the favorite game of Americans, and have steadily widened the margin ever since. It is estimated that fifteen million boards have been sold since 1967. Just a game? Perhaps, for some. But for others, using a ouija board has become a substitute for authentic prayers for guidance—and a vulnerable opening for Satan!

But nothing has gripped the American mind quite so much as the fascination, now grown into fanaticism, with the influence of the stars upon our lives. The astrology industry makes the cultists and spiritualists look like back-street peddlers. In a recent year, twenty-five million people spent over two hundred million dollars on personal horoscope materials, all to find out what "fate" a particular day holds for them according to their sign. We are told that we are in the "Age of Aquarius." There are twelve signs of the Zodiac, the imaginary belt of the heavens, for the paths apparently taken through space by the sun, the moon and principal planets. The eleventh of these signs is Aquarius, Latin for water-bearer. The idea is that every two thousand years we enter into a new astrological age which is named for one of the Zodiac symbols. We supposedly have passed through Pisces and the age of Aquarius is upon us. It is predicted to be an age of peace, freedom, and universal brotherhood. Better hurry! The signs of the time do not meet the astrological sign of the age, although the "Dawning of the Age of Aquarius" from the Broadway hit musical *Hair* made some bold promises.

The "Age of Aquarius" is now a household term. Everything from billboards to embroidered bikinis won't let us forget. What does it all mean? The richest nation on earth is emaciated spiritually for lack of hope.

Recently a deeply committed Christian woman who dabbles in the "both/and" of astrology and prayer for the guidance of her life said to me, "Don't worry about anything tomorrow. I

have checked your sign and your horoscope and you are going
to have a great day!" My response exposed my growing alarm
over people's oblation to the daily newspaper's horoscope page
or dedicated study of the millions of astrology how-to books
and magazines published each year. "My dear distracted friend,"
I said, "my fate is not in the stars, but my faith is in the
Superstar, Jesus Christ. I do not live under the sign of Virgo,
but under the sign of the Cross!"

The woman was shocked by my answer. That's exactly what
I had intended. I wanted to alert her to the danger of putting
her trust in anything or anyone except Jesus Christ. Astrology,
fortune-telling, or any of the spiritualistic experimentations put
us in touch with forces which not only distract us from but distort our life in Christ and our absolute dependence on him. He is
all we need!

That same issue faced Paul when he arrived on the scene in
Ephesus for nearly three years of penetrating ministry (Acts
20:31). We should have no trouble understanding that marketplace of Asia Minor. All we need do is look at what is going
on in our own cities and we will have captured the mood and
muddle of Ephesus. Superstition, sorcery, spiritualism, star worship, and sophistry pervaded the city. What a place to preach the
gospel. Not so—what a gospel to preach in such a place!

Ephesus had been built at the mouth of the Cayster River.
The city became known as the "Treasure House of Asia" because she commanded the trade into the river valley of the rich
province of Asia Minor. Voluptuous sensualism dominated the
city. It was called an "assize town" because the Roman governor
tried cases there and brought with him the pomp and pageantry
of Rome. The Pan-Ionian Games were held there and afforded
not only recognition but revenue for the city.

We may be troubled with the false hopes of the age of
Aquarius, but in Ephesus every age was the age of Artemis.
The opulent Temple of Artemis was one of the seven wonders
of the then-known world. One hundred and twenty-seven Parian
marble pillars distinguished its exterior, some of them inlaid with
gold and precious jewels. A study of its architecture reveals that
it was four hundred and twenty-five feet long, two hundred and
twenty feet wide and sixty feet high. Inside was the pride of
Ephesus—an altar carved by the famous Greek sculptor

Praxiteles. On it was the black, multi-breasted image of Artemis, supposed to have fallen from the stars and to assure fertility and prosperity.

That kind of superstition will always be capitalized on, and the silversmiths of Ephesus did just that. They made silver shrines of Artemis and sold them for a profit that brought them great wealth.

The city became a cesspool, sucking into its foul spiritual pollution every kind of magic worker and cultist in the region. In addition there were criminals of all types—murderers, swindlers, and con artists—who were given asylum if they could reach the precincts of the temple.

Superstition was not limited to the temple or the powers of Artemis. Charms and spells from Ephesus were sold all over the world, among them the "Ephesian grammata," or Ephesian letters, charms that were supposed to guarantee safety, fertility, success, and love.

With this background on Ephesus, we can better understand the triumphs and the tragedies of Paul's ministry there. He began his ministry in the synagogue, but the stubbornness and disbelief of the Jews drove him to the Gentiles. With them his preaching and teaching of Christ had a great response. Luke tells us that he taught in the lecture hall of the philosopher Tyrannus daily from 11:00 A.M. until 4:00 P.M. Those were customarily hours of rest when all work stopped, and people rested—but not the Holy Spirit. He gave Paul great power, and news of the Christian movement spread all over the province of Asia.

It wasn't long before the gospel came into direct confrontation with the culture of Ephesus. Evil had a death grip on the city and was not about to let go without a desperate battle. Then, as now, conflict with the Lordship of Christ is generated by superstition, spiritualism, and sophistry.

The power of Paul's message produced hundreds of new Christians, but the extraordinary miracles he performed agitated the superstitious. The Apostle worked at a trade while in Ephesus. The handkerchiefs and aprons he used as a workman were carried away to be placed on the sick; his sweat-band and tentmaker's apron were believed to have the Apostle's power. New grammata, the people thought. And they worked. People were healed of diseases and evil spirits left them. How gracious

of God! He met the people where they were. The name of
Jesus alone had power over sickness and possession. But we
suspect that Paul did not allow the name of Jesus to be a new
form of superstition. He helped people to know the One who
was the source of the miraculous power.

Itinerant Jewish exorcists who neither knew the Savior nor
had surrendered their lives to his Lordship tried to use the
name of Jesus to exorcise people of evil spirits. Their formula
was to say, "I adjure you by the Jesus whom Paul preaches, come
out!" (Acts 19:13). The seven sons of a priest named Sceva got
an answer they had not expected. The evil spirit they were trying to cast out responded, "Jesus I know, and Paul I know, but
who are you?" Who indeed! The only one who can use the
name of Jesus is one in whom the Spirit of Jesus dwells. The
exorcists wanted to exploit the power they had observed in
Paul without having a relationship with the Savior he preached;
they were selling a religion. But Paul had not come to spiritualistic Ephesus for the purpose of adding one more mysterious
spirit to the constellation of spirits which demanded no moral
responsibility.

The same is true today. When people use the name of Jesus
carelessly for personal gain without personal commitment to
him, they call forth not Jesus, but the forces of evil. He will
not be manipulated! Yet for some people, the Christian faith
represents little more than the imagined answer to their desire
for magic. We want what we want when we want it, and on our
terms. But Jesus is not an errand boy. He works miracles, not
tricks of magic. And the greatest miracle is the transformation
of a human heart by the power of love. Anything after that is a
blessing we gratefully receive with thanksgiving, but can never
demand.

The exorcists and magic workers of Ephesus had not listened
and responded to the gospel. Because they did not know Jesus
whose name they used, they were attacked by the very spirits
they wanted to exorcise for profit. Luke tells us vividly that the
sons of Sceva were overpowered and beaten by the demons they
tried to cast out.

Seeing what happened to Sceva's sons brought about a moral
revolution in Ephesus. Those who practiced magic and sorcery
brought their manuals of the black arts and burned them so that

everyone could see. The implication is that they turned from
magic to Christ. Luke says that "the word of the Lord grew
and prevailed mightily" (Acts 19:20). That's always the result
of confession, repentance, and a radical change of lifestyle. It
makes me wonder what kind of fire we could have in the
Church today if all of the manuals of magic, horoscopes, cult
books, and occult literature were gathered and burned in the
name of Jesus.

In Ephesus, the moral reformation was far-reaching. It cut
right to the heart of the silver shrine business and into the
pockets of the silversmiths. The worst manifestation of evil
which confronted Paul and the followers of the Way was the
sophistry of the silversmiths. Every fallacious argument was
mustered to expose Paul and his followers as the cause of
the diminishing trade in silver icons of Artemis. They were not
far from the truth: the new converts to Christ did not need the
grotesque figures to manipulate their destiny. The silversmiths
reached the height of their sophistry to the people of Ephesus
for the preservation of the worship of Artemis when it was their
profit that concerned them most. A near riot ensued. The silversmiths chanted, "Great is Artemis of the Ephesians!" What they
really were saying was, "Our livelihood is being threatened by
the Way! Get rid of these Christians at all costs!" Many of the
Way barely escaped with their lives. But the Lord intervened.
Little did the town clerk who brought order know that he was
being used to speak for the Savior of the world.

We are left to ponder the implications for our cities of the
sophistry of these Ephesians. Christian history is filled with
bloody memories of what happens when the gospel confronts
vested interests, political pride, or economic investments. Now
many of the silversmiths are in the Church! How often we practice the clever art of sophistry when we resist change, the impact
of the gospel on prejudice, or Christ's judgments of social practices which cripple people. It's a demanding and dangerous
business to spell out the love of Christ in practical ways. One
man told me that he made two resolutions in response to the
call to allow Christ to guide his life and his business. Resolution
one: to obey Christ at all costs; resolution two: to do it even
if no one else does. Only that kind of action will liberate us
from equivocating sophistry.

The fires of conflict in Ephesus had forged a great church. Paul pressed on to visit the churches in Macedonia and Greece, but he could not forget the Ephesian followers of the Way. They were on his mind and heart throughout the rest of the third missionary journey. On his way back to Jerusalem for final confrontation with the Hebrew authorities, his ship made a stop at Miletus, about thirty miles from Ephesus. Luke tells us that Paul had decided not to visit Ephesus again. But his concern for the new Christians and the struggling church there made it impossible to resist seeing his friends once more. He sent for the elders of the church so he could express a final word of encouragement and affirmation. How he loved those saints! He wanted to be sure that they continued to grow in Christ as they lived in Ephesus. He knew that they could not survive the latter without the first.

The meeting of Paul with the elders was an occasion of mixed joy and sadness. The Ephesians were delighted to see their beloved friend again, but they knew that his determination to go to Jerusalem would surely mean persecution and trial, perhaps death.

I can imagine the pathos in Paul's heart as he looked into the Christ-illuminated faces of his converts. Among them must have been some of the now Spirit-filled disciples of John on whom he had laid his hands at the beginning of his ministry in Ephesus; some transformed exorcists now liberated; a magician or two who had found a power greater than magic; a silversmith who no longer made silver images of Artemis to sustain his worship of the god of wealth; several leaders of the city who had found a Leader for their souls; criminals who had come to the city for asylum and discovered an eternal haven in Christ; and many cultists who had learned that Christ alone could satisfy. Paul wanted all these new men in Christ to lead a movement. To do so they had to keep on growing and to stay constantly open to the Holy Spirit's power over all the forces of evil in their city. What they needed to lead the Church was also the most profound need in their own lives. The greater the difficulties they would face, the more power would be given them. The Church would never be out of danger.

Paul's message to the elders was filled with love and affection. He gave them an admonition and an assurance. "Take heed to yourselves and to all the flock, in which the Holy Spirit has made you guardians, to feed the church of the Lord which he obtained with his own blood" (Acts 20:28). A warning followed for the unique problems of Ephesus. "I know," he said, "that after my departure fierce wolves will come in among you, not sparing the flock; and from among your own selves will arise men speaking perverse things, to draw away the disciples after them." The perverse forces which had resisted Paul's ministry would persist against the church and from within it. The new people in Christ must be fed spiritually, built up in the faith and kept close to Christ and the fellowship if they were to survive the threatening superstitions, pagan cults, and materialism of Ephesus.

The tedious situation in that snake pit of dangerous influences is not different in your Ephesus and mine today. The struggle of the Church to be authentic is no less demanding. The more spiritually powerful our churches become, the more they will be the target of satanic attack. The forces of evil are not concerned with bland, culturally captured churches.

Today, as in Ephesus, the external influences must be counteracted with the internal power of the Holy Spirit. Paul's final word to the elders is an assurance of the resources for the battle: "And now I commend you to God and to the word of his grace, which is able to build you up and give you the inheritance among all those who are sanctified." The source of power and the result belong to God. He will finish what he has begun. The Apostle wanted the Ephesians to claim the implications of that inheritance of sanctification, and we have the same need today. It is the only antidote for satanic influence. What is holy belongs to God and bears his nature. The inheritance of sanctification means that we are joint heirs with Christ, and we are to become like Jesus. His living Spirit is instigator and enabler of the process. In our sanctification we grow in the image of Christ in our thoughts, feelings, words, and actions—but as a gift, not an achievement of our efforts. We can love with his love and are able to forgive by his grace. We are energized by his power and are released to face the future with his hope. We won't make it in our Ephesus without that!

One Sunday afternoon not long ago, my son Andy went out in our backyard to take a nap in the sun and fell deeply asleep

Drumbeat of Love

in the warm afternoon temperature. He was sleeping so soundly that he was not awakened by a small helicopter which slowly descended over our home. When it was about twenty feet over him, the playful pilot leaned out and shouted over a megaphone, "Hang in there!" Andy awoke with a frightened start, leaped up, and ran into the house.

The family all laughed, but then we decided this was a good message for all of us. We had not been asking King Zedekiah's question of Jeremiah, "Is there any word from the Lord?" (Jer. 37:17). But it was a word that we needed to hear even if it came from a very unexpected and unusual messenger. "Hang in there!" now has a very special meaning for us.

In a way, that's what Paul was saying to the Ephesian elders. But he wanted them to know that "hanging in there" in Ephesus would be possible because the Lord would never let go of them. That's all I need to know for life in my hometown or wherever I find myself in this distorted and disturbing world.

CHAPTER 23

Tender Toughness

Acts 21:1–16

The other day I heard a man's maturity in Christ described as tender toughness. At first the words seemed contradictory. How could this person be tough and tender at the same time? Wouldn't one cancel out the other?

We all know tender Christians. They are warm, emotional people whose love enables them to express assurance and compassion. Easily impressed by the concerns of others, they are sensitive and supple. Gentleness guides their judgments and pathos pulses through them. We all need a greater measure of that tenderness for others as a result of the graciousness of Christ towards us.

But there is also a toughness we admire in some followers of the Master. They are distinguished by determination and directness. They seem to know who they are and where they are going, because they know whose they are and what they are to be and do. They are on the move toward a clearly defined goal. They speak the truth boldly, without equivocation, in words congruent with their character, and they make each decision as if it were part of a predetermined destiny. We admire that kind of tough Christian. Most of us long to have more of such vision and pertinacity.

The problem is that most tender Christians need more toughness and most tough Christians need more tenderness. The man whose maturity was complimented had both. My experience of him confirmed the accolade. He had the tenderness of grace.

Life had pounded softness into him. He had been hard and judgmental until successive failures and tragedies had brought him to the healing love of our Lord. The "new creation" gave him a capacity to affirm and encourage others. His own brokenness and sense of fallibility was expressed in gracious sensitivity to others. But, thank God, he has never lost the other half of grace. He is a man under orders who is determined to seek and do God's will as he sees it. No one dissuades him from his direction. He sees reality as it is, and when it comes to following Christ, living in the Scriptures, and spelling out the implications for his life and society, he is tough. This unpurchasable man has tender roughness. We are all meant to be like him.

Many of the tender Christians we observe are far too soft. They find it difficult to speak bold truth with love. Afraid of hurting people, they seldom help them. Peace and pleasantness become so important that battling for the best is abhorrent. The soothing words "Now, now, everything is all right and will all work out" often become a prison door which locks people in their condition. Equally uncreative is excessive toughness which objectifies truth with little empathetic feeling for what people face in living it. Many tough people deny the process by which people can develop the same convictions they hold so tenaciously. The toughness of the Savior was never hardness. He was always tender toward people who were in need and tough with those who needed to grow. His love was never sloppy nor simplistic. It did not approve anything people were or did that was destroying them. Rather his affirmation of people included creative and constructive correction. The woman by the well of Jacob was never approved for having a multiplicity of husbands. The rich young ruler was never assured that he could keep his love of riches. Peter was not encouraged in his efforts to press the Master to turn away from the sacrifice of the Cross. Herod was exposed as "that fox!" the Pharisees as whitewashed tombs, the scribes as nitpicking legalists, Judas as the betrayer. Jesus knew what was in people. He was tough in being about his Father's business, which eventually meant the Cross. Our Lord is the magnificent example of the blend of tender toughness.

In Acts 21:1–14 we see the Apostle Paul at his tenderest and toughest. We feel his parting anguish at leaving his friends and fellow believers along the way en route to Jerusalem. Yet, at the same time we sense an undissuadable determination to follow his conviction, to press on even though it will surely mean imprisonment, suffering, and eventually death. We empathize with the tenderness of Paul's beloved friends and admire his tough directness. The account seems to contrast the two qualities sharply, but then shows us how both can be blended by the guidance and power of the Holy Spirit.

In the previous chapter we felt the depth of Paul's love for the elders of the Ephesian church. He seemed to sense their agony when he said, "And now, behold, I am going to Jerusalem, bound in the Spirit, not knowing what shall befall me there; except that the Holy Spirit testifies to me in every city that imprisonment and afflictions await me. But I do not account my life of any value nor as precious to myself, if only I may accomplish my course and the ministry which I received from the Lord Jesus, to testify to the gospel of the grace of God" (Acts 20:22–24).

The people knew what was waiting for him in Jerusalem, for word of the hostility of the Jews there had reached Ephesus. A death warrant was out on the Apostle's life. That's why he said they would see his face no more and why when he parted from them it was so heartbreaking. Acts 21:1, "When we had parted from them and set sail," in the Revised Standard Version does not catch the wrenching emotion expressed by the Greek, which actually says, "We tore ourselves away from them." The basic verb used here means "to draw a sword from its scabbard, pull something apart, or separate." Paul and his company had to wrench themselves loose from their friends, whose love wanted to keep them from sailing into danger.

It would be no different at the two major stops on the voyage from Miletus to Jerusalem. But Paul could not be deterred. Later, from prison, he clarified his indomitable purpose. "One thing I do, forgetting what lies behind and straining forward to what lies ahead, I press on toward the goal for the prize of the upward call of God in Christ Jesus" (Phil. 3:13–14).

Luke's description of the voyage reads like a nautical account, as if he had one hand on a map retracing the voyage while with the other hand he wrote the chronicle of the journey. From the port of Miletus, one day's journey brought them to Cos, where they dropped anchor before going on to Rhodes. From Rhodes

Drumbeat of Love

they sailed for Patara on the Lycian mainland. There they changed to a larger ship for the long 350-mile journey on the high seas of the Mediterranean to Tyre on the Syrian coast. The vessel landed there to unload cargo. The week's wait was profitably spent with a small cluster of believers who made up the church at Tyre.

What happened at Tyre is a vivid description of the difference between tenderness and toughness and the need for both. As soon as Paul's ship was in port, he sought out the Christian disciples. Perhaps he had known some of them before, but most of them were new friends. The week of fellowship that followed galvanized them to Paul with affection and love. Surely this is why they were so alarmed when they learned of his unshakable determination to go to Jerusalem as the result of the Spirit's guidance in his prayers. They too prayed and came up with a very different answer. "Through the Spirit," Luke tells us, "they told Paul not to go to Jerusalem" (Acts 21:4). The same Spirit seemed to be giving two different directions. How could this be? Think of how unsettling that must have been for Paul. His friends were clear in their conviction that he should not go to Jerusalem. But he pressed on.

The drama in the tender scene of his departure from Tyre grips us. All of the believers and their children came down to the beach at the harbor. Along with Paul, Luke, and the others in the party, the people got on their knees and prayed together. Yet Paul was still determined to move on to Jerusalem. Parting was not "sweet sorrow" but an expression of tender love rubbed raw with the certainty that Paul's fate was sealed in Jerusalem. Sense Paul's tender response to the people's love, but also feel the toughness of his vigilance.

The counterconvictions of differing guidance were even more intense at the next stop. From Tyre Paul sailed the twenty miles south to Ptolemais and then traveled overland forty miles to Caesarea. There he was greeted by Philip, the deacon and evangelist. Strange twist of providence! The same Philip who was forced from Jerusalem years before by the purge of the Church by Saul of Tarsus was now the gracious host of the Apostle. The inclusive spirit which Philip expressed in preaching to the Samaritans and in proclaiming Christ to the Ethiopian was lavished on his old enemy, now a beloved brother in the Lord.

Philip, along with his four daughters, made Paul welcome in his house and relished the days of fellowship with him. Philip's daughters had the gift of prophecy, which enabled them to discern what the Lord was saying about present circumstances and the implications for the future. It was while Paul was staying at Philip's house that powerful pressures were mounted to keep him from doing what he believed was the will of the Lord for him.

A Christian prophet named Agabus came down from Judea to meet with Paul. He had fresh information about the gathering storm of hostility against Paul in Jerusalem. This knowledge, coupled with his own prayers for the guidance of the Spirit, prompted him to sound his alarm in a very dramatic way. Like the Old Testament prophets Isaiah, Jeremiah, and Ezekiel, he acted out his prophecy. He took Paul's girdle, a belt which gathered an outer tunic about the waist, and bound his own hands and feet. Then he said these frightening words, "Thus says the Holy Spirit, 'So shall the Jews at Jerusalem bind the man who owns this girdle and deliver him into the hands of the Gentiles' " (Acts 21:11). Powerful prophecy, indeed!

Now add to that Philip's concern, a prophecy of danger undoubtedly voiced by his daughters, and the resistance of Luke, Silas, Timothy, and all the rest—and you have a formidable force to unsettle Paul's conviction to press on to Jerusalem. Imagine how we might have reacted if people with the gift of prophecy tried to dissuade us in a direction we felt was clearly Spirit-guided. That, along with the uncertainty of trusted friends, would make any of us wonder if we were wrong.

Let's pause at this juncture of our exposition to reflect on the question of differing guidance. Good men and women, all who loved the Lord, all who prayed to know God's will, seemed to get different guidance. What had happened at Tyre was repeated now at Caesarea. What does this mean?

Paul, the Christian prophets, and his friends had several things in common. They all had prayed. And they all had received the same revelation from the Holy Spirit, that suffering and imprisonment lay ahead for the Apostle in Jerusalem. The difference in their conclusions about their prayers resulted from what they added to the basic revelation they had received. Paul added toughness; his cherished friends added tenderness.

The amazing love that the people felt for Paul was both a delight and a difficulty, and it adds a dimension to our portrait of the Apostle. Apparently he was not only a vigilant communicator of revealed truth but a participant in a relational fellowship. He was free to let people love him. It was their tender love, however, which eventually confused what they understood the Spirit to be saying about his destiny. Their deep affection and warm affirmation would not let them abide the thought of Paul's being sacrificed to the stupidity of the prejudices of the Jews at Jerusalem. Sentimentalized love twisted the guidance of the Spirit about their friend's fate. There was nothing to do but weep and try to change his mind.

Paul had added something to the same revelation about his future: the ultimate passion to live and die for Christ, if need be. Like his Master before him, he "set his face to go to Jerusalem" (Luke 9:51). And like Jesus' disciples, Paul's friends were filled with amazement and anguish. The difference between Paul's understanding of what he should do and the advice of his friends was in the different levels of love. They loved Paul and wanted his safety; he loved Christ and thought nothing of physical suffering. Safety was no longer his primary concern.

Toughness and tenderness are sublimely blended in the Apostle's response to the importuning of his friends to stay out of Jerusalem. He seems to have caught the full impact of their anxiety for him. It was wearing on him, troubling his spirit, unsettling his vision. His answer was an explosion of emotion, "What are you doing, weeping and breaking my heart?" (Acts 21:13). Misguided tenderness was getting at him and pressing him dangerously close to denying the heavenly vision. The Greek word *sunthruptō*, "to break," from *apothruptō,* meaning "to crush together," translates Paul's implication that his friends were trying to crush his guidance from God. They were breaking his heart because they were trying to bend it. Instead of vigor he was beginning to feel vacillation in his purpose. His faithfulness to Christ was being enervated and his clarity of direction was being clouded. Another way of putting Paul's response is: "My dear friends, what are you trying to do? Do you realize what you are doing to me with your weeping? It's making me question my own heart's desire to obey the Master!"

Now Paul must restate his steadfast resolve, as much for him-

self as for his friends. "For I am ready not only to be imprisoned
but even to die at Jerusalem for the name of the Lord Jesus."
Despite the warnings, he felt it was the Lord's will, as before, to
go on regardless of cost. He interpreted the tender love of his
friends as information and warning, something he had had from
his own prayers. The disciples had added the prohibition themselves, but his own conviction was louder than their concern
about safety. He survived the menace of clinging, sentimental
love. Tender sentimentality is usually the same: enjoyment without responsibility.

That forces us to go deeper. Could it be that in addition to
love there was a frightened concern in the disciples for their own
safety? We cannot encourage another person in a direction we
are not able to go ourselves. Often tender love keeps people from
those very things for which they were born because we cannot
imagine ourselves doing what they seem determined to do.

Jesus' own response to his disciples' fear has fired the courage
of saint and martyr in every age, right down to our own, and to
you and me. The frenzied fear in the disciples burst out, "Rabbi,
the Jews were but now seeking to stone you, and are you going
there again?" (John 11:8–10). His answer cut through the air
and then to the taproot of their apprehension. "Are there not
twelve hours in the day? If anyone walks in the day, he does not
stumble, because he sees the light of the world. But if anyone
walks in the night, he stumbles, because the light is not in him."

Following his Lord, Paul was marching to Jerusalem in the
light of clear guidance. The darkness of his friends' protective
affection could not put out the light of Christ in his soul.

But note that the motives of both Paul and his friends were
pure. The difference was that they wanted to save Paul; Paul
wanted to save the world! The Spirit hadn't told them that he
should not go to Jerusalem, but what would happen if he did
go? How easily we can distort the Spirit's revelation of reality
with our determined efforts to shape reality for the welfare and
comfort of people we love. Paul's loved ones had a high motive,
but his was higher: love for Christ and passion for the fulfillment
of his purpose. That is the final and ultimate test of our motives.
After we have prayed our prayers and sought the Spirit's guidance, we must be sure that our answer stands the test of utmost
loyalty to Christ. It is so easy to project our will and perception

of what is best into our prayers and to come out with what we wanted all along, with what we wish to think is the Spirit's confirmation. But this is not confirmation at all; it is rather an effort to make the Lord conform to our preconceptions. There is only one pure motive: the desire to know and to do the Lord's will, regardless of cost to us or to others. Be sure of this: the Holy Spirit will never guide us to give advice to others which, if obeyed, would be an escape from faithfulness.

Now look at the naïveté in Luke's confession in verse 14: "And when he [Paul] would not be persuaded, we ceased and said, 'The will of the Lord be done.' " What did that mean? Had he and Paul's friends believed all along that it was God's will for Paul to go to Jerusalem and still persisted in dissuading him? Were they intentionally standing in the way of Paul's obedience? Or does it mean that, as so many of us do, they used the phrase, "The will of the Lord be done," out of habit, after having tried to get their way and failing? I wonder if Luke's account doesn't simply mean that as long as Paul's friends could not get him to do the safe and sane thing, God would have to work out the implications of the Apostle's unswerving determination.

This passage leaves us with some disturbing questions. Do we have Paul's toughness to follow as much guidance as we have been given? How do we handle the protective affection of people around us? Can we say, "I must . . . see Rome! " even if it means tragic difficulties in Jerusalem on the way?

Those questions press me on to others. Am I more like Paul's friends than like Paul? I wonder whose vision I have bent or reshaped because I could not imagine or grapple with a similar vision for myself. What is my point of resistance in faithfulness to Christ? When do I say, "Lord, anything you want, but not that! I'll do anything for you Lord, but this is ridiculous!"

Often we are like the young man who wrote his loved one: "I'll do anything, go any place for you. I will swim the broadest ocean, climb the highest mountain, fight the fiercest enemy—all for you. P.S. I'll see you next weekend if the blizzard doesn't block the road."

Halford Luccock tells a story of a football referee's analysis of a certain player. "I can only say this, I have never had to pull him out from the bottom of a scrimmage. I have often found him on top of a pile of players, where he had jumped on after the man with the ball had been stopped by another player. He was never the first to make the tackle." Only the people who would be courageous enough to make the tackle could encourage someone else to do it.

Could it be that, like Paul's friends, we are tripping up the steps the Lord has guided for some person we profess to love?

Think of people in our families. Husbands and wives can muffle the call of the Master in each other. As parents, our love of our children can be so protective that we clutch them to us and refuse to allow them to grow through facing difficulties and frustrations. Before my mind's eye flash the faces of countless teenagers who have taken Christ seriously and outdistanced their parents, only to find that their parents' reservations kept them from being obedient disciples. One young man said to me recently, "I can't figure my parents out. They took me to church school for years. They were anxious for me to confess Christ and join the church. Then I began to read the New Testament and follow Christ seriously. Now my parents are afraid I'm going overboard. All I'm doing is putting into action what I thought they believed all along. I have begun to wonder if we believe in the same Christ. All they want is my safety, success, and prosperity. But anything that gets in the way of that they resist, questioning my guidance from the Lord."

And what about our friends? Have we been tough Christians in helping them to reshape their lifestyle around Christ and the gospel? Has softness kept us from asking the challenging questions and exemplifying for them the surrendered and obedient life of contemporary discipleship? Proverbs 3:6 sets the bench mark: "In everything you do, put God first, and he will direct you and crown your efforts with success" (*The Living Bible*). That success is always to be measured by the goals of the Kingdom.

Spalatin begged Luther not to go to the Diet of Worms. Luther's response was, "Though devils be as many in Worms as tiles on the roofs, yet thither will I go!" In spite of resistance and danger, he finally said, "Here I stand; I can do no other!"

It is shallow love which desires to keep life smooth and easy for people. By word, suggestion, or outright resistance, we can keep people from doing what God has willed for them. That's frightening. Not one of Paul's associates, fellow-disciples, prophetic seers, or faithful prayer-partners volunteered, "Paul, I affirm your vision. I know what will happen in Jerusalem, but I am for you and willing to go with you. Don't turn back or stay here in safety. I would not bend your heart or crush your determination. Praise God, you know what you are to do, and I am for you!" But Paul's friends never said anything like that. How very tragic, after all they had seen the Lord do in them and around them.

Tender toughness, that's what spurred on the indomitable Apostle. His purpose was clear. What he would be called to do and suffer in Jerusalem was "for the name of the Lord Jesus." That means literally, "under the guidance of, in keeping with, and for the sake of, the Lord." When a person exposes any vision, dream, or plan to the pure illuminating light of that perspective and it stands the test, he can seek to fulfill it with joy and courage.

All this centers on a serious analysis of our own relationship with the Savior. Has his love made us creatively tender toward others? Has his indwelling Spirit enabled us to be tough about ultimate issues? Tenderness without toughness is sloppy sentimentality. Toughness without tenderness is harsh intractability. But together, they make the courage-producing combination of Christian maturity. Thank God, he gave Paul both. He would never have made it to Jerusalem and on to Rome without them! We may have more of one than the other; only the Lord can tell us. And he alone can tenderize the tough and toughen the tender. He is ready to do both.

CHAPTER 24

The Resiliency of the Resurrection

Acts 21:17–26:32

Last year, on the Monday after Easter, a Los Angeles
newspaper carried a story about the Easter services in
Hollywood Bowl. The opening sentences were both true and very
false. "The Hollywood Presbyterian Church held Easter services
for the Los Angeles community yesterday in the Hollywood
Bowl. The celebration of the resurrection began at 10:00 A.M.
and ended at 11:15."

But Hollywood Presbyterian Church's celebration of the Resurrection did not end at 11:15 A.M. on Easter. It goes on all
through the year. Every Sunday is a triumphant festival of hope
because Christ lives, and every day is a diminutive Easter. Our
congregation is made up of many "Easter people" who could not
live through an hour of any day of the year without the courage
which comes from knowing that Christ's Resurrection has defeated death, frustration, and despair. Christ's death on the Cross
assures us that we are forgiven and can live a life of freedom and
joy, but it is the Resurrection which gives us the power to live
that new life in daily pressures. The celebration of Christ's victory is for every moment, relationship, situation, or problem.
The realization of Christ's Resurrection has enabled our own.
We are alive forever and therefore truly alive right now; we have
died to our own control of our lives and have been resurrected
to a new dimension of living; we have become the post-
resurrection dwelling of the living Lord; we will never be alone

again, for he is with us and in us; we can face anything because the same power which raised Jesus from the dead is at work in us!

That was the emancipating drumbeat which sounded in the soul of the Apostle Paul as he strode courageously into Jerusalem and the clutches of his enemies. The Resurrection was his only reason for going, his only hope of power to withstand what he knew would happen there, his only message to proclaim. There is no other way to explain the audacity we feel in the brave Apostle. He lived in two realms: the visible, transitory world of change, hatred, corruption, negativism, and death; and the invisible realm of the Resurrection in fellowship with a risen Savior who had defeated death, sin, the powers of darkness, and discouragement. That's why he could write the Roman Christians: "May the God of hope fill you with all joy and peace in your faith, that by the power of the Holy Spirit, your whole life and outlook may be radiant with hope" (Rom. 15:13, Phillips).

The center of Paul's radiant hope was the Resurrection. It was the heart of the gospel for him. A few months before entering Jerusalem, at Ephesus, he had written the Corinthians that without the Resurrection there would be no hope. "If there is no resurrection of the dead, then Christ has not been raised; if Christ has not been raised, then our preaching is in vain and your faith is in vain. . . . If Christ has not been raised, your faith is futile and you are still in your sins. . . . If for this life only we have hoped in Christ, we are of all men most to be pitied" (1 Cor. 15:13–19). The Cross without the Resurrection is just another tragic death of a good man; faith is empty; the Christian life is a pitiful, self-generated wish-dream. But crowned by the Resurrection, and enabled by the resurrected Lord, the daily life of a Christian is liberated by the Cross and has abundant assurance, now and forever.

That fact alone enables us to understand the emotional stability, mental outlook, and incredible confidence in Paul when his faith was under fire in trial and imprisonment. Anyone with a lesser hope would have been despondent and despairing. Not Paul. He had known persistent sickness, rejection by his people, resistance from fellow Christians, and constant physical persecution. Something he wrote just before the trial by fire in Jerusalem gives us the key to understand how the Resurrection and the present, powerful Savior kept him from giving up. "We are pressed on every side by trouble, but not crushed and broken. We are perplexed because we don't know why things happen as they do, but we don't give up and quit. We are hunted down, but God never abandons us. We get knocked down, but we get up again and keep going. These bodies of ours are constantly facing death just as Jesus did; so it is clear to all that it is only the living Christ within [who keeps us safe]" (2 Cor. 4:8–10, *The Living Bible*). That's the reality of the Resurrection!

Acts 21:15 through chapter 26 gives us Luke's dramatic account of Paul's arrest, imprisonment, and repeated trials in Jerusalem and Caesarea on the way to Rome. I have found it helpful to deal with this passage as a whole. The central theme is the Resurrection: The hope of the Resurrection brought Paul back to Jerusalem; the truth of the Resurrection was the conclusive thrust of his witness in each trial; the power of the Resurrection was his source of strength in prison. Through the events of Luke's account in these chapters I want to show how the resiliency of the Resurrection we see in Paul's faith can be ours today. I believe that the same uncrushable courage which springs back after difficulty is available to us today because Christ lives.

The first aspect of Resurrection resiliency is shown when Paul arrived in Jerusalem and went to the leaders of the church. His report of what had been happening in his ministry is filled with joy—amazing, after all he'd been through. With excitement he told James and the church fathers what the uplifted, ubiquitous Lord had done among the Gentiles. They rejoiced with Paul, but he also presented them with a problem. They were disturbed about the conflict which was raging over his ministry and the rumors which were flying everywhere that he was telling Jews among the Gentiles to forsake the Law of Moses. The particular concern of the Church was for the converted Jews who had swelled the ranks of Christians in Jerusalem. Something had to be done to clarify the Apostle's position. What they recommended may have helped the Jewish Christian, but it brought Paul into direct conflict with the Sanhedrin. But note how Paul's resiliency through the resurrected Christ released him to comply with the request of the Church. The Living Christ enabled freedom in Paul to participate in a compromise for unity. After all he'd been through it must have seemed silly, if not stupid. But the Resurrection had made Paul responsive. Everything mattered because nothing mattered except the Easter miracle.

Following the instructions of the church leaders, Paul gave support not only with his physical presence but his money to four Jewish Christians who were taking the Nazarite vow in the temple. An expression of gratitude, the vow involved abstention from eating meat, drinking wine, and cutting of hair. The final seven days were to be spent in the temple courts. At the conclusion of the time, offerings were to be made of a year-old lamb as a sin offering, a ram as a peace offering, a meat-and-drink offering, and a basket of unleavened bread and cakes. (No wonder a sponsor was needed to pay for their time away from work and for the expensive offerings.) Finally, the supplicant's hair was to be shaved as an outward sign of the inner oblation. Paul's participation was meant by the Church to be a final and vivid affirmation of the Law of Moses for both the confused Hebrew Christians in the Church and the priests in the temple.

Paul's resilience seemed to have no limits as he cooperated wholeheartedly in the efforts at reconciliation. The Resurrection does that to a person. We are free to be flexible and adjustable as a part of the fellowship. That kind of maturity comes from ultimate trust in the present Savior. Paul did not demand to do things his way. Liberated by the expulsive power of a great vision, he was on his way to Rome for the Risen Master! His winsome willingness to do anything which would strengthen the ministry of the Church in Jerusalem was a direct result. What the Sanhedrin did to distort his obedience to the fellowship would not in any way diminish the evidence of the freedom of the Resurrection in his witness.

But the Church's reconciliation strategy backfired. It was Pentecost time and Jerusalem was filled with Jews. Some had come from the Roman province of Asia that Paul had just left. They were more than pilgrims to the Holy City; they were determined to destroy the Apostle Paul, once and for all. They had seen him in the temple but had also watched him in Jerusalem with a Gentile convert from Asia named Trophimus. They put the two things together to make an untrue but inflammatory accusation: they charged Paul with taking Trophimus into the sacred precincts of the temple. They were sure they had the ancient Law on their side: "No man of alien race is to enter within the

balustrade and fence that goes around the temple, and if anyone
is taken in the act, let him know that he has himself to blame
for the penalty of death that follows." It was a lie, of course, but
the Jews knew that the Romans allowed them to carry out the
death sentence for the offense.

The Asian Jews incited a riot, supported by the leaders of
Israel, crying out, "Men of Israel, help! This is the man who
is teaching men everywhere against the people and the law and
this place; moreover, he also brought Greeks into the temple,
and has defiled this holy place" (Acts 21:28). Taking "justice"
into their own hands, they seized Paul and dragged him out of
the temple and proceeded to try to kill him with beating and
stoning. Jerusalem was thrown into confusion, which brought
out the Roman tribune, Claudius Lysias, with centurions and
soldiers. Seeing that Paul was about to be beaten to death but
unable to make out the charge from the angry, jeering mob,
Lysias interceded and arrested him. His soldiers chained the
Apostle and actually had to carry his broken and bleeding body
out of the mob. The tribune quickly ordered him taken to the
Tower of Antonia, connected to the outer court of the temple
on the northwestern side. The crowds followed with bloodthirsty
cries, "Away with him!"

But now look at the physical resiliency of the resurrected
Lord in Paul! As he was being carried away, under the immediate protection of the tribune, who had mistaken Paul for an
Egyptian leader of the Assassins, Paul identified himself as a
Jew, a citizen of Tarsus, and begged to speak to the people again.
Lysias must have had mingled feelings of amazement and admiration at that. What grit, courage! The power of the Lord
living in Paul is shown not only in physical endurance and spiritual courage; but in charismatic prowess when he is blessed to
speak again. When Paul stood on the steps and motioned with
his hand for attention and began to speak in Hebrew, a great
hush fell on the crowd. His body was swollen from beating and
blood streamed down his face, but his full powers quickly sprang
back to full force.

There is an indomitable, artesian physical resiliency in those
who have realized the Resurrection. It has been true through
Christian history. Not only does the indwelling Lord release
latent, untapped energies, he miraculously infuses us with strength

beyond our own. I have known this repeatedly. When I am too
exhausted to move, the Lord provides the strength to do what
he has willed. When I feel beaten by circumstances or problems and the courage to go on seems to have run out, I realize
that I have used only the surface resources of human energy,
and beneath are the limitless powers of the Lord.

Paul knew this better than any man who has ever lived. When
Lysias watched his prisoner hold the crowd in rapt attention,
he wondered how Paul could do it, beaten as he was. The
tribune realized that this was no ordinary man he had arrested.

Paul's defense quickly outlines his heritage as a Jew, his training as a Pharisee under Gamaliel, his zealous vigilance of the
observance of the Law, and his persecution of the Way. Then he
boldly told the crowd of his encounter with the resurrected
Messiah and his commission to bear witness to all men. Resilience grew as he spoke. But when he stated that "all men" included Gentiles, the mob's wrath blazed up again. "Away with
such a fellow from the earth! For he ought not to live." They
expressed their rage according to Oriental custom: shouting,
waving garments, and throwing dust into the air.

Once again Lysias had to step in to save his prisoner. This
time he took no chances. To obtain a confession of what Paul
had been up to in Jerusalem, he ordered Paul imprisoned and
scourged. (Scourging was beating with leather thongs inter-
twined with bone and metal.) In preparation Paul was stretched
out and tied. But what well-timed sagacity Paul displayed.
Believing himself destined for Rome, he had no intention of
surrendering his life-verve in this manner. Just as the thongs
were lifted for the first strikes, Paul cried out something which
turned the centurion extortioner pale with fear: "Is it lawful for
you to scourge a man who is a Roman citizen and uncon-
demned?" (Scourging a Roman citizen could mean death to the
one inflicting the punishment). The centurion dropped his whip
and ran to the tribune's chambers. "What are you about to do?
This man is a Roman citizen." Now Lysias and the soldier were
both frightened. The tribune was further amazed at his prisoner
when he questioned Paul with the respect due a Roman citizen.
How could Lysias explain the resourcefulness of this man of
Tarsus? He was not physically powerful, his physique was not

impressive, and yet he seemed unconquerable by the emotional and physical strain he'd been through.

Lysias, determined to get to the bottom of the charge against this remarkable prisoner, arranged a hearing before the Jewish rulers of the Sanhedrin. Perhaps he hoped that would end his responsibility for this strange mixture of Jew and Roman he had in chains. But once again Paul astounded him. Completely unafraid and unimpressed with the imposing array of rulers, Paul strode in before them and began to speak. "Brethren, I have lived before God in all good conscience up to this day." The tempers of the Sanhedrin were raw, and Paul barely got the words out before Ananias ordered him to be struck on the mouth for blasphemy. Now we see the fearlessness of his resiliency. With prophetic boldness like that of an Old Testament prophet he faced his accuser. "God will strike you, you whitewashed wall! Are you sitting to judge me according to your law, and yet contrary to the law you order me to be struck?" Paul could not have used a more inflammatory term. A whitewashed wall! It was the custom to whitewash tombs containing dead bodies to alert an Israelite of the danger of ceremonial defilement incurred by touching the dead. Ananias deserved the defamatory appellation. He was a glutton, an unjust ruler, and a capricious quisling in league with Rome. Yet, Paul had overstepped. In the intervening years since Paul had been employed by the Sanhedrin to persecute the Christians in Jerusalem, Ananias had risen to power. The law forbade speaking evil of the high priest, and Paul was unaware of Ananias's new position. Paul quickly acknowledged his indiscretion, but he did not retract his accusation! The record stood.

Now Paul presses on to his real purpose and passion. He knew that the Sanhedrin was made up of Sadducees who did not believe in resurrection or a life beyond death, and that the Pharisees did. He wanted them to know exactly where he stood. The unmistakable certainty in the Apostle's faith not only of resurrection, but Christ's Resurrection, is stated pointedly. He would return to the confidence and courage of that unvarnished verity again and again in the months ahead. Here before the Sanhedrin, the highest court of his people, he wanted to expose the vibrant pulsebeat of Christianity: "With respect to the hope

and the resurrection of the dead I am on trial." Two inseparable
realities: Jesus the Christ was the fulfillment of the messianic
hope; he had been raised from the dead and was alive. Paul's
own experience of this tandem truth gave him assurance that
because Christ was alive, he was a recipient of eternal life that
death could not end. He could take anything with that hope.

The Sanhedrin was thrown into new conflict over an old
dispute. The Sadducees and Pharisees lined up on different sides
of the issue. Old loyalties brought some of the Pharisees to Paul's
defense, embittering the Sadducees. The truth had divided to
conquer. The dissension between the rulers took the heat off
Paul, but once again violence ensued and the tribune had to
step in to protect his Roman citizen prisoner. But Paul had made
his point. He had accomplished the purpose for which he had
come to Jerusalem: to witness to the power of Christ's Resurrection.

Back in the barracks the following night Paul received Resurrection resoluteness again from the Living Jesus. He had held
the line in his belief that Jesus was alive and now the same
Jesus came to him to give him assurance. Unswerving witness
to the truth was rewarded by undeniable experience of the
reality. Luke tells us that "the Lord stood by him." What more
did Paul need than that? What greater help can any of us have
than that when our faith is under fire? What the Lord said to
Paul he says to us. "Take courage, for as you have testified about
me at Jerusalem, so must you bear witness also at Rome" (Acts
23:11). The words are drenched with dynamic strength. "Stay
in there, Paul; I am with you, this is neither the worst nor the
last of it. We're going to Rome together! Keep your attention on
that! Don't give up. We are going to penetrate the center of
political power at Rome and change the world. I am in charge;
trust me!"

With that assurance the drumbeat of the Master was quickened in Paul. He could face anything knowing he was not alone.
After that Paul was all the more determined.

But so were the Jews. Forty of them banded to keep the
pressure on the rulers who had briefly lost their determination
in internal conflict. Hatred has its twisted vows, and they made
one now, swearing not to eat or drink until Paul was dead. A
hunger strike is a powerful pressure ploy. This one brought the

Sanhedrin back into line as they devised a clever scheme to get
Paul back before them so that the forty vigilantes could ambush
and kill him as he was being brought from the prison. But the
resurrected Lord's network of people in Jerusalem were also at
work. When word of the intrigue reached the church, Paul's
nephew was dispatched to warn Paul. He in turn sent the young
man directly to the tribune. This settled it for Lysias. Paul was
too hot to handle in Jerusalem. There was nothing to do but send
him to Caesarea to be judged by Felix, the Roman governor.
We are amazed by the precautions the tribune took to protect
his prisoner, assigning two hundred soldiers, seventy horsemen,
and two hundred spearmen as guards for the journey. Actually, there were four hundred and seventy-one watching over
this Roman Jew who would not give up his belief that Jesus
was alive and loved all men, Jews and Gentiles alike: the soldiers,
spearsmen, horsemen and the Savior of the World! The Lord of
Paul's Resurrection message was keeping watch over his own.
No wonder his faith was resilient!

The account of Paul's repeated arraignments and trials in
Caesarea is a study in lugubrious Roman jurisprudence and
human befuddlement. First one governor and then another
tried to handle the case, while still seeking to maintain the
Roman law and keep peace with the rebellious Jews. None succeeded.

Felix, the first to try, was a complex, ambitious man with a
distorted record. It was through the influence of his brother
Pallos, a favorite of Nero, that Felix had risen from being a
slave to a powerful governor. He never lived down his humble
origins, however. The Roman historian Tacitus said of him, "He
exercised the prerogatives of a king with the spirit of a slave."
His lust for power had moved him through three propitious
marriages, the last to Drusilla, the daughter of Herod Agrippa I.
His record of intrigue and greed places him in sharp contrast
to the brilliant Pharisee of Tarsus he was destined to try to judge.
Little did the unscrupulous Felix know that he, not Paul, was on
trial—and before eternal court.

It took only five days for Ananias and the Jews to track Paul
to Caesarea. They brought with them Tertullus, one of the most
eloquent and clever trial lawyers of Jerusalem, to present their
case before Felix. But neither Tertullus's flattery of Felix nor

his flagrant demeaning of Paul was a match for the Apostle's brilliant witness. Paul stated his case flatly: "With respect to the resurrection of the dead I am on trial before you this day." He held the line, however great the forces opposing him in the verbal tug-of-war.

Paul won the day: the governor returned him to custody and showed his partiality by allowing Paul's friends the privilege of visiting him. Felix was obviously moved and bargained for more time. He was knowledgeable about Christianity and apparently well aware that he should be cautious in any quick decision. More than that, he wanted to learn more about this strange hope in the Resurrection Paul talked about. Along with his wife Drusilla, he listened to Paul privately on several occasions although his capacity to hear the clear message about Christ was muddled by the dubious quality of his own moral life and his mixed emotions. His interest was piqued by the power of Christ, but punctured by incisive justice, self-control and future judgment Paul proclaimed. His adulterous relationship to Drusilla was now under question, something the governor had not bargained for in what he thought would be an entertaining encounter. But beyond that, his capacity to hear the gospel was blocked by his hidden agenda of hoping to be able to barter Paul's freedom for money. He missed a God-given opportunity to experience the abundant life and live forever because he did not want his past disturbed nor his motives purified. How sad. Two years later his attempts at clever intrigue got him into trouble with Rome over the way he handled a conflict between Jews and Greeks in Caesarea. He was deposed and transferred, leaving his post without either political or spiritual power.

Festus, a different breed of governor, replaced Felix. A much more honest and just man, he was nevertheless no more successful in resolving the sticky case. He had hardly set foot on his new territory as governor when he was besieged by the leaders of the Jews. Over two years had passed and still their anger burned white hot. Eight days' visit in Jerusalem convinced the new governor that he had better try the case in the relative safety and sanity of Caesarea, but the trial brought no more resolution than before. There were the same absurd charges from the Jews and the same assured courage from Paul. In one momentous difference this time, however, Paul's declaration of innocence

ended with an appeal to be tried by Caesar. Every Roman citizen
had that right. And Paul was under orders from his Master to go
to Rome. Festus seemed relieved. He would get out of responsibility to judge the nasty mess much more easily than he thought.
"You have appealed to Caesar; to Caesar you shall go."

But one further scene remained in the dramatic act exposing
Paul's resurrection resiliency in Caesarea, one further encounter
that would fulfill the Lord's prophecy and promise for his followers: "Beware of men; for they will deliver you up to councils,
and flog you in their synagogues, and you will be dragged before
governors and kings for my sake, to bear testimony before them
and the Gentiles. When they deliver you up, do not be anxious
how you are to speak or what you are to say; for what you are
to say will be given to you in that hour; for it is not you who
speak, but the Spirit of your Father speaking through you"
(Matt. 10:17–20). Paul had known all things that the Lord
predicted and promised, except one. King Herod Agrippa II was
now to fulfill that prophecy, and the Lord's promise of Holy
Spirit–inspired eloquence would never be more evident.

Agrippa II and incestuously dependent Bernice arrived in
Caesarea to welcome Festus. What happened to him there
would almost persuade him to become a Christian.

The Herods had had a strange entangling relationship with
Christ. Herod Agrippa II was the last of the Herods to meddle
with Christ or his followers. His great-grandfather was the King
Herod who had feared the birth of the Christ-child and murdered the male children in the vicinity of Bethlehem. The grand-
uncle of Agrippa II had murdered John the Baptist; and his
father, Agrippa I, had executed James, imprisoned Peter, and
been eaten with worms as a punishment for allowing people to
worship him as a god right there in Caesarea (Acts 12:20–23).
Bernice was a sister of Drusilla, Felix's wife, and therefore
actually sister of Agrippa II. What a sick, infested family tree!

After Festus briefed the king on general affairs, he brought
his attention to the strange case before him concerning Paul of
Tarsus. He knew that Agrippa had personal knowledge of the
Jewish religion and supposed he might help him in dealing
with the complexities of the troublesome Pharisee. The problem
was clear: the Sanhedrin would not relent and Paul would not
recant. To complicate matters, Festus told the king, Paul had

appealed to Caesar. Like his family before him, Herod could not resist the impulse to get involved in something to do with Christ or his followers.

The sheer drama of Paul's appearance before Agrippa and Bernice grips our imagination. The king and his sister were arrayed in the splendor of the purple robes of royalty. Festus, in honor of the king, was probably wearing his scarlet governor's robe. The court was decorated for the occasion and guarded by captains, centurions, and legionnaires. Now picture the Apostle as he is brought before these imposing earthly powers. He is stooped, small in stature, and physically unimposing. The chains dangle about his gnarled hands. But the expression on his face is magnetic and his eyes glint in majesty. When he speaks, his voice cuts through the pretentious elegance of the Hall of Audience built by Herod the Great. Paul was neither impressed by Agrippa nor afraid of the Roman power.

After Festus stated the case and Agrippa gave his permission to speak, Paul rose to the occasion with soaring rhetoric. He retold his story and once again proclaimed the power of the Resurrection. "And for this hope I am accused by Jews, O king! Why is it thought incredible by any of you that God raises the dead?" His heavenly vision was not denied. "To this day I have had the help that comes from God and so I stand here testifying both to small and great, saying nothing but what the prophets and Moses said would come to pass: that the Christ must suffer, and that, by being the first to rise from the dead, he would proclaim light both to the people and to the Gentiles."

It was obvious that Agrippa was moved and disturbed by the gospel. The resurrected Lord drove Paul's words like arrows into the king's heart. He was convicted and unsettled. But what could he say before that auspicious gathering in the magnificence of his grandfather's Great Hall? He must uphold the dignity of his depleted family name! Festus realized how rattled the king had become with the situation. "Paul," Festus said, "your great learning is turning you mad."

Paul, unimpressed with Festus' ridicule, did not take his eyes off Agrippa. Holding intense eye-to-eye contact with the king, he responded to Festus. "I am not mad, most excellent Festus, but I am speaking the sober truth. For the king knows about these things, and *to him* I speak freely; for I am persuaded that none of these things has escaped his notice, for this was not done in a corner" (26:25, emphasis mine).

Now note how Paul moves in on Herod. "King Agrippa, do you believe in the prophets? I know you believe." Agrippa knew where Paul was leading. If he believed in the prophets, he would believe in the Messiah, and that would demand a decision about Jesus and the Resurrection. What could he say? Paul was leading him up to an encounter with the Lord and he knew it. What could he do? The gift of faith was leaping within him, but then he remembered who he was and where he was. Enough of this! "In a short time you think to make me a Christian!"

Paul's response is the result of the Resurrection resiliency in him, the undeniable desire for all to find what he has found: "Whether short or long, I would to God that not only you but also all who hear me this day might become such as I am— except for these chains." That's the power of personal witness, the dynamic of relational evangelism. Unless we can say that we want everyone to know what we know and become what Christ's Resurrection has done for us, we have missed the excitement of the Christian life. Can we say that we want people to become what we are? Many of us would shrink from that, unsatisfied by what we have allowed Christ to do in us. We would not want others to have the same incomplete, unsatisfying, inadequate experience of Christ we have! Be as we are? Do we want a duplication not just of our convictions, but our character? Paul wanted both for Agrippa. If we do not want to multiply what we are, there is something wrong with what we are!

Though Festus and Agrippa did not have the courage to respond to Paul's challenge, they could not deny the admiration they felt for him. The impact of the gospel was upon them. They did not have courage enough to believe in his Christ, but they did have conviction enough to resist pressure from the Sanhedrin, saying to one another, "This man is doing nothing to deserve death or imprisonment." Festus even went so far as to say, "This man could have been set free if he had not appealed to Caesar." Roman law required that once the appeal had been made by a Roman citizen, it must be carried out. Paul must go to Rome. But only Paul knew the real reason—

not Roman law or even his appeal: Christ had destined him to go to Rome, and neither the angry Jews nor all the legions of the emperor could keep him from his heavenly vision.

Getting Paul in and out of Jerusalem and Caesarea has renewed my desire never to let the celebration of the Resurrection close at 11:15 A.M. on Easter Sunday. Something has happened to me as I have lived in the Apostle's skin through his two years in prison and on trial. It has reminded me of the ebullient power of the Resurrection. Christ is alive! His words echo in my heart: "Because I live you shall live also." His Resurrection makes possible my own. Nothing's impossible now. The crushed hopes and dreams, the depleted energy and vision, the collapsed determination and daring all spring back to life. I have rediscovered the resiliency of the Resurrection. My deepest prayer now is that you have too!

CHAPTER 25

Anchors in the Storm

And fearing that we might run on the
rocks, they let out four anchors from the
stern, and prayed for day to come (Acts 27:29).
Acts 27

Picture the situation; catch the moving drama. Paul is
the only courageous man on the bridge of the ship. The
captain is frozen with fear; the centurion assigned to get the
Apostle to Rome is immobilized by anxiety. Paul alone has
the presence of mind to calm the crew, the soldiers, and the
other prisoners. He has taken command of the ship because he
knows the Lord is the Captain of their fate.

The cumbersome grain ship was being driven before the wind
across the Adriatic. Though she was one hundred and forty
feet long, thirty-six feet wide and took a draught of over thirty-
three feet, she was out of control. The two paddle rudders
were impotent against the raging sea and the relentless wind.
The one mast with the square sail could not head into the
wind. To try to save the ship, they had strapped the hull with
hawsers and drawn them up tight with winches, making of the
ship a wrapped-up package.

But still they were in danger. The wind seemed merciless.
The sun had not shown through the winter clouds for days
and the stars were hidden by the black mists of the night. The
ship tossed helplessly in the unknown sea. The tumult of the
sea matched the raging storms of fear, both in the seasoned
sailors and the battle-hardened Roman soldiers. Only Paul's
soul was as calm as a windless pond. The prisoner had become
the fearless captain because of his faithful trust in the One who
is Lord of land and sea.

Paul had warned them not to set out to sea. But Julius the centurion had wanted to get his prisoner to Rome before winter, and the captain of the ship he had requisitioned was determined to get his cargo to Italy for high profit. Caution had been thrown to the winds. Now the winter winds were making their reply.

Weeks before, Paul, with Aristarchus, his personal servant, and Luke, his beloved physician, had boarded a ship at Caesarea under the careful guard of Julius and his especially selected legionnaires. Julius must have been impressed that Paul was permitted to have his friends accompany him. Only special prisoners were allowed such privilege. Aristarchus, who had distinguished himself for his devotion to Paul and his loyalty to Christ in the disputation with the silversmiths of Ephesus, had never left Paul's side through the two and a half difficult years in Jerusalem and Caesarea. Luke attended to the Apostle's physical and spiritual needs. His faithful friendship enabled him to see Paul through each difficulty and to be eyewitness to this most dramatic sea voyage in Scripture.

The journey was difficult from the beginning. From Caesarea, they coasted up the ragged Mediterranean coast to Sidon. After a brief stop, the west wind made the journey along the coast of Cilicia possible only by moving under the protection of Cyprus. At Myra, a port on the coast of Lycia, they transferred to the Egyptian grain vessel bound for Italy.

The normal course straight across the Aegean was impossible because of the treacherous winter winds which were already evident. It was a poor time to be at sea. Luke tells us (Acts 27:9) it was after the Feast of Atonement, making it the first half of October. Sailing was difficult after September and almost impossible by November. Ships seldom sailed the area until after March. The cloudy weather made charting a course almost foolhardy. The lack of either sextant or compass at this time made the sun and stars absolutely necessary for navigation.

Paul advised that they stop and stay at a harbor called Fair Havens on the Island of Crete and trust the winter wind no further. But the centurion and the captain could not be dissuaded. They wanted to strike out for Phoenix, also a harbor on Crete, to winter there. A brief southerly wind gave them false confidence and they coasted along the shores of Crete.

Then the ill wind Paul had predicted hit them. It was a greatly feared northeaster called the *Euraquilo,* well known to ancient sailors. For days the gale tossed the ship like a twig in the sea. Gear and cargo were thrown overboard in a frantic effort to stabilize the ship. Crew and passengers were willing to give up anything to stay alive. But at last, they even gave up hope. Crashing into the Syrtis Sands, a graveyard of many ships off the coast of North Africa, was a fate accepted as inevitable. Terror pervaded the ship, gripping all on board.

All except Paul. The resurrected Lord was his helmsman. Christ had brought the bow of his life around into the wind of conflict before and given Paul his expert guidance through tempestuous seas. The treacherous winds at sea hardly matched the voyage of vicissitudes he had been through already. And he was sure of one thing: at the right time, when he needed the Master most, he would come with assurance and protection.

The Apostle was not disappointed. He knew that he was as close to the ever-present Savior at sea as on land. When all on board had given up hope, a messenger of the Lord gave him what he needed: courage, assurance that his heavenly vision of going to Rome would be accomplished, and that all those with him would be saved. The message of the Lord was clear and undeniable: "Do not be afraid, Paul; you must stand before Caesar; and lo, God has granted you all those who sail with you." His prayers were answered!

Then Paul took command of the ship, his words ringing above the howling wind. Look at his face, his immovable stature, his radiant, commanding leadership as he stands before the cowering seasick crew and the fear-racked legionnaires. Now listen to his voice, clanging like a harbor bell: "I now bid you take heart; for there will be no loss of life among you, but only of the ship. For this very night there stood by me an angel of the God to whom I belong and whom I worship, and he said, 'Do not be afraid!' "

Like the assurance of a guiding foghorn the words pierced the souls of all on the ship. They had been aware that they were carrying a most unusual passenger, but none had expected this. Who was this Jew in chains? As they listened in rapt attention his words made their confidence leap. "So take heart, men, for I have faith in God that it will be exactly as I have

been told. But we shall have to run on some island." Better
than death in the Syrtis Sands, they thought!

Now they were on their feet. Paul's faith had quickened
them, and in renewed hope they began listening for the sound
of the sea against the breakers of a shore. Soon the most experienced among them shouted with almost inexpressible excitement that they were indeed nearing land. That gave them
new energy to sound the depth of the sea. Paul was right! They
sounded twenty fathoms; then soon, fifteen. Then the captain,
now back on his feet and alert, cried out, "The rocks! We're
heading for the rocks. We can't make it at night. Throw out the
anchors over the stern so the bow is heading for shore if we
have to beach her!"

Actually, though they did not know it, they were off the
coast of the Island of Malta and not the Syrtis Sands, as they
had feared.

Now follows one of my favorite passages in Acts. Luke's nautical account spares no detail, but the symbolism of his next
sentence explodes my mind. "And fearing that we might run on
the rocks, they let out four anchors from the stern, and prayed
for the dawn to come" (27:29). Paul already had given them
anchors for their souls in the words of the angel. Now they let
out four anchors to save the ship and prayed for day to come.

When I put the angel's message and the stern anchors together, I find an amazing message of hope and courage for the
dark night of difficulty and the restless seas of life. An exposition of the Lord's message to Paul provides me with anchors
to hold my ship off the rocks as I pray for the darkness of any
impossible situations to lift and for morning to break. I want
to share with you the anchors the Lord has given me out of
his encouragement to Paul that stormy, windswept night.

The first anchor is the intervention itself—a messenger from
the Lord, perfectly timed to arrive when all human resources
had run out. That anchor had kept Paul off the rocks before.
In fact, all of Acts is filled with the stabilizing anchorage of
the propitious presence of the Lord. He was always as close as
the cry for help. Throughout Acts, Luke's interchangeable terms
for the Presence—the Lord, the Spirit of Jesus, the Holy Spirit
or angelic messenger—tumble forth with little thought of carefully ordered theological formulation. The Lord had many

ways of getting through to his people. Fellow believers, circumstances, difficulties, and even enemies were used by the omnip-
otent, omnipresent Savior to guide his people. Paul's life was
punctuated by penetrations of his power. He had learned that
tragedy was but the prelude to a new intervention of the Presence. He depended on the Lord, not only for his salvation by
grace, but for his protection by providence.

The anchor of the presence of the Lord was held by the inter-
twining, unbreakable cable of his love and forgiveness. To know
that Christ is with us is a beautiful thing, but to know that he
holds us secure with unfaltering acceptance and forgiveness is
sublimely something more. The anchor is shaped in the form
of the Cross, and the cables which hold us are his own words,
"I love you and cannot, will not, let you go."

This anchor stabilizes us in any storm because it reminds us
that we are loved eternally, that this life is but a brief interlude
in forever, that death has no power over us, and that nothing
can separate us from our Lord. That's why Paul could write,
"I know the one in whom I trust, and I am sure that He is
able to safely guard all that I have given Him until the day of
His return. Hold tightly to the pattern of truth I taught you,
especially concerning the faith and love Christ Jesus offers you.
Guard well the splendid, God-given ability you received as a
gift from the Holy Spirit who lives within you" (2 Tim. 1:12–
14, *The Living Bible*).

There's an anchor to throw to the depths of life's difficulties!
Cast it overboard at the first sound of the rocks. When your
sounding rope signals danger, get it into the sea. Love alone
will hold us off the rocks! Then we can say with Paul, "This
doesn't mean, of course, that we have only hope of future joys—
we can be full of joy here and now even in our trials and
troubles" (Rom. 5:3, Phillips).

But the Lord's messenger gave Paul more than one anchor
that night. The anchor of faith was also offered. "Do not be
afraid!" was also the courage-instilling word. He had been told
that before, repeatedly. It was Jesus' constant anchor offered
to his disciples for the storms without and within. The Lord's
whole ministry had been announced by the angels' words, "Fear
not: for, behold, I bring you tidings of great joy!" (Luke 2:10,
KJV). Faith as abandoned trust was the anchor he lived, died,

and rose to offer his people. It was this anchor which enabled Paul to say to the Philippians, "I can do all things through Christ who strengthens me" (Phil. 4:13).

We all know fear. It's a part of living. Some of it is creative. But the anguished fear which grips us in life when we worry about people, present happiness or lack of it, and the uncertain future, can be released only by faith. Our Lord comes on board a turbulently tossed life and says, "All right, what's the worst that can happen? If it happened, would you in any way be separated from me? Do you think that this thing has more power than I? Throw over the anchor of faith. Have no fear!" When the anchor sinks to the deep and we feel it catch hold securely, we know that peril must always be measured against the promises and power of the Lord.

> No water can swallow the ship where lies
> The Master of ocean and earth and skies.*

The anchor of faith can be tested. Pull on the cable. Don't you feel its security? The psalmist knew what that taut, tough cable felt like.

> Then they cried to the Lord in their trouble,
>   and he delivered them from their distress;
> he made the storm be still
>   and the waves of the sea were hushed.
> Then they were glad because they had quiet,
>   and he brought them to their desired haven.
> Let them thank the Lord for his steadfast love,
>   for his wonderful works to the sons of men!
>   (Psalm 107:28–31)

But the anchor of faith holds even when the waves splash over the hull and there is no haven in sight. The Lord does not allow us to drift in the storm which seems never to end. The secret of the anchor of faith is that stillness invades our souls and the true haven is given within.

The third anchor the Lord offered gave Paul his incredible confidence. It was the anchor of a sense of destiny. "Paul, you

---

* Mary Baker, "Peace! Be Still."

must stand before Caesar!" He would be protected for the fulfillment of the Lord's purpose.

The anchor of destiny is offered to each of us. It is the reason
we were born. When we hold it before us and then cast it into
the raging sea, it too catches us and holds us off the rocks
of discouragement and despair. Purposelessness always causes
a dangerous drift. But once we become sure of why we are
alive, we can take any storm. The holding, anchoring power
of purpose is liberating. It takes our attention from present
trouble and frees us to get back to essentials. Often we become
more aware of problems than our purpose. Those are the dangerous times. Life is more than solving problems; it's grasping
opportunities the Lord has made available. Our purpose is both
general and specific. The reason we have been given new life
in Christ is to introduce him to others. The specific focus of
that is our unique assignment from the Lord.

I talked to a Christian businessman recently whose life was
full of difficulties to be sorted out. His business was demanding all of his energy and time. One upset was quickly followed
by another. "When's the last time you spoke to someone about
Christ?" I asked. "Months!" was his response. "I don't have
time or opportunity with all these problems." I suggested that
he put renewed focus on communicating Christ and trust that
the problems would work out. It made all the difference for
him. He had gotten so bogged down that he was missing the
adventure for which he was born and reborn. Then he adopted
a slogan that's worked for me. "Find an ultimate purpose—
give yourself to it and let it use you!" Robert Louis Stevenson
caught the power of the anchor of purpose: "To be what you
are, and to become what you are capable of becoming, is the
only end of life." For me that means to live in Christ, to be
filled with Christ, and to be used by Christ. To know the Lord
and make him known is a stable anchor. Michelangelo said, "It
is only well with me when I have a chisel in my hand." It is
well with a Christian when he is sharing his faith.

Paul's recall to go to Rome did two things for him. It reminded him that he had something bigger to do than survive
that storm at sea. But also it convinced him that he would
survive to serve the Lord in Rome.

The final anchor this passage suggests is a combination of

the promise of God and prayer which grasps it. It is the anchor of peace. The angel specifically promised safety, so "they let out four anchors and prayed for day to come." There are times when there is nothing to do but claim the promises and pray for dawn to break. This kind of prayer is sustenance as well as survival. It infuses power to wait patiently with endurance. That's not easy, especially for one who wants solutions and resolutions yesterday. One of the greatest gifts of the Holy Spirit is calm resignation during periods of waiting. Paul spoke of the word of God dwelling in us richly. His word in the storm, "Peace I give to you," anchors our turbulent hearts. But peace is inseparable from hope. When our hope is in our Lord, we can be at peace. The author of Hebrews said it plainly: "We who have fled for refuge . . . have strong encouragement to seize the hope set before us. We have this as a sure and steadfast anchor of the soul, a hope. . . ."(Heb. 6:18–19).

The anchor of prayer really makes all the other three anchors secure. Through prayer we are put in touch with the Presence and we experience love; we are liberated from fear by the displacing power of faith; we rediscover our destiny and purpose.

But the night can seem long. All of us have had times when we wondered if dawn would ever come. Then we come to a crucial discovery. The long night is bright with the Light of the World. And to those in whom Christ dwells night is not the darkness of absence of light. Morning has broken in Christ. He greets us across the wild and tempestuous sea. "Peace, be still; it is I!"

We all have the same anchors which made Paul the captain of the ship. Morning did come. The ship's passengers and crew were not on the sands of the seaman's graveyard but the rocks of Malta. All made it to shore safely. The Lord was faithful to his promise and Paul could go on to Rome. And so can we.

CHAPTER 26

The New Chapter on the Book of Acts

Acts 28

When I did graduate studies in Scotland, I had the thrilling experience of sailing on the *Queen Mary* from New York to Southampton. She was a magnificent ship. Though my student's budget allowed only double "D" deck, I used to spend most of my time up on the top deck walking with the cold salt winds blowing in my face. I can remember admiring the gallant determination with which the historic craft cut through the high waves. With typical British efficiency the perfectly organized crew kept everything working in perfect order to achieve the destination. As I walked on deck I would try to recapture the feeling of what it must have been like aboard the "Mary" as a lovely pleasure vessel and then as a troop ship carefully evading the German submarines. I couldn't help comparing that beautifully built craft to the church for which I was preparing myself to be a pastor.

The next time I saw the *Queen Mary* was as a museum piece, docked in the Long Beach harbor. Her last voyage had been around the world and then into the harbor, where she was stripped of her vitals. The gigantic engine had been removed as well as most of the sailing equipment. She sat there motionless, attached tightly to the dock. Shops now line the decks to sell souvenirs to visitors. The dining and lounge areas provide meeting places for groups and the cabins have been refurbished as hotel rooms for conventions. Actors have been hired to act out the parts of officers and crew with carefully

studied British accents. The one thing the *Queen Mary* can't
do now is to fulfill the reason for which she was built: to sail the
high sea. I couldn't help feeling disappointed. Everything was
the same, yet nothing was the same. The vessel had become a
monument to past glory.

While on board the motionless *Queen* I reviewed a documen-
tary movie about how she was built and the way she had served
through wars and changing history. The movie ended with a
triumphant but somehow tragic statement, supported by an up-
sweep of dramatic music: "The greatest ship that ever went to
sea is now the greatest ship to come and see."

The words were still on my mind the next day when I greeted
the congregation of my Hollywood Presbyterian Church after
worship. A woman visitor from Iowa made a comment she
meant to be a compliment. The similarity to the closing lines
of the movie made it just the opposite. She had heard about
the Hollywood Church for years and had been inspired by the
influence of its preaching and program upon America. With
excitement she said, "I have waited for years to visit Hollywood
Presbyterian Church to see all the great things that *used to
happen here!*" The great church that went to sea was now a
memorable church to come and see.

Like the *Queen Mary,* my church and yours were meant for
the adventure of the high seas. Our congregations are not museum pieces of past glory, but restored and refurbished ships
to sail in the turbulent waters of our own time. Our organiza-
tions are not meant to be like souvenir shops to keep alive a
memory, but members of a crew to sail with a mission. We are
not actors pretending to sail, but experienced seamen to get out
of the harbor and back to sea. The great task for the Church
in our time is to put the engines back into the ship, clear the
decks of impedimenta, and start sailing again.

The last chapter in the Book of Acts thunders for me with
the challenge that we are to write the new chapter in the Book
of Acts in our time. In the closing paragraphs of Chapter 28,
Luke gives us a picture of life and the Church of the Holy
Spirit which is meant to be rediscovered and lived in each new
age. Acts ends abruptly, like an unfinished symphony. I think
that's exactly what Luke intended. He did not want to give the
impression of the closing of an age but the beginning of the era

of the Holy Spirit. What he described of the power available then, of the energetic Church on the move at that time, of the quality of contagious new life exposed in the first century, is to be the blueprint and handbook for every generation. Acts closes with the impression, "Well, it's up to you now to continue; what you have learned about the early Church is to be a challenge for the Church always; dare to measure the Church in every age by the vision and vitality of the Church empowered by the acts of the Holy Spirit."

Acts is the chartbook and sailing instructions for getting your *Queen Mary* and mine back to sea. We are heading back out to sea at the Hollywood Church. The great ship of our historic Church is on the move! The challenge with which we began in the first chapter of this book has charted our course: we are not to be a religious memorial society of the past, but a vigorous movement in the present.

The last chapter of Acts has been both compass and sextant for me and our church officers. In our untiring efforts to be more than a religious institution, we have found Luke's comparison between the church at Rome and the religious leaders of the synagogue there to be a guiding star. The Church clustered about Paul gives us the image of what we are to be and do; and the religious leaders who troubled Paul give us the danger signal of what we are constantly tempted to drift off course and become.

In the closing paragraph of Acts we are confronted with two very different pictures of God's people. One is cautious and constricted, and the other is challenging and contagious; one is limiting and legal, the other is loving and living; one is exclusive and judgmental, the other is inclusive and joyous.

How clever of Luke! He closes his exciting account of the birth and growth of the Church with a vivid portrayal of the Church set in bold contrast to the life of the Jewish leaders. In it is given an example and a warning. We are shown the spontaneous quality of life of the Church as it met in Paul's quarters under the surveillance of his guards. But we are also shown the careful, cautious attitude of the Jews who came to interrogate the Apostle. Here is an unforgettable picture of the Church we are to emulate and the religious institutionalism we are to avoid.

The last days of the sea voyage had brought Paul from Malta to the Italian port of Puteoli. Under the guard of Julius and the Roman legionnaires, he and his friends traveled along the Appian Way, which led from the coast to Rome. The Christians at Rome had received word of Paul's arrival and could not wait to see him. They sent a deputation to meet him and welcome him with joy. The Greek uses the same word as is used for a welcoming party sent out to meet a conquering general or king. The jubilant greeters met the honored Apostle at the Forum of Appius and the Three Taverns, stops along the Appian Way. The underground communications network of the Christians had kept them informed about all that Paul had been through. Life had not been easy for the church at Rome either. Some historians suggest that the fellowship had grown from a small nucleus of Jews who had been in Jerusalem at that historic Pentecost when the Church was born. The infant church at home had expanded as Hebrew-Christian travelers and merchants settled there. Many Jews were of the Liberti, those who had been slaves and had purchased their freedom. Added to converts from among the Jews were Roman believers who were secret followers of the Lord. There was a strong church anxiously waiting for the Apostle. Christianity had become a vital movement.

The long-awaited visit of the famous leader had finally become a reality. The pent-up joy exploded when they embraced and greeted his hero of the hope they shared. Their love and affection drenched the parched, weary spirit of the exhausted traveler. We can only imagine the excited conversation among Christ's people as they walked the final miles to Rome. How much the Roman Christians needed the Apostle! Their need was matched by his own. The fellowship of "the Way" made a triumphant procession along the old Appian Way to Rome.

In the imperial city, Paul was treated with respect by the Roman authorities while he waited for trial. He was given quarters under the surveillance of the praetorian guard, the private troops of the emperor. Luke tells us that he lived for over two years "without let or hindrance." He was able to have visitors, and his quarters became the center of fellowship and study among the Christians of Rome.

The first thing Paul did in Rome was consistent with his

usual practice of over thirty years of apostleship. He never lost his urgency to communicate Christ to his fellow Jews and never tired of their resistant response. That's why he began his ministry in Rome by calling for the leaders of the seven synagogues in the Trastever, the Hebrew colony. He wanted to speak to them first. He was not free to go to the synagogues as had been his habit in every other city. No word had arrived from Jerusalem about him, and they had heard nothing bad about him. But they had nothing good to say about the "sect" of which he was a leader. They were suspicious of him because of their encounter with the Christians at Rome. They were willing to listen, but with reservations. They came to Paul's quarters with minds made up. Paul expounded the truth of Jesus as Messiah and the reality of the Kingdom of God from morning until night, but only a few responded. Luke speaks succinctly of their bland, unimpressionable religiosity: they disbelieved, disagreed, and departed. But before they left, Paul had the last word. He used Isaiah and Psalm 67 to give his diagnosis and prognosis of spirituality gone stale. His quotation of the Lord in Acts 28:26–27 was pointed:

> "Go to this people, and say
> You shall indeed hear but never understand,
> and you shall indeed see but never perceive.
> For this people's heart has grown dull,
> and their ears are heavy of hearing,
> and their eyes they have closed;
> lest they should perceive with their eyes,
> and hear with their ears,
> and understand with their heart,
> and turn for me to heal them."

What a dreadful picture of religious people who have missed the point and the glory! They had come to the place through religious activity, where they heard words but did not understand; they saw truth but refused to perceive; their emotions were dull and their ears were weary of the repetition of great things. The result is disturbing: they could no longer see truth, discern its implications, or order their lives around it. They no longer needed or wanted God!

As I picture that group of self-righteous, judgmental Jews

crowded into Paul's quarters in Rome, I see much of the Church in America today. The legacy of religion is spiritual lethargy! What the rules and regulations, prejudice and preconceptions did for those Jews then, happens to churchmen today: we get bored. Our ears are closed, our eyes are shut and our hearts are cold. Faith is not something we lose; we merely stop shaping our lives around it. Like the docked *Queen Mary,* our churches become dry-docked memories of days gone by.

Now look at Luke's contrast with the Church. The quarters are the same, Paul is the same, and the climate in Rome is the same. But something has happened that makes all the difference. When the Christians and their inquiring friends crowded that room it was radiant with joy and vitality. In a final sentence Luke portrays the true Church: "And he [Paul] lived there two whole years at his own expense, and welcomed all who came to him, preaching the kingdom of God and teaching about the Lord Jesus Christ quite openly and unhindered."

Catch the dynamics of a great Church in that statement. It was a Church focused on Christ, the Kingdom of God, and an inclusive fellowship—the irreducible maximums of a truly great Church. *The Living Bible* translation catches the viable joy: "Paul lived for the next two years in his rented house and welcomed all who visited him, telling them with all boldness about the Kingdom of God and about the Lord Jesus Christ; and no one tried to stop him." Let's move backward from finish to start of this great sentence and spell out the meaning for us today.

First, the Lord Jesus Christ is the focus and force of a great church. We exist to know him and make him known. When Luke tells us that Paul taught about the Lord quite openly and unhindered, that not only clarifies for me the conditions in which he taught but the quality of the content he taught. Because he was unhindered, he was uninhibited. The ambience of freedom enabled abandoned sharing of what Christ meant to the Apostle and what He could mean to His listeners. The King James Version says he taught "with all confidence." The truth of the person of Christ thundered through the personal experience of the liberated Pharisee.

A woman whose husband claims he is a "recovering alcoholic" says she's a "recovery Pharisee." Christ is at work setting her free. Her witness is not what happened, but what's happening. I believe Paul was like that. His teaching was the penetrating pulsebeat of the Church because it was fresh with recent and present experiences.

That's always the key to a great church. Relational preaching and teaching is revelational truth exposed in our relationships. Christ is not a theological formulation nor just a historical figure; he is a living Person. When a church not only talks about what Christ did, but what he's doing in our lives, dynamic power is released. Our life "in Christ" as recipients of the salvation of his death and Resurrection must be coupled with his life "in" us as the motivating, engendering Holy Spirit. The finest compliment I ever heard given to a clergyman was, "He talks about Christ as if he knew him!" When Christ is taught and preached that way, and all the life of the Church is a fellowship in the presence of the Lord, the world will be startled and attracted. Christ alone can satisfy human hunger; he alone can sustain in pressure; he alone can liberate people to love; he alone can enable us to face death and be assured of eternal life.

A church focused on Christ is a personal church. Christ frees us to be personal. By that I mean we are released from privatism to talk about what Christ means to us in the personal struggle for identity, security, affirmation, purpose and self-worth. When we talk about Christ theoretically, we zoom over the heads and hearts of most people. When pastor, officers, and members are open to talk about what a difference Christ has made in their inner attitudes and outer feelings, others will listen and want to become part of their fellowship. Many people have gone to church for years with broken relationships, hidden guilt, unconfessed fear, and anguished hurt lurking beneath the surface of their "church faces." They get the feeling that they alone face those problems. If the pastor in the pulpit and the people in the pews could be honest, they would find they are all alike in the human struggle. A vital church presents Christ as the vanquisher of death, but also as the liberator from all the things which keep us from living while we are alive!

That leads to the second thing which Luke tells us about the viable church in Paul's quarters in Rome. Paul told them "with all boldness about the Kingdom of God." Christ was not only the answer for personal needs, but the Kingdom of God was the blueprint for what the Church was called to do in society. Preaching and teaching of the Lord Jesus Christ must be followed by communicating the adventure of the Kingdom of God. That means the reign of the Lord in our hearts, in our relationships, and in our society. Preaching Christ is the call to new life; preaching the Kingdom is sounding the marching orders to spread his plan and purpose into every facet of our existence. Jesus taught that the Kingdom is within, between us, in the midst, and coming in all of life. The little church in Paul's room really believed that it had been called to be part of God's strategy of restoring his damaged and perverted creation to its original destiny. Audaciously they sought the will of the Lord for their total life. Elton Trueblood said, "We are told to pray for the Kingdom, which is defined as that situation in which God's will is made manifest on earth."

A truly great church lives under the mandate of the Kingdom of God. That defines its strategy. The repeated question is: "Lord, what do you want us to do to realize your reign in our church and the society around us?" A church grows in power as it orders its life and ministry around the mandate of the Master.

That's when an exciting church comes alive. It is electrified by seeking the situational guidance of our Lord and then reporting back to the fellowship what is happening. The reign of Christ is sought for our relationships, our families, our places of work, our community and our nation. The world and its problems become our parish. We need not apologize to anyone. We have the secret of the abundant life: Christ is the answer to the world's complexities. Two thousand years have slipped by without much change in the world not because the gospel is impotent, but because the people of God have been too imprescriptible to follow guidance.

There is an adventuresome excitement which pervades a church on the move. When people have followed guidance to share Christ with others and work for his justice in the structures of society, and then support each other's vision, a fellowship is galvanized. Some of the most memorable moments of my Christian experience have occurred in groups where people report in on areas surrendered to our Lord and what he has done with the raw material of their willingness.

The other day I sat in with a group of couples in our church who meet weekly to discuss the implications of the Kingdom for their marriages and family life. As each person spoke of the delights and difficulties, I had the feeling I was back in Paul's quarters in Rome!

An intercessory prayer fellowship in our church is being captured by the adventure. They intercede for people and problems and keep in touch by telephone between meetings. The charter of the Kingdom of God is constantly before them. They seek the Lord's guidance on how to pray and then claim the answers which come. Christ is forging ahead on all fronts with these people.

Another group has zeroed in on the gigantic social problems of Hollywood. Their influence accounts for the passage of ordinances which will eventually cripple and then destroy the sexual massage parlors. They are working on housing and education. When a breakthrough comes, they thank the Lord for the courage to keep trying and for the results of their efforts.

Our enabler groups which cluster our congregational family all over Los Angeles pump life into our whole church. The key to the vitality of these groups is the way each person is challenged to seek out the implications of the Lordship of Christ for personal and social problems and then support the others in being faithful. The reports on the results bring joy and thanksgiving. Without the mandate of the Kingdom these groups would be pious evasions of obedience. When each person is helped to picture his life, relationships, responsibilities, and realms of social need under the infusing power of Christ, then he knows what he is to say and do. Life really begins when we meet Christ, but it gets exciting when we follow him. That means that the King's people dare to discover the Kingdom.

But there is a third reason the Church was alive and dynamic there in Paul's quarters. It was an inclusive fellowship. And what an unlikely mixture of people it was! First, there were the saints who had been faithful to Christ through the years in Rome. They had kept the church together with little support or help against the difficulties and dangers in Rome. Added to these were Paul and his friends. We are told in corollary Scriptures in the letters Paul wrote during his imprisonment that he was surrounded by his friends. Mark was there, indicating it was a fellowship of forgiveness. His defection at

Perga years before had been forgiven, and Paul had called for him to be at his side. We can imagine the hours of conversation, confession, and reconciliation which took place between those two.

It was also a fellowship of encouragement, for Timothy was there. He meant a great deal to the Apostle. He was his "child in the faith" (1 Tim. 1:2), his "brother" in the Lord (1 Thess. 3:2) and "fellow worker" (Rom. 16:21). Timothy had a special gift of encouragement to the Apostle.

It was Luke who kept the challenge alive. There is a winsome quality to the words "Luke alone is with me" (2 Tim. 4:11). He had never failed Paul. The brilliant physician could provide intellectual stimulus. I believe Luke was writing Acts during these years at Rome. Can you imagine the delight they had together as they reminisced over what the Holy Spirit had done throughout their journeys? I believe Luke pressed the Apostle to crystallize and synthesize the implications of what they had seen and heard. And there were others: Aristarchus, Tychicus, Epaphroditus, and many others—a supportive, affirming fellowship.

No picture of that church with Paul is complete without the Roman guards. Read between the lines of Philippians and check historical accounts and you will find that the very guards who were assigned the duty of guarding Paul were magnetically drawn into the inclusive fellowship. Paul says he is thankful for his imprisonment because it seemed to advance the gospel; he goes on to tell the Philippians, "so that it has become known throughout the whole praetorian guard and to all the rest that my imprisonment is for Christ" (Phil. 1:13). There are historians who suggest that the guards had to be changed repeatedly because of the rapid rate of their conversion. The reason that news spread through the praetorian guard so quickly was that converted guards could not resist telling what had happened to them.

Picture a guard watching the Church in action; feel the warm, accepting fellowship pierce and penetrate his heart. Knowing what we do about the church in Paul's quarters, a guard could not last very long without meeting the Lord of the fellowship and seeing his own life in the light of the Kingdom. There was a contagious quality of life which few guards could resist. The cross-cultural, interracial fellowship was made up of all ages, both sexes, different backgrounds, and a multiplicity of personality types. That's always a sign of a great church.

But the mark of a vital church is that it exists for those beyond it. Luke tells us that Paul welcomed all who came to him. *The Living Bible* says that all who visited were welcomed. Word had spread throughout Rome that something was happening! Inquirers were included with acceptance and affirmation. The quality of life not only attracted them, but showed them how they too could live. Evangelism is not only going out; it's modeling life as it was meant to be for those the Lord has brought in to observe.

Every contemporary church must ask, "If an outsider, an onlooker, were to observe the life of our church, would he be impelled to want to find our Lord and become one with us in an adventure?" Any church that's writing the new chapter of Acts in our time is living so close to Christ that it is open to others. People should be able to see in our churches saints whose lives are so radiant with joy, so filled with the Holy Spirit, and so responsible for people's needs, that they are irreversibly drawn into the fast-moving currents of the congregational life. Unless the quality of a church's life is a contrast to the dull, drab sameness of the world, we deserve to be dry-docked for- ever, like the *Queen Mary!*

Luke has taken us on an eventful, exciting adventure. His ending may seem abrupt, but his task is finished. The purpose dramatizing the Acts of the Holy Spirit, the birth of the Church and strategy for changing the world is complete. The next chapters were written by other generations who dared to follow the Master. The new chapter is being written by you and me. The same power through the Holy Spirit is available. The same miraculous life can be everyday Christianity. The same quality of a church can be born in Hollywood and in your town. We can never be the same as we were before being gripped by Acts. The bland, religious life is no longer tolerable. We are disturbed and alarmed by what life and the Church were meant to be. We can never be easily satisfied again. And that's exactly what Luke wanted to accomplish.